Centro de Estudios Puertorriqueños

CENTRO JOURNAL
VOLUME XXXIII • NUMBER II • SUMMER 2021

Cover: Ashes for your tenement sky: Piñero 2021, *by Miguel Trelles. Charcoal, ink, and acrylic on canvas, 29" x 27 1/2". Photograph by David Troncoso; Photoshop by Tatiana Ronderos. Reprinted by permission from Miguel Trelles..*

ISSN: 1538-6279 (Print); ISSN: 2163-2960 (Online)
978-1-945662-51-5 (print) 978-1-945662-53-9 (ebook)
©2021 Centro de Estudios Puertorriqueños
Hunter College / City University of New York
695 Park Avenue, E-1429, New York, NY 10065
212.772.5690 • Fax 212.650.3673 • http://centropr.hunter.cuny.edu

CENTRO Journal is indexed or abstracted in: Academic Search Complete (EBSCO host); Alternative Press Index; America: History and Life; Cabell's Whitelist; Caribbean Abstracts; CONUCO–Consorcio Universitario de Indización; Gale; HAPI—Hispanic American Periodical Index; Historical Abstracts; Left Index; MLA International Index; OCLC PAIS; Pro Quest; Scopus; Social Services Abstracts; Sociological Abstracts; Ulrich's Periodicals Service; H.W. Wilson Humanities Abstracts; Worldwide Political Science Abstracts.

Journal of the Center for Puerto Rican Studies
VOLUME XXXIII • NUMBER II • SUMMER 2021

Abject Failure and Utopian Longing in the Lower East Side: The Poetry and Performance of Miguel Piñero

CHARLIE GEYER

ABSTRACT

This article explores the presence of utopian imaginaries in the poetry and performance of Miguel Piñero. Departing from the work of Arnaldo Cruz-Malavé on the colonial abjection of Puerto Ricans, I examine the manner in which Puerto Ricans exist as abject bodies in the cultural imaginary of late 20th-century New York, and the way in which a utopian politics arises out of the abject in *Short Eyes* and "A Lower East Side Poem." I read alongside José Esteban Muñoz, Jack Halberstam, Ernst Bloch, and Theodor Adorno in order to examine both the positivity and negativity of utopian longing in Piñero's work, in other words, the tension between future utopian possibility and its present inability to be realized. I ultimately argue that Piñero's writing straddles these two poles, locating radical utopian potential within sites of abject failure, while remaining open to the possibility that this potential may never be realized. [Keywords: Miguel Piñero, *Short Eyes*, Nuyorican, abject, utopia, queer theory]

The author (chgeyer@bsu.edu) is a Teaching Assistant Professor of Spanish at Ball State University. In his current book manuscript he studies the way in which marginalized groups are represented in public discourse as grotesque, revolting, or threatening, and the manner in which literature in Spanish America, Brazil, and the Latinx United States offers a contestatory discourse through finding beauty in stigmatized bodies and spaces.

Miguel Piñero's literary oeuvre is marked by a continual return to scenes of violence and oppression that demonstrate the abjection of Puerto Ricans in New York City during the latter half of the twentieth century.[1] This marginalized status becomes especially visible in his lyric, "A Lower East Side Poem," in which Piñero's poetic speaker asks that, after his death, his ashes be scattered among the "hustlers and suckers" and "faggots and freaks" (2010, 4) in the streets of his home, the Puerto Rican cultural haven of the Lower East Side.[2] The Lower East Side is the setting for many of Piñero's poems and plays, and an environment that is typified by crime, drug addiction, poverty, neocolonial and capitalist exploitation, homophobia, misogyny, and sexual and racial violence. And yet, within this abject zone, Piñero's poetic speakers and the characters of his plays sporadically happen upon some glimmer of social alternative to suffering and violence, some regenerative possibility springing forth from abjection.

Both Piñero's writing and his life bespeak an intimate relationship with the abject. The poet and playwright, who was born in Puerto Rico in 1946 and moved to the Lower East Side with his family in 1950, was incarcerated at Riker's Island at age eighteen, where he became addicted to heroin (Bernstein 2010, 134). He remained actively addicted to drugs for the majority of his adult life and spent extended time in prison, writing much of his first play, *Short Eyes*, in one of Marvin Felix Camillo's prison theater workshops while incarcerated at the Sing Sing Correctional Facility in New York (Hart 1981). He died in 1988 at forty-one of cirrhosis of the liver. In short, he was a writer who remained always enmeshed in a life of crime and addiction, and inscribed within the scenes of suffering, oppression, and violence that are the focus of his literary works.

Despite winning the 1973-1974 New York Drama Critics' Circle Award for *Short Eyes* and being awarded a Guggenheim Fellowship in 1982, Piñero's other plays and poems have not received much critical acclaim, leaving some critics to grieve a sense of untapped potential—of possibility that is interrupted by the tragic death that cut short his artistic career (Iglesias 2010, xxiv) and the drug-fueled lifestyle that led many of his poems and plays-in-progress to be lost to posterity (Kanellos 2010, vii). While it is likely that greater literary output and distinction, financial stability, physical health, and other external markers of "success" would have graced Piñero's life if he had renounced a criminalized and marginal lifestyle, Piñero as both writer and historical subject seems to have been more invested in a different value system—one that finds promise in losing, straying, and failing, and in a general praxis of unruliness, anti-normativity, and revolt that has been united in other contexts under the banner of "queer failure" (Halberstam 2011) and "wildness" (Halberstam and Nyong'o 2018). Indeed, Piñero is a subject who refuses to "live up to his potential" as determined by dominant logics of success, and who, by enacting this refusal, provides a glimpse of another sort of potential, a radically outside and socially illegible one, that speaks to new ways of living and being in society. His work gestures toward the productive possibility and utopian longing that can arise from those marginal zones of society that are marked as abject.

The purpose of this essay is to return to the scenes of loss, failure, and abjection that populate Piñero's work, in order to recover the utopian possibility that arises within them. This multilayered argument will unfold over several steps. I will first examine utopian imaginaries within diasporic Puerto Rican literature and activism of the same time period, to distinguish the radical utopianism of Piñero's work from that of his contemporaries. Secondly, I will enter into dialogue with the work of Arnaldo Cruz-Malavé (1995; 1997), who recognizes an empowering or restorative effect of giving form to the abject for Puerto Rican authors, and I will continue in this vein, with the caveat that I find within Piñero's work a distinctly queer component to the politics of his writing. Following in the footsteps of José Esteban Muñoz (2009) and his queer reading of Amiri Baraka's *The Toilet*, I will argue that the stigmatized, abject practice of queerness as it appears in *Short Eyes* does the work of imagining an unrealized order of social relations, and of gesturing, to use Ernst Bloch's term, toward the "not-yet-here." Thirdly, through engagement with Halberstam's (2011) concept of queer failure, I will explore how the queer utopianism of *Short Eyes* opens up to a wider abject utopianism in "A Lower East Side Poem," in which the poetic speaker's act of opening to a collective of abject bodies proposes a new mode of sociality through being with the abject, rather than enacting its violent exclusion. Finally, I will consider the relations between utopia and failure—its hopeful promise and its continual disappointment—and the manner in which the abject bodies of Piñero's work—the queer, addicted, criminalized, colonized, and racialized bodies of the Puerto Rican diaspora—look hopefully beyond the horizons of present failure to imagine something different.[3]

I. Diaspora Dreams: Abjection and Utopianism in New York City

Utopian dreaming amid abjection within the context of Puerto Rican communities in 1960s and '70s New York is not unique to Piñero's writing. Rather, his work comes into being within a rich milieu of community organizing, activist efforts, and artistic production, many of which coalesce around a sense of utopian longing. In order to situate Piñero within this sociocultural landscape, and to identify how the utopian imaginaries that glimmer at the margins of his work differ from those of his contemporaries, it is useful to briefly survey this political context.

As Puerto Ricans were driven to the northern urban centers in search of jobs that never fully materialized on the Island under the economic reforms of Operation Bootstrap (Scarano 1993, 749-64), they were met with a declining industrial sector and limited economic prospects. A pair of 1968 Department of Labor reports found that "in East Harlem, the percentage of Puerto Ricans who were unemployed, underemployed, or permanently out of the labor force for lack of success in finding employment was approximately 47 percent," and that "[t]he majority of the Puerto Ricans in the metropolitan area—over 50 percent—relied on jobs that were increasingly disappearing" (Fernández 2020, 55). This economic disenfranchisement was accompanied by popular discourse among white, dominant groups that characterized Puerto Ricans as an abject mass invading their city. The "Puerto Rican problem," as it was frequently termed in public discourse (Fernández 2020, 56), characterized the new migrants as "abusing the welfare roles, carrying infectious diseases, exhibiting criminal behavior, and 'suffocating the culture of their adopted city'" (Fernández 2020, 53). The Lower East Side in the 1970s, a majority Latinx neighborhood by the end of the decade (Mele 2000, 195–7), came to exist as an abject zone in the cultural imaginary of New York, occupied by a threatening, racialized Other associated with drug sales, addiction, violence, and petty crime (Mele 2000, 186–7). These stigmatizing representations fueled disinvestment in the neighborhood, which in turn facilitated a housing crisis and further impoverished the community (Mele 2000, 180–219).

Structural racism and disenfranchisement of Puerto Ricans were met with resistance by a variety of community action groups, the most visible of which was the Young Lords. The New York Chapter of the Young Lords was established in 1969, and immediately began a series of direct actions with the aim of forcing local government to address the overwhelmingly neglected needs of the Puerto Rican community.[4] As outlined in their 13-Point Program and Platform (Young Lords 2010, 11–3), the Young Lords' long-term political goals centered around Puerto Rican independence, an end to American hegemony in the Global South, and the establishment of a socialist society. Embracing a revolutionary nationalism centered in antiracist, anticapitalist, and decolonial ideals, the Young Lords married grassroots activism with the utopian vision of Third World Socialism.

Concurrently with the work of the Young Lords, centered predominantly in East Harlem and the South Bronx, community organizers in the Lower East Side also sought to address the social abjection of Puerto Ricans. A group first known as the Real Great Society (RGS) and later reorganized under the name CHARAS (an acronym for the group's six founding members) administered a wide variety of programs throughout the late 1960s and '70s, designed to combat derelict housing conditions, poverty, and lack of access to education. Their activities included founding the University of the Street, which provided a series of academic, arts, and job training classes to neighborhood residents; building geodesic domes as temporary housing alternatives; re-appropriating and refurbishing abandoned or neglected buildings for community housing; starting a recycling center; building community gardens; and rehabilitating the abandoned PS 64 building and to establish the El Bohio Community Center (Bagchee 2018, 102–51). While always grounded in the steady pragmatism of trying to make the lives of Lower East Side residents materially better, the efforts of CHARAS also frequently hinted at utopian underpinnings. The urban homesteading, or "sweat-equity," projects that the group organized along with the Interfaith Adopt a Building (AAB) organization put community members to work to renovate abandoned buildings and then gave full control and management over to the residents as limited equity cooperatives (Bagchee 2018, 117–8). Communal solutions to public housing, coupled with community garden and alternative energy initiatives—including installing solar panels and an electricity-generating windmill on the roof of an East Eleventh Street homesteading project—led sociologist Daniel Chodorkoff to find within the CHARAS-led homesteading movement "the lived reality of [Murray] Bookchin's socioecological utopia" (Bagchee 2018, 126). Similarly, earlier attempts by CHARAS to provide temporary housing to displaced residents by building geodesic domes on abandoned lots came about through collaborations with utopian architect and environmentalist Buckminster Fuller (Bagchee 2018, 107–14; Mottel 1973).

Miguel Algarín explicitly acknowledges the manner in which Nuyorican literature is enmeshed in this particular social and political fabric in his introduction to *Nuyorican Poetry: An Anthology of Puerto Rican Words and Feelings* (1975), which he edited with Piñero. His embrace of nationalism as a productive means of identity formation (1975, 13–4) echoes the Young Lords' revolutionary nationalist cause, and his call for New York Puerto Ricans to generate "alternative behavior habits" (1975, 9)—which involves a precarious blend of living inside and outside the law in order to, ultimately, "transition from organized street hustling to coordinated alternative street government" (1975, 10)—evokes CHARAS's delicate dance to work with governmental institutions in order to receive funding and negotiate the bureaucratic labyrinth of building ordinances and property law, while simultaneously contesting the racist and neoliberal values that drive these institutions. Utopian imaginaries frequently surface in other ways in Nuyorican literature and arts of the era: in actor/director Eddie Figueroa's concept of the Spirit Republic of Puerto Rico—a transnational, multicultural, multiracial homeland of the spirit that blends Eastern religion, New Age psychology, and Spanish Caribbean *espiritismo* (Morales 2002, 90–2)—and in the recurring motif of the idyllic return to the island homeland that other critics have noted among Nuyorican authors (Campa 1988; Esterrich 1998).

The politics of the Young Lords, the community work of CHARAS, and the ideals of the Spirit Republic and the restorative return to the lost island home are all fundamentally driven by the concept of positive uplift of the Puerto Rican community, which is predicated upon a movement away from the abject position that Puerto Ricans occupy in the New York cultural imaginary.

While drawing its political force from the same abjection of Puerto Ricans as the utopian imaginaries outlined above, the utopianism that arises from the abject in Piñero's work is different in kind. The politics of the Young Lords, the community work of CHARAS, and the ideals of the Spirit Republic and the restorative return to the lost island home are all fundamentally driven by the concept of positive uplift of the Puerto Rican community, which is predicated upon a movement *away* from the abject position that Puerto Ricans occupy in the New York cultural imaginary. In other words, imagining utopia in each of these cases requires an explicit or implicit process of boundary setting: of invoking a set of *positive* ideals—socialist egalitarianism, economic opportunity, racial pride, cultural autonomy, etc.—to be embodied within the utopian space, and a set of *negative* ideals—the junkie, the criminal, the vagrant, and, in some cases, the queer subject—to be discarded outside upon entry. While the value and political force of these approaches, which Leticia Alvarado refers to in her study of Latinidad and abject performance as "a counterstrategy of creating distance between abjection and minoritized communities through respectability" (2018, 11), is undeniable, they also run the risk of rendering invisible or further excluding certain marginal bodies in the name of respectability, or of establishing a new form of normativity—in Alvarado's words, "[a] normative inclusion that will require repudiation of other abjects if seeking out proper subject status" (2018, 11). In other words, these types of utopian imaginaries run the risk, sooner or later, of reifying their borders in opposition to a newly defined excluded and abject outside. Such potential pitfalls can be seen in the heteronormativity of the Young Lords' revolutionary nationalist project,[5] as well as in the binarism of CHARAS' commitment, in Bagchee's (2018, 149) description, to changing the material conditions of the Lower East Side community "from negative (disinvested, demolished, abandoned) to positive (cared for, rebuilt, enlivened)."

The intention of this essay is certainly not to devalue these positively oriented utopian imaginaries, nor to dismiss them as, due to their potential shortcomings, destined for inevitable failure. As we shall see, utopia by nature is always courting failure. Rather, my purpose is to recover what lies beyond the boundaries of these other utopian visions—to examine what happens in Piñero's work when utopia is evoked through a *negative* motion into the abject terrain of addiction, criminality, and, indeed, queerness, and the manner in which this "deviant," pathologized space offers a different political promise, which challenges all normativizing gestures through remaining radically open to the abject body.[6] Alvarado describes this productive engagement with abjection as having a "world-making potential" (2018, 10), which communicates "an ungraspable alternative social organization illuminated by the aesthetic" (2018, 11), and I conceive of it here as a radically inclusive social vision that finds the key to utopian possibility in the act of opening to the abject Other. The work of Cruz-Malavé coupled with reflections on the intimate connection between queer utopianism and queer failure of Muñoz and Halberstam will help us to elaborate the particulars of the utopian possibility within the abject in a specifically Nuyorican context.

II. Abject Politics in Puerto Rican Literature

Cruz-Malavé's work (1995; 1997) is indispensible to understanding the points of intersection between abjection and literature in a Puerto Rican context. Broadly, he argues that colonial domination is a form of abjection, to which Puerto Rican literature responds in various ways. On one hand, he notes the continuously failing attempt on the part of certain canonical authors (especially Antonio S. Pedreira and René Marqués) to establish a dominant national literature, which consolidates its phallic power through the abjection of the feminine and the queer (1995). On the other, he brings critical attention to a queerly valenced writing (evidenced primarily, in his view, by the work of Luis Rafael Sánchez and Manuel Ramos Otero) that refuses the paternal project of forming national identity by means of abjection, and instead willfully occupies a space of abject queerness (1995).

In "'What a tangled web!': Masculinidad, abyección y la fundación de la literatura puertorriqueña en los Estados Unidos," Cruz-Malavé (1997) seeks to delimit the place of Nuyorican literature within this theoretical schema, arguing through analysis of Piñero's *Short Eyes* and Piri Thomas' *Down These Mean Streets* that Nuyorican literature renders visible the homoeroticism that underlies colonial power relations, while ultimately attempting (albeit unsuccessfully) to re-inscribe itself within the project of forming heterosexual national identity through abjection of the queer. Before offering my own alternative interpretation of the power of the abject and of queerness in Piñero's work, this complex argument requires elaboration.

Cruz-Malavé begins the essay with an analysis of Sanchéz's story "¡Jum!" ([1966] 1985), which dramatizes the sacrificial murder of a gay man in a small (presumably Puerto Rican) town. He finds within this story the allegorical tale of the construction of Puerto Rican national identity. Here, the abjection of queerness serves as a metaphor for the way in which the colonial subject purges himself—I say "himself" intentionally, because this is, indeed, a phallic fantasy—of the homosexual erotic charge that underlies the relationship between colonizer and colonized, in order to form a virile, patriarchal national identity. Following the schema of colonial relations theorized by Frantz Fanon in *Black Skin, White Masks*, Cruz-Malavé argues that the white fear of colonized and hyper-sexualized black bodies carries within it desire in equal measure, that negrophobia and homosexual desire are inextricably linked to one another: "[e]n el fondo, el hombre blanco que le teme al falo erecto que es el hombre negro en la cultural occidental, argumenta Fanon, también lo desea; así como el hombre blanco que se imagina perseguido por el hombre negro, también lo persigue, lo invoca" (1997, 331). Thus, the abjection of homosexuality in "¡Jum!" serves as a strategy by which racialized colonial subjects attempt to escape the homo-erotics of colonial power relations, and form a collective identity outside of the colonizer/colonized binary. However, Cruz-Malavé also notes that the action of abjecting the queer is never truly completed, that the "constitutive outside," to use Judith Butler's term (1993, 3),[7] against which the heteronormative colonial social structure defines itself is always present, lurking at the porous boundaries of the social margins. In a similar way, the figure of the queer subject in "¡Jum!" is also marked as a constitutive presence in the formation of the communal body in the story; as he is ritualistically drowned in the river that runs alongside the town, his corpse becomes the fragile border that delimits the collective identity, the "contrapunto [a] su identidad" (Cruz-Malavé 1997, 329).

    After elucidating how the abjection of homosexuality becomes a ritual of social purification that structures identity in "¡Jum!" Cruz-Malavé theorizes a different trajectory that abjection could follow. Considering whether the abject could suffer a fate other than that of ritual sacrifice, finding "una respiración que no sea aprovechable para ese contrapunto," (1997, 329) he wonders if there could exist:

¿[...] [O]tras vías —vías propias— por medio de las cuales resistir la abyección? Y si pudiera salir del río y desplazarse por canales previstos, recorrer nuevamente la ruta de su crucifixión, ¿lograría él [lo abyecto] subvertir entonces la estructura que lo repudia y lo absorbe? ¿O caería él nuevamente en las redes imbricadas de la expiación? (1997, 329)

The "otras vías" that Cruz-Malavé cautiously suggests here propose a subversion of the binaries of colonizer/colonized and inside/outside through channeling the return of the abject into the dominant social sphere, a crucifixion in reverse that renounces sacrifice and, like a drowned corpse rising to the surface, returns to perturb, disrupting both the dynamics of colonial subjugation and the fragile boundaries of identity. He then notes that the Puerto Rican literature written in the United States—in other words, outside of the porous borders that demarcate the Commonwealth of Puerto Rico as nation—tends to itself occupy the position of Sánchez's drowned protagonist, and thus embodies the various possibilities of subversion and resistance that the Puerto Rican literature of the abject may offer: "[g]ran parte de la literatura puertorriqueña en los Estados Unidos, tanto la llamada "nuyorican" como la de los escritores homosexuales exiliados de la generación del '70, está escrita desde este destierro, desde ese río de la abyección" (1997, 329).

Within this corpus (corpse?) of abject literature, Cruz-Malavé identifies a key similarity between the way that the Nuyorican writers and the homosexual Puerto Rican writers in exile mentioned above approach the dynamics of abjection, concluding that authors from both groups reveal the aporias and the fragility of heterosexual masculinity and, by metaphorical extension, national identity construction. Yet he also argues that this work in the Nuyorican context is fraught with ambivalence and paradox—that these writers generally seek to maintain a brittle heterosexual masculine identity through the abjection of queerness at the same time that they reveal the impossibility of such a project—whereas the gay male writers he invokes delve more openly into the radical and subversive power of queerness.

Ambivalence toward homosexuality marked both Piñero's writing and his life. His bisexuality was an open secret before his death, and Lee Bernstein writes that, "[a]lthough Piñero did not define himself as gay and was briefly married to a woman, he did have same-sex encounters throughout his life and lived with painter Martin Wong" (2010, 132). In an interview with *The Advocate*, Benjamin Bratt, who played the leading role in the 2001 biopic *Piñero*, said the following regarding the author's sexuality:

He was most certainly a practicing bisexual. But I think he, like many other cons, didn't really play that sexual identity political game. Sex is sex, and even within a prison system, what you are and how you should be labeled depends on whether you're giving or receiving. And many of his friends have told me that if you called him gay to his face or even called him bisexual, he'd probably stab you. (2002, 42, 45)

Thus, one can observe in Piñero's life the same aporia that Cruz-Malavé locates in his writing. His lived sexuality performs both queerness and the abjection of queerness—the willful abandon to socially abject sexual practices (especially within a heteronormative nationalist context) as well as the violent repudiation of identification with such practices. While it is undeniable that Piñero's relationship with homosexuality remained always a conflictive one, I would like to argue that the moments of queerness in his work do more than reveal the aporias of heteromasculinist identity projects—as argued by Cruz-Malavé—and propose instead that expressions of queer desire in Piñero's writing serve the critical purpose of gesturing toward homoerotic alternatives to queer abjection.

III. *Short Eyes*: Queer Abjection, Hidden Utopias
Critical engagement with *Short Eyes*, first performed in 1974, reveals an intricate display of the colonial abjection that Cruz-Malavé so eloquently elaborates, as well as the utopian possibility offered within the abjected practice of queerness. The play tells the story of the murder of a child molester inside a New York pre-trial detention facility, and the title derives from the prison slang term, "short eyes," used among inmates to refer to pedophiles. The work also displays a deep ambivalence toward practices of homosexuality, "frequently switch[ing] between violence and intimacy, uncritical homophobia and repudiations of contemporary morality" (Bernstein 2010, 132).

Within the play, the carceral environment becomes a privileged site upon which to examine the force of abjection in American society of the late twentieth century—a microcosm of the manner in which colonialism, racism, capitalism, and queer stigma operate intersectionally to form the structural hierarchy of the body politic. The prison is not only the site where the criminal, the violator of the Law, is deposited after his/her excision from the social body; it is also the place where the social forces that mark certain racialized and colonial bodies as abject are rendered fully visible. In other words, the prison reveals the manner in which the forces of white supremacy and neocolonialism are woven into the fiber of the carceral institution, influencing which bodies are judged as criminal and designated abject.[8] The makeup of the population on the cellblock in *Short Eyes* bears this out: three are Puerto Rican (Juan, Paco, and Julio, a.k.a. "Cupcakes"), three are African American (Ice, El Raheem, and Omar) and one is white (Longshoe), until the later introduction of the pedophile, Clark Davis, who is also white. As a result, the colonial dynamics of desire and repudiation, of homoerotic yearning and abjection, that Cruz-Malavé identifies are very much present in the prison setting of *Short Eyes*. All prisons to some degree function as penal colonies, and prisoners may be thought of as existing in a colonial relationship with their overseers, in which they are often required to perform poorly or unpaid labor for the benefit of the state or private company that maintains authority over them. Adding another layer to this colonial relationship, the majority of the occupants of American prisons are to some extent postcolonial subjects (or colonial subjects, in the case of Puerto Ricans), who exist as abject bodies in the cultural imaginary of the dominant white, middle-class society.

The body of the prisoner—literally, the ass—becomes the feminized, homosexual object of desire and repudiation for the patriarchal authority figure, as the sexual domination implied by "taking the ass"—dominating it, planting a phallic flag within it—implies desire as much as violence.

The homoerotics of this colonial relationship become apparent in first lines of the play, in which a guard addresses the inmates before roll call, saying, "your soul may belong to God, but your ass is mine" (Piñero 2010, 194). The body of the prisoner—literally, the ass—becomes the feminized, homosexual object of desire and repudiation for the patriarchal authority figure, as the sexual domination implied by "taking the ass"—dominating it, planting a phallic flag within it—implies desire as much as violence. The inmates, in an attempt to escape from the passive position of abject homosexual, repeat the same abjection they have suffered, enacting sexual violence against other prisoners in a precarious effort to reclaim a space of dominant masculinity, thus forming, "una cadena jerárquica, unilateral de abyección" (Cruz-Malavé 1997, 333).

However, in these moments of homosexual contact between inmates, Cruz-Malavé also notes that the ambivalence between desire and revulsion, the ease with which one can transform into another, threatens to shift the balance of power between active and passive, between colonizer and colonized. The most memorable moment of this inversion comes between Paco and Cupcakes, who Piñero refers to as a "Puerto Rican pretty boy" in the description of the characters that precedes the script of the play (2010, 193). When Cupcakes is in the shower in Act II, Paco gets in with him and kisses him, offering even to "go both ways" (2010, 221). At this moment in the bathroom—the site of the most universal form of abjection, the evacuation of bodily waste—the two inmates threaten to transform violent expulsion into pure erotic desire. Paco tells Cupcakes that he is, in fact, in love with him, and lavishes him with amorous and seductive supplications:

Óyeme, negrito ... déjame decirte algo ... tú me tiene loco ... me desespera ... nene, estoy enchulao contigo ... Yo quiero ser tuyo y quiero que tú sea mío ... ¿Y qué tú quiere que yo haga por ti? [...] te quiero y que te adoro ... nene [...] Tú va a ser mío ... mi nene lindo ... Cupcakes, que dio bendiga la tierra que tú pise. (2010, 220)

However, the moment of queer romance never fully manages to escape the threat of violent abjection, as in response to Cupcakes' resistance, Paco tells him, "[p]ush comes to shove, I'll take you. But I don't wanna do that 'cause I know I'm gonna have to hurt you in the doing" (2010, 221). The subtext of the play, as well as suggestive statements by other characters, insinuates that Cupcakes is also attempting to work out a conflictive relationship between homosexual desire and homosexual repudiation. Various inmates besides Paco (Omar, Longshoe, El Raheem, and Ice) express explicit or implicit sexual desire for Cupcakes (231), and Cupcakes' behavior—doing pushups in front of the other prisoners with his buttocks ostentatiously thrust up into the air (2010, 217)—suggests that, to some degree, Cupcakes enjoys being an object of desire. When Omar gives voice to this suspicion—"You's a fine motherfucker, Cupcakes. Like I said, I ain't the smartest guy in the place. But I get the feeling you like being a fine motherfucker" (2010, 222)—Cupcakes does not deny it, but instead attempts to deflect Omar's desire toward Clark: "Look, look ... we're gonna do it to the white freak" (2010, 222). Yet the displacement of desire onto another object (Clark), and its transformation into violence, does not erase or resolve the ambivalence that arises in the shower scene between Paco and Cupcakes, in which the faltering repression of desire on the part of both is expressed in repudiation. For Cupcakes, this takes the form of deflecting of Paco's advances, and for Paco, it is the unrealized threat that his expression of love will turn into the most extreme form of sexual violence—into rape.

In the end, Cupcakes is successful in diverting the erotic interest of the other inmates toward Clark, thus fully transfiguring this latent, collective homosexual desire into violent repudiation, and reestablishing the colonial system of abjection that defines the prison structure. Much like the homosexual protagonist of Sánchez's "¡Jum!," Clark is thrust into the position of abject pariah, and cast out of the society in the perverse purification rite of ritual murder. When all of the inmates (except for Juan, who serves as a sort of voice of moral conscience in the play) put into practice their plan to gang rape Clark, he threatens to tell the authorities. The prisoners respond by collectively holding Clark down while Longshoe cuts his throat. If we imagine that the community in "¡Jum!" is a Puerto Rican one, then we can read both "¡Jum!" and *Short Eyes* as allegories of collective colonial identity formation. The colonized communal body, rendered abject through colonial domination, repeats abjection through the violent exclusion of a stigmatized other, in order to purge itself of a perceived homosexual passivity and establish a heterosexual patriarchal collective identity. If in "¡Jum!" we are presented with a Puerto Rican communal body, in *Short Eyes* we are shown the members of a penal colony, cut off from society by the walls of a New York correctional facility.

One thing *Short Eyes* makes particularly clear is the spatialization of the abject in the construction of the social body. While the prison becomes the colonial repository for the abject figure of the criminal—revealing also the manner in which racialized colonial and postcolonial subjects are criminalized and rendered abject—certain spaces within it also serve as privileged sites in which the system of abjection threatens to unravel and manifest as its inverse: queer desire. After the inmates learn what Clark has been accused of (raping a young girl), they immediately begin to associate him with the abject space of the toilet. When none of the inmates will give him space to stand in the common area, Cupcakes suggests that he stand by the toilet: "[h]ey, Clark ... that spot's not taken ... right over there ... Yeah, that's right ... the whole toilet bowl and you go well together" (2010, 212). Shortly thereafter, Longshoe demands that Clark hold his penis while he urinates, and when he refuses, the inmates stick his head in a urine-filled toilet and flush it. Finally, after Clark is murdered, his body is left in the shower, and the space of the bathroom becomes his final resting place, acquiring both a literal and metaphorical sense of evacuation and cleansing in the penal colony.

Conversely, the bathroom is also the site of the shower scene between Paco and Cupcakes, which reveals a moment in which abjection tends on the verge of transgressive eroticism, yet never manages to transcend colonial dynamics of repression and violence. Regardless of the impossibility of abandon to homoerotic desire that is expressed in this scene, the encounter between the two men does tender the possibility of *going both ways*, of opening—with all of the queer, sexualized valences of the term—within the site of abjection— the prison, the bathroom, the anus itself—to an eroticism that, perhaps only for a moment, could liquidate the colonial hierarchy into the horizontality of queer egalitarianism. While Cruz-Malavé focuses on the foreclosure of the ephemeral moment of queer possibility, and the resumption of the oppressive hierarchy of abjection, I propose to linger a moment longer with the ephemera, and to explore its political value, namely, that within the abject scene of the prison bathroom, amid the threat of rape and murder, there lies latent an as-of-yet-unrealized potential for an alternative social order—that the bathroom serves as a stage for an abject performance of queer eroticism, which enacts a rupture in the order of colonial domination, opening it to new valences of utopia that might otherwise be expelled in the toilet.

IV. Utopia in *The Toilet*
Muñoz's reading of Amiri Baraka's *The Toilet* provides a roadmap for recovering utopia from the scene of abjection. Baraka, formerly known as LeRoi Jones, was a contemporary of the New York School poets, and an active participant in this literary circle during the late 1950s and early 1960s. He would later renounce this bohemian aesthetic scene to become one of the founders of the Black Arts Movement, and embrace Black Nationalism.[9] Baraka also expressed an ambivalence to homosexuality that is similar to Piñero's, and before this transition away from the New York School scene, it is known that Baraka engaged in homosexual encounters, and that one of his partners

was the poet Frank O'Hara (Muñoz 2009, 85–6). Debuting in 1964, *The Toilet* deals explicitly with the topic of queer abjection and, in a manner very similar to *Short Eyes*, gestures toward alternative possibility arising out of the abject.[10]

The Toilet tells the story of two high school boys, Jimmy Karolis (who is white) and Ray a.k.a. "Foots" (who is black), who are bullied into fighting one another in a school bathroom. The impetus toward conflict arises when Foots' friends find a note that Karolis sent to Foots, in which Karolis tells him that he's beautiful and that he wants to give him a blowjob. The subtext of the play to this point suggests that the interest is not one sided, and that a sexual relationship between the two boys has been going on for some time. Foots' friends have already badly beaten Karolis by the time they drag him into the bathroom. The first time that Foots sees Karolis during the action of the play, he is lying bloodied on the bathroom floor, and the stage directions describe Foots' reaction as one of "horror and disgust," which he struggles to conceal as he lingers over his body, "threatening to stay too long" (Jones 1966, 52). While Foots initially declines to fight, in his first lines of the play Karolis accepts the challenge, and in doing so reveals that the toilet exists for him and Foots not only as a space of violence, but also as one of desire:

Karolis: I'll fight you Foots! (*Spits the name.*) I'll fight you. Right here in this same place where you said your name was Ray. (*Screaming. He lunges at Foots and manages to grab him in a choke hold.*) Ray, you said your name was. You said Ray. Right here in this filthy toilet. [...] You put your hand on me and said Ray! (1964, 60)

The fight ends as Karolis chokes Foots into unconsciousness and the other boys intervene and beat Karolis together. Queer desire is thus repressed into violence and abjection until the very last moment of the play, when the other boys leave and Foots wakes up, walks over to Karolis, and "kneels before the body, weeping and cradling the head in his arms" (1964, 62).

Fred Moten describes *The Toilet* as "a homosexual, interracial seizure" (2003, 168) on the part of Baraka, which contains within it both an avowal and a disavowal of homosexuality. He argues that, "Baraka's work, over the course of the early 1960s is, in large part, the struggle to embrace such seizure, to think and renew its political content and force" (2003, 169). Moten's articulation of the nature of the "political content and force" of this seizure is quite nuanced and complex, but generally revolves around a resistance to racialized subjection, a radical cut or break in systems of subjugation, that is realized in the black avant-garde. Moten also emphasizes a definitively homoerotic element in this "break," and while noting that some black performers, such as musician Cecil Taylor, embrace this homoerotic radicality, for Baraka, this embrace remains a struggle. Thus, while on one hand *The Toilet* serves an attempt to hold on to (to seize) this moment of seizure, "Baraka's work is also, at the same time, a massive disavowal of such an embrace, a disavowal continually given in his desire for a purified racial and sexual self-referentiality" (2003, 169). Moten sees this disavowal as a "violent purification" of the productive "frenzy or rapture" (2003, 169) that is this moment of seizure. The language of violent purification is, of course, the language of abjection, and the end game of this abjection is the establishment of a "black heterosexual maleness," which is "the path that Baraka must always take toward this purification" (2003, 169). Thus, in *The Toilet*, as well as in the toilet of *Short Eyes*, the purification of heterosexual masculinity rests upon the ambivalent abjection of queerness. Similarly, Baraka's disavowal of queerness, which happens a few years after the production of *The Toilet* (Muñoz 2009, 90), parallels the adoption of a Black Nationalist ideology, which carries within it an echo of the formation of heterosexual national identity through queer abjection that Cruz-Malavé finds in various Puerto Rican works.

Despite the homophobic violence that pervades *The Toilet*, Muñoz locates within the work a critique of masculinity that constructs itself via abjection, and a gesture toward queer alternatives that could exist in the future. It is important to understand that this queer futurity does not recast the play as a present utopia. Muñoz is clear that he is not interested in re-signifying "the gesture of tenderness as redemptive," nor in "cleansing the violence that saturates every move and utterance of the play" (2009, 90). Instead, he sees the final movements of the drama as speaking to what is absent in the violent present, and to an interracial homosexual relationality that could be realized in the future:

This moment nonetheless tells a story that suggests some kind of futurity, a relational potential worth holding on to. Battered and bruised, shattered by internal and external frenzies of homophobic violence, the combatant lovers nonetheless have this moment of wounded recognition that tells us that this moment in time and in this place, the moment of pain-riddled youth, is not all there is, that indeed *something is missing*. The gestural speaks to that which is, to use Bloch's phrase, *not-yet-here*. (2009, 90—emphasis added)

It is the something that is missing, the yet-to-arrive, toward which utopian thinking gestures for Ernst Bloch and, following him, Muñoz. For the function of utopia is double: it enacts a critique of the present while at the same time pointing out alternative possibility. Bloch and Theodor Adorno tease out this dialectical essence together in a conversation that takes place in 1964, later transcribed under the title "Something's Missing: A Discussion Between Ernst Bloch and Theodor W. Adorno on the Contradictions of Utopian Longing." Bloch posits that "the essential function of utopia is a critique of what is present. If we had not already gone beyond the barriers [of the present], we could not even perceive them as barriers" (Bloch and Adorno 1988, 12). In other words, the function of utopia is simultaneously to demarcate the boundaries of the possible within the current society, and to look beyond those barriers to imagine what might be. Adorno agrees, and elaborates this idea:

Yes, at any rate, utopia is essentially in the determined negation, in the determined negation of what merely is, and by concretizing itself as something false, it always points at the same time to what it should be. Yesterday you quoted Spinoza in the passage, "Verum index sui et falsi" [The true is the sign of itself and the false]. I have varied this a little in the sense of the dialectical principle of the determined negation, and said Falsum—the false thing—index sui et veri" [The false is the sign of itself and the correct]. That means that the true thing determines itself via the false thing, or via that which makes itself falsely known. And insofar as we are not allowed to cast the picture of utopia, insofar as we do not know what the correct thing would be, we know exactly, to be sure, what the false thing is. That is actually the only form in which utopia is given to us at all. (1988, 12)

Thus, utopia, by presenting itself in the form of the negative—*not this* form of subjugation, *not that* instance of violence—critiques the present and its limits, while at the same time invoking the something that is missing, which lies beyond society's grasp. As such, utopia is a double sign, signaling the problems of the present while simultaneously gesturing toward a ghostly future that is caught only in glimpses—the something still missing toward which humans may continue to strive.

In the end, desire does not persist, and returns to its inverse of repudiation.

Applying this theoretical perspective to *Short Eyes*, the shower scene between Paco and Cupcakes can also be read as a gesture toward queer utopia—a possibility that is foreclosed by the colonial dynamics of the violent present, but that remains open, latent in unrealized form. Similar to the final moments of *The Toilet*, Paco's expression of love and his willingness to *go both ways* suggest a future possibility for queer relationality that can only appear in the present as an ephemeral vision. This vision is marked as the negation of the violence of homosexual abjection, and of the repudiation of queer desire that subtends the heterosexual nationalist project. The something missing toward which this negation points is an egalitarian queer relationship that renounces subjugation, and in doing so, puts forth an alternative to the social structure of the prison, which is predicated upon a hierarchical chain of abjection. In the end, desire does not persist, and returns to its inverse of repudiation. Nevertheless, the something missing that arises in the abject space of the prison bathroom remains as a specter of possibility that haunts the play, an unconsummated future in the process of arriving.

V. Hope and Failure in Utopian Longing

Reading *Short Eyes* through the lens of Muñoz allows us to see how both the abjected practice of queerness and the abject spaces of the prison and the bathroom become staging grounds for utopian imagining. Furthermore, reading the play through Cruz-Malavé reveals the manner in which racism, colonialism, heterosexism, and capitalism work in concert to produce the abject bodies that populate the prison, and how queerness as practice offers a contestatory response to these intersecting forces. Finally, the text displays for the reader the vexing futurity of the utopian gesture—the manner in which the "not-yet-here" implies both a tangible future possibility and its failure to be realized in the present. Piñero's "A Lower East Side Poem," the last text that I will examine in this essay, expands upon the utopianism of *Short Eyes* in several important ways, showing how utopian vision arrives not only from queer praxis, but from the various forms that the abject body may take in the Puerto Rican diaspora. Additionally, the text demonstrates utopian possibility arising from a new space—the abjected neighborhood that serves as one of the centers of the "Puerto Rican problem" in New York City: the Lower East Side. Finally, the poem renders even more visible the bipolar nature of the utopian gesture—the manner in which hope and failure coexist in utopian thinking.

Halberstam's reflections on failure help to bridge the gap between the two texts, showing the value of the utopian imaginary despite its failure to be realized, as well as suggesting the manner in which queer utopianism opens up to a wider utopianism of the abject body. Whereas Muñoz spends less time dwelling on the negativity implicit in utopian thinking in *Cruising Utopia,* emphasizing instead the futurity envisioned in queer art, in *The Queer Art of Failure* Halberstam embraces both the positivity and the negativity of queerness and follows how both trajectories are realized, sometimes simultaneously. When analyzing the seascapes painted by artist Judie Bamber in 2004, he engages explicitly with Muñoz's conception of queer futurity, and questions whether or not it is possible to move beyond the boundaries of the social to realize that "something missing" which lies beyond:

For [Bamber] the thematics of losing and failure appear within visuality itself as a line or threshold beyond which you cannot see, a horizon that marks the place of the failure of vision and visibility itself. While José E. Muñoz casts queerness as a kind of horizon for political aspiration [...], Bamber's horizons remind that possibility and disappointment live side by side. (Halberstam 2011, 105)

The link between failure and the abject pervades Halberstam's book. Especially in chapter three—also titled "The Queer Art of Failure"—he identifies a series of subject positions that are generally associated with failure and negativity in dominant social discourse, which include not only queer subjects, but also those that suffer abjection under the rubrics of race, class, and colonial/postcolonial status. He describes these histories of failure that are abjected from dominant discourse as, "a hidden history of pessimism, a history moreover that lies quietly beyond every story of success" (2011, 88), and notes that these narratives display a wide range of political valences—from those that forcefully gesture toward positive social alternative, to those that remain firmly grounded in the realm of negation and refusal. While suggesting that this history can be told in a number of ways, he characterizes his own narration in the following manner:

I tell it here as a tale of anticapitalist, queer struggle. I tell it also as a narrative about anticolonial struggle, the refusal of legibility, and an art of unbecoming. [...] The queer art of failure turns on the impossible, the improbable, the unlikely, the unremarkable. It quietly loses, and in losing it imagines other goals for life, for love, for art, and for being. (2011, 88)

Here, Halberstam elegantly captures the polarized trajectories that the art of abjection may follow. It is an art that is as much about illegibility and unbecoming as it is about imagining alternative social configurations, an aesthetic practice that allows hope and disappointment to cohabitate in the same space. Finally, he identifies the political force of this aesthetic practice as transcending the borders of a merely queer politics, and engaging in anticapitalist, anticolonial, and antiracist resistance.

In "A Lower East Side Poem," the Lower East Side becomes the abject staging ground for an intersectional utopian critique—a site of failure that offers a narrative of alternative social possibility. Urayoán Noel also notes the spatial importance of the Lower East Side in Piñero's work, finding in the 1980 collection *La Bodega Sold Dreams* (the only collection of poems published during Piñero's life) a "spatial poetics" that depicts the Lower East side as "a space of simultaneous lawlessness, beauty, freedom, and despair, reminiscent of William Burroughs's trope of the Interzone" (2014, 52). In Noel's analysis, the concept of the Interzone maintains a close kinship with the theory of the abject (2014, 51–9), and in the poem this space becomes a stage upon which an abject collective of "hustlers & suckers," "faggots & freaks," "dope wheelers & cocaine dealers," thieves, and junkies (Piñero 2010, 4) enacts the critique and refusal identified by Halberstam while also engaging in utopian dreaming, suggesting how a reconfiguration of the oppressive present might arise out of the abjected neighborhood. Furthermore, in this poem the simultaneity of pure negation and positive possibility reaches its apotheosis, as both poles become fully elaborated, and neither is subordinated to the other.

VI. Longing and Death in Lower East Side

The poem's lyric subject, who is identified with the recurring figure of the "junkie Christ" in other poems in *La Bodega*,[11] in a sense performs his own crucifixion within the text, as he imagines his own death, and the scattering of his ashes in the Lower East Side. However, the result here is different from the metaphorical crucifixion that takes place in "¡Jum!" Whereas in Sánchez's story the abject body is violently sacrificed in order to reify the borders of the heteronormative nation, here we see a radical opening to the abject that occurs in the moment of death. The poem begins as the speaker recites his last will and testament:

> Just once before I die
> I want to climb up on a
> tenement sky
> to dream my lungs out till
> I cry
> and scatter my ashes thru
> the Lower East Side (2010, 4)

This first stanza locates the tenement sky as a horizon of possibility similar to that which Halberstam finds in Bamber's paintings. The negative ideal of the Lower East Side tenement as a site of poverty maintains its pejorative connotation, but nevertheless becomes the horizon that the speaker must approach ("climb up on") in order to engage in the act of dreaming. The phrasing of "dreaming the lungs out" locates the dream imaginary within the breath and the poetic word of the lyric "I," while simultaneously showing how dreaming draws the speaker outward, beyond this horizon/limit of the tenement rooftop, and beyond the limits of his own corporeal boundaries, leaving only his ashes to be scattered through the streets.

Julia Kristeva refers to death and the corpse that represents it as "the utmost of abjection" (1982, 4), and the imagined crossing of the final boundary of life and death produces a dual scattering of the lyric subject: his voice/ dream outwards, beyond the body, and his material remains into the Lower East Side. Yet, in keeping with the tendency that I have noted in Piñero's work, the utopian motion here does not lie in movement *away* from the abject—neither the material residue of the ashes, nor the marginalized neighborhood and its inhabitants—toward the paradisiacal, salvific vision of the hereafter invoked by the archetype of the sky. Rather the dreaming voice of the disarticulated lyric subject leaves the body to follow the ashes, and disperse *within* the abject space depicted in the poem. In other words, the lyric "I" opens its borders to the abject Others of the Lower East Side, and this act of radical opening to form community within the abject space is the essence of the speaker's utopian dream.

> The scene of the Lower East Side is set as:
> Jews and Gentiles...bums and men
> of style...run away child
> police shooting wild...
> mother's futile wails...pushers
> making sails...dope wheelers
> & cocaine dealers...smoking pot
> streets are hot & feed off those who bleed to death... (2010, 4)

Piñero's use of ellipses in this stanza evokes a sense of fluidity, as the subjects that populate the abject space bleed into one another, and into the scene itself. This intersubjective and spatial porosity mirrors the poetic speaker's own act of scattering and border opening, as the lyric voice, the ashes, the abject subjects, and the neighborhood itself intermingle to form a collectivity that coalesces into a feeling of community and home. Piñero writes:

> I am [...]
> a dweller of prison time
> a cancer of Rockefeller's ghettocide
> this concrete tomb is my home. (2010, 5)

"Rockefeller's ghettocide" refers to the Rockefeller Laws passed in New York in 1973—which imposed extraordinarily heavy sentences for nonviolent drug offenses and served as a harbinger of the mass incarceration movement—and the concept of "ghettocide" speaks to the intersections of race and class that render abject the subjects within the poem, and the space that they inhabit as one of social and material death. Nevertheless, equating the figure of the tomb with that of the home identifies the abject space as one of solace and refuge, to which the speaker relates with care and longing, in which a community that remains open to abject otherness rather than closing off from it becomes not only possible, but desirable.

The sense of finding home among an impossible collective, defined by porous borders, intersubjective blending, and opening to the abject perdures through the poem's last stanza, as the speaker re-states his preference for abject scattering over the fixity of a final resting place:

> I don't wanna be buried in Puerto Rico
> I don't wanna rest in long island cemetery
> I wanna be near the stabbing shooting
> gambling fighting & unnatural dying
> & new birth crying
> so please when I die...
> don't take me far away
> keep me near by
> take my ashes and scatter them thru out
> the Lower East Side... (2010, 5)

In these verses, there is no moment of refusal or repudiation that re-institutes a hierarchical structure of abjection, as occurs between Paco and Cupcakes. Rather, the boundaries that separate the speaker from the abject disappear altogether, as his ashes become subject to perpetual dispersal in the Lower East Side streets. Perhaps the "runaway child" is the key figure of the poem, as the lyric subject in the last stanza embodies the unruly, runaway children of the diaspora that reject both the idealized return to the island homeland—coming to "rest" both literally and metaphorically in Puerto Rico—and the confines of Long Island Cemetery which, in Pedro Pietri's earlier "Puerto

Rican Obituary," is emblematic of the assimilationist dreams of the Puerto Rican working class—their daily social death from racist, capitalist, and neocolonial oppression that becomes material death in the "long ride/ from Spanish Harlem/ to long island cemetery [sic]" (Pietri 2020).[12] Indeed, the speaker seems to reject the proposition of a stable identity altogether, as the scattering of the ashes, confusion of subjective boundaries, and the refusal to cohere within confines of a stable lyric "I" imply a choice for abject dispersal in the "stabbing shooting/ gambling fighting & unnatural dying/ & new birth crying" of the Lower East Side and, by extension, the diaspora. And what is the "new birth crying" that appears in the abject scene? Is it the possibility of a new sociality, of a new collectivity formed by and within the abject bodies of the Puerto Rican diaspora? Is it a proposition that by relaxing our borders and opening to the abject body, that we can envision a new utopia that is borderless, open to all and excluding none? In keeping with Bloch and Adorno's prohibition against naming the positive utopia, the poem merely suggests, and does not say. Rather, the speaker's words evanesce into the white horizon of the page's margin, as the final ellipsis gestures toward the unspeakable. The reader is left with only the sense of promise within the violence and suffering described in the poem—that perhaps by resisting the urge to recoil, we may find unthinkable possibility in opening to the abject.

Nevertheless, as our theoretical survey has shown, utopian promise always comes with the possibility of disappointment, and the vexing bipolarity of the utopian gesture—its positive possibility and its present negation—seems to reach its climax in Piñero's gesture of embedding a utopian vision within the speaker's fantasy of death. In his conversation with Bloch, Adorno remarks that without a consciousness of death, a concept of utopia cannot exist:

To be sure, I believe that without the notion of an unfettered life, freed from death, the idea of utopia, the idea of *the* utopia, *cannot* even be thought at all. [...] Wherever this is not included, where the threshold of death is not at the same time considered, there can actually be no utopia. And it seems to me that this has very heavy consequences for the theory of knowledge about utopia—if I may put it crassly: One cannot cast a picture of utopia in a positive manner. Every attempt to describe or portray utopia in a simple way, i.e., it will be like this, would be an attempt to avoid the antinomy of death and to speak about the elimination of death as if death did not exist. (1988, 10)

Here, Adorno makes the case that death is itself a condition for utopia. It is the paradigmatic example of the negativity through which, and only through which, utopia can be conceived—the boundary that must be crossed in order to get at that which is missing.

The Lower East Side in Piñero's poem presents a series of thresholds that all figuratively or literally invoke the experience of death: the scattering of the ashes of the lyric subject; the speaker's crossing of the horizon of the tenement sky and the confines of his own body, which sends the boundless subject outwards into the abject collective; and finally the geographic space of the Lower East Side itself, which marks the boundary of social death that is the lived experience of abjection. As such, the Lower East Side signifies in the text as the essence of a utopian double sign, revealing the capitalist, colonialist, and racist systems that enact the abjection of Puerto Ricans in late twentieth-century New York, while also gesturing beyond this reality to an ideal of community and hope within violence and death. Yet in the poem, as within *Short Eyes*, the moment of definitive arrival at utopia is withheld. We are left instead within the frozen moment of ellipsis, of gesture beyond the threshold of death to something inaccessible that cannot be realized at the present time. As such, in Piñero's poem the Lower East Side becomes the point at which the antinomies of death and utopia coincide, allowing utopian possibility and abject suffering to coexist, and speaking to the promise of utopia that has yet to arrive, and may never come.

VII. Utopian Failures

Perhaps utopia is always about failure. Certainly, Bloch, Adorno, Muñoz, and Halberstam all recognize the negativity of the not-yet here, and its continual deferral to another time and place. The positive Nuyorican utopias from which I distinguish Piñero's abject utopianism do not escape this fate. The Young Lords' rapid ascension onto the national stage in 1969 was followed by an equally precipitous decline—internal destabilization by the FBI's COINTLEPRO program, internecine disputes, and a hard turn toward authoritarianism left the group all but finished as a political organization by 1976 (Fernández 2020). Whereas CHARAS was quite successful during the 1970s in working with local government and non-profit entities to raise the quality of life of the Lower East Side community, by the 1980s governmental and economic tides had turned, and activist groups were locked in an increasingly losing battle with the forces of gentrification (Mele 2000, 220–310; Bagchee 2018, 138–47). Re-appropriated lots were sold to developers, community gardens were bulldozed (Bagchee 2018, 138–7), and the displacement of the Puerto Rican community began in earnest, as the Lower East Side Latinx population dropped by 14.5 percent from 1980 to 1990 (Mele 2000, 250). The socialist revolution did not come to pass, the triumphant national return never materialized, Puerto Rico remains a colony, and although Puerto Rican literature in the United States continues its legacy of political resistance to the shifting conditions of the diaspora (Noel 2014), the utopian dreams of the first generation of Nuyorican writers and activists largely seem to have failed. Perhaps Piñero's most powerful contribution to a conversation about failed Nuyorican utopias is his manner of intimating that within each site of failure there lies a subtle promise. His work suggests that perhaps by opening further, by delving *in* to the scenes of abject failure that birthed the utopian imaginaries listed above, we might recover an even more radical utopia, one that finds utopian promise in queerness, in scattering, in diaspora, and in rendering porous the borders that define normativity and exclude its abject opposite.

Or perhaps not. Regardless, impelled toward an alternative future by hope and inscribed in the present by disappointment, both *Short Eyes* and "A Lower East Side Poem" locate the site of abject failure as a propitious staging ground for utopia. Whether in the prison bathroom or on the streets of the Lower East Side, Piñero shows how the radical negativity of the socially abject simultaneously criticizes the present and gestures toward alternative possibility—how the abject outside of criminals, junkies, queers, gangmembers, the homeless, and the welfare-dependent may become a source of hope and renewal. Consequently, his writing engages in a project that is more radical than the positive utopian idealism of his contemporaries: the project of refusing social legibility, of finding within the abject a form of social death that, by means of its radical negativity, indicates something missing that lies beyond the porous boundaries of the present social order. These utopian gestures not only point toward queer transformations of hegemonic power dynamics, as in *Short Eyes*, but also toward an abject collective that challenges anticolonial, anticapitalist, and antiracist imaginaries, as is seen in "A Lower East Side Poem." By revealing the disruptive political possibility that is dormant within the abject, Piñero unveils the utopian promise that undergirds its negativity, gesturing toward the unfathomable potential of the not-yet-here. Similarly, by highlighting the oppression, violence, and, indeed, death that also mark the abject, he simultaneously emphasizes the postponement of the utopian promise, and the suffering that marks its distance from the present. Thus, *Short Eyes* and "A Lower East Side Poem" perform the full paradox embedded in the contradiction of utopian longing alluded to by Bloch and Adorno: locating death within utopia, and disappointment within hope. Nevertheless, the texts continue to insist on abject failure, on the critique that this failure offers, and on the vague and murky hope that we might someday, with enough persistence, fail our way into utopia.

NOTES

[1] The conceptualization of abjection that I deploy in this essay is a synthesis of the work of a wide number of theorists and cultural critics. I define abjection in the broadest of terms as a psychic phenomenon of *excluding threatening otherness* that functions on both an individual and a sociocultural level. For Julia Kristeva, who is the first to provide a rigorous theory of abjection in *Powers of Horror* (1982), the abject represents the contamination of the self by otherness, a certain confusion of subjective boundaries in which the self can no longer clearly distinguish itself from the other, which in turn threatens the subject with the possibility of its own dissolution and annihilation. Following Kristeva, abjection is, in the most general terms, the violent exclusion of otherness by which the subject establishes its more or less stable borders. Judith Butler uses abjection in more explicitly social context in *Bodies that Matter* (1993), arguing that gender binaries and heteronormativity are produced through the repudiation and exclusion of queer expressions of gender and sexuality, which, in essence, blur the boundaries of the male-female gender binary and disrupt the play of opposites upon which heterosexual attraction and traditional gender roles rely. Due to the ambiguity and confusion that they introduce into heteronormative social structures, queer bodies become abject in the dominant cultural imaginary, and are thus subjected to stigmatization, marginalization, and violence. David Sibley, in *Geographies of Exclusion* (1995), demonstrates how the mechanics of social exclusion follow the oppressive logic of abjection with respect not only to queer groups, but also to a wide variety of intersecting social bodies (see especially chapters 1 and 2). In Sibley's elaboration of abjection as social exclusion, any group that deviates from dominant social norms—based in race, class, sexuality, religion, immigration status, etc.—may be seen from the dominant perspective as a contaminating form of otherness, in other words, as introducing a form of social heterogeneity that threatens to destabilize existing social structures. Additionally, Arnaldo Cruz-Malavé (1995; 1997), whose work I will engage with extensively in this essay, sees colonialism as a form of abjection that Puerto Rican subjects continue to suffer throughout the twentieth century. All of these critical perspectives come to bear on understanding the abjection of Puerto Ricans in New York during the period in which Piñero is writing. The diaspora that followed Operation Bootstrap brings Puerto Ricans to the city as a racialized, colonized Other, as immigrants despite their status as American citizens, and as members of a subordinated working class to be mined for cheap labor. All of these intersecting forces of abjection factor into the creation of Puerto Ricans as abject bodies within the sociocultural cityscape of New York, and it is this abjection that Piñero explores in his writing.

[2] I use the term "Lower East Side" and not "Loisaida" as the neighborhood commonly came to be known among its Puerto Rican residents, out of a desire to maintain consistency with Piñero's work, in which the former name appears more frequently.

[3] The scope of this essay is limited to the historical context of the first generation of Nuyorican writers, which roughly spans the late 1960s to the mid-1980s, and is not meant

to be a prescriptive evaluation of a static relationship between abjection, queerness, and utopianism in later generations of Puerto Rican writers in the US. Nevertheless, Noel (2014, 123-63) notes a recurring preoccupation with both the abject and the utopian in Puerto Rican poets of the slam era, observing both continuity and deviation from earlier Nuyorican traditions, and a larger study of abjection and utopianism across generations of Puerto Rican writers in the US is undoubtedly an area of critical inquiry worth pursuing.

⁴ See Fernández (2020) for an in-depth historical accounting of the actions taken by the Young Lords related to environmental racism, childhood lead poisoning, healthcare discrimination, prison reform and prisoner rights, and the various social programs that the group offered through its occupation of the First Spanish United Methodist Church in East Harlem.

⁵ While the Young Lords' nationalist program was quite ahead of its time in its effort to dismantle patriarchy within its leadership (Fernández 2020, 233–70) and in its rejection of "machismo and male chauvinism" in its party platform (Young Lords 2010, 12), Fernández nevertheless notes that "the issue of gender equality remained a contested terrain throughout the organization's life" (2020, 263). Similarly, although the Young Lords also showed some level of openness to queer solidarity— forming an unofficial "gay caucus" and offering protection to queer Puerto Rican activist Sylvia Rivera after she received death threats (Fernández 2020, 263–5)— LGBTQ issues still "remained shrouded in taboo within the organization" (Fernández 2020, 264) and the project of dismantling heteronormativity never entered meaningfully into the party's platform. Finally, a logic of abjection shows itself most clearly in the organization after its definitive turn to Maoism, when a rigid focus on ideologically purity on the part of party leadership led to authoritarianism and purges of perceived counterrevolutionary elements (Fernández 2020, 367–77).

⁶ It should be noted that Piñero does write some overtly nationalistic poems—see "La Cañonera del Mundo" (2010, 22) and "Vente conmigo" (2010, 52)—and at least one poem that communicates an empowering vision of Latinx identity —see "Obreras" (2010, 43–4). Neverthless, I claim that the overwhelming body of his work maintains an investment in staying with the abject, rather than turning away from it in order to adopt a more normative contestatory stance.

⁷ "[The] exclusionary matrix by which subjects are formed thus requires the simultaneous production of a domain of abject beings, those who are not yet 'subjects,' but who form the *constitutive outside* to the domain of the subject" (Butler 1993, 3—emphasis added)

⁸ The language that Alexander (2012) uses to diagnose the mass incarceration movement as the latest instantiation of a racial caste system in the US follows the logic of abjection invoked here. Specifically, she refers to the social exclusion of incarceration and the "shame and stigma of the 'prison label'" (2012, 17) as a means to materially disenfranchise the "undercaste" of black and brown subjects, who form "a population deemed disposable" (2012, 18), thus showing how the racialized stigma of criminality is a key mechanism in the production and regulation of abject bodies. While *Short Eyes* predates the true advent of the mass incarceration move-

ment, Fernández (2020, 305–34) notes how an oppressive carceral state in 1970s New York disproportionally affects black and brown people, and how the activism of the Black Panthers and the Young Lords foreshadows the contemporary activist response to mass incarceration.

[9] In the 1970s, Baraka also frequented the Nuyorican Poets Café, and was present at Piñero's funerary performance.

[10] The play was published before Baraka's name change, and thus appears in the References section under the name LeRoi Jones.

[11] See "Jitterbugging Jesus" (2010, 13–4) and "New York City Hard Time Blues" (2010, 40).

[12] I owe recognition of the intertextual resonance between Piñero and Pietri to Sandín (2004, 106–7).

REFERENCES

Alexander, Michelle. 2012. *The New Jim Crow: Mass Incarceration in the Age of Colorblindness*. New York: The New Press.

Algarín, Miguel. 1975. Introduction: Nuyorican Language. In *Nuyorican Poetry: An Anthology of Puerto Rican Words and Feelings*, eds. Miguel Algarín and Miguel Piñero. 9–20, New York: Morrow.

Alvarado, Leticia. 2018. *Abject Performances: Aesthetic Strategies in Latino Cultural Production*. Durham, NC: Duke University Press.

Bagchee, Nandini. 2018. *Counter Institution: Activist Estates of the Lower East Side*. New York: Fordham University Press.

Bernstein, Lee. 2010. *America is the Prison: Arts and Politics in Prison in the 1970s*. Chapel Hill: University of North Carolina Press.

Bloch, Ernst and Theodor W. Adorno. 1988. Something's Missing: A Discussion between Ernst Bloch and Theodor W. Adorno on the Contradictions of Utopian Longing. In *The Utopian Function of Art and Literature*, translated by Jack Zipes and Frank Mecklenburg. 1–17. Cambridge, MA: MIT Press.

Bratt, Benjamin. 2002. Unspoiled Bratt. Interview by Alonso Duralde. *The Advocate* 5 March, 41–6.

Butler, Judith. 1993. *Bodies That Matter: On the Discursive Limits of Sex*. New York: Routledge.

Campa, Román de la. 1998. En la utopía redentora del lenguaje: Pedro Pietri y Miguel Algarín. *The Americas Review* 16(2), 49-67.

Cruz-Malavé, Arnaldo. 1995. Toward an Art of Transvestism: Colonialism and Homosexuality in Puerto Rican Literature. In *¿Entiendes? Queer Readings, Hispanic Writings*, eds Paul Julian Smith and Emilie L. Bergmann 137–67, Durham, NC: Duke University Press.

_____. 1997. 'What a Tangled Web!': Masculinidad, abyección y la fundación de la literatura puertorriqueña en los Estados Unidos. *Revista de Crítica Literaria Latinoamericana* 23(45), 327–40.

Esterrich, Carmelo. 1998. Home and the Ruins of Language: Victor Hernández Cruz and Miguel Algarín's Nuyorican Poetry. *MELUS* 23(3), 43–56.

Fernández, Johanna. 2020. *The Young Lords: A Radical History*. Chapel Hill: University of North Carolina Press.

Halberstam, Judith. 2011. *The Queer Art of Failure*. Durham, NC: Duke University Press.

Halberstam, Jack and Tavia Nyong'o. 2018. Introduction: Theory in the Wild. *South Atlantic Quarterly* 117(3), 453–64.

Hart, Steven. 1981. The Family: A Theatre Company Working with Prison Inmates and Ex-Inmates. Ph.D. dissertation, City University of New York.

Iglesias, Jorge. 2010. Introduction to the Drama of Miguel Piñero. In *Outlaw: The Collected Works of Miguel Piñero,* Miguel Piñero. xv–xxvi. Houston: Arte Público Press.

Jones, LeRoi. 1966. *The Toilet*. In *The Baptism & The Toilet*. 33–62. New York: Grove Press.

Kanellos, Nicolás. 2010. Introduction to the Poetry of Miguel Piñero. In *Outlaw: The Collected Works of Miguel Piñero,* Miguel Piñero. vii–xiii. Houston: Arte Público Press.

Kristeva, Julia. 1982. *Powers of Horror: An Essay on Abjection*. Translated by Leon S. Roudiez. New York: Columbia University Press.

Morales, Ed. 2002. *Living in Spanglish: The Search for Latino Identity in America*. New York: St. Martin's Press.

Mele, Christopher. 2000. *Selling the Lower East Side: Culture, Real Estate, and Resistance in New York City*. Minneapolis: University of Minnesota Press.

Moten, Fred. 2003. *In the Break: The Aesthetics of the Black Radical Tradition*. Minneapolis: University of Minnesota Press.

Mottel, Syeus. 1973. *CHARAS: The Improbable Dome Builders*. New York: Drake Publishers.

Muñoz, José Esteban. 2009. *Cruising Utopia: The Then and There of Queer Futurity*. New York: New York University Press.

Noel, Urayoán. 2014. *In Visible Movement: Nuyorican Poetry from the Sixties to Slam*. Iowa City: University of Iowa Press.

Pietri, Pedro. 2020. Puerto Rican Obituary. *Poetry Foundation*. Accessed 10 July 2020. <https://www.poetryfoundation.org/poems/58396/puerto-rican-obituary/>.

Piñero, Miguel. 2010. *Outlaw: The Collected Works of Miguel Piñero*. Houston: Arte Público Press.

Sánchez, Luis Rafael. 1984. "¡Jum!" In *En cuerpo de camisa*. 53–60. San Juan: Editorial Cultural.

Sandín, Lyn Di Iorio. 2004. *Killing Spanish: Literary Essay on Ambivalent U.S. Latino/a Identity*. New York: Palgrave Macmillan.

Scarano, Francisco A. 1993. *Puerto Rico: cinco siglos de historia*. San Juan: McGraw-Hill Interamericana.

Sibley, David. 1995. *Geographies of Exclusion: Society and Difference in the West*. New York: Routledge.

Young Lords Party 13-Point Program and Platform (Revised November 1970). 2010. In *The Young Lords: A Reader*, ed. Darrel Enck-Wanzer. 11–3. New York: New York University Press.

Nuyorican *mestizaje* or *la gran familia neorriqueña* in Piri Thomas's *Down These Mean Streets*

MARISSA L. AMBIO

ABSTRACT

In keeping with a transinsular approach, this paper proposes that the narrative of the "Great Puerto Rican Family" informs *Down These Mean Streets* (1967) and Piri's conception of race and gender. Piri's interactions with his mother and her representation throughout the novel are of central interest since she is Piri's most immediate connection to the Island. Through their conversations, Piri hears his mother's recollections of the Island, which, in turn, are appropriated and transformed by Piri in the creation of his own memories and thoughts. *Down These Mean Streets* thus rewrites the *gran familia puertorriqueña* within the U.S. context, making it, as one might propose, the *"gran familia neorriqueña."* This new rendering of a traditional literary trope offers a paradigm of the diaspora that exposes earlier misconceptions. And while not devoid of contradictions, the *gran familia neorriqueña* offers insight in approaching representations of race and gender in the novel. [Keywords: Nuyorican literature, Puerto Rican literature, Latino literature, race, *mestizaje, la gran familia puertorriqueña*]

The author (mambio@hamilton.edu) is Assistant Professor of Hispanic Studies at Hamilton College and specializes in U.S. Latinx literary and cultural production from the 19th century to the present. She has expertise in Cuban émigré periodicals of the Ten Years War (1868-1878) with a focus on nation, transnationalism, and visual culture. Her research on contemporary U.S. Latinx literature explores race, gender, sound studies, and ChYA Literature.

In the autobiographical bildungsroman *Down These Mean Streets* (1967), Piri Thomas recounts the struggle to reconcile his cultural identity, largely informed by his Puerto Rican family, with his racial one, defined on New York's city streets. In the early scenes, Piri repeatedly rejects his identification as a black man, asserting instead his Puerto Rican heritage. Whether a show of ethnic pride or to ensure superior placement on the U.S. ethno-racial hierarchy, Piri's claim to his Puerto Rican heritage functions as a denial of blackness. Yet, with a light-skinned mother and dark-skinned father, Piri and his four siblings are of varying skin tones and phenotypes. Piri thus finds that the multiracial make-up of his family belies the notion of a Puerto Rican cultural identity exclusive of blacks, and is also at odds with the U.S. racial binary. In an attempt to resolve the competing notions of Puerto Rican and U.S. racial paradigms, Piri journeys down South where he explores the origins of the U.S. racial divide.

Piri's ultimate conception of racial identity, however, appears problematic:

*Really, God, run it to me. Are we really all in Your image? I mean, so many different kinds of us, all colors, all shapes? Hey, Baby, that's it. You look like us, all right, but only in the – what's the word? – in the "psyche" – the breath, life, soul, spirit....*Some souls are worse than others, but they all look the same; they gotta, 'cause nobody's seen them, so nobody can say differently. The soul and spirit is blood with blue eyes, dark skin, and curly hair...We're all the same in our souls and spirits and there's nobody better than anybody else, only just maybe better off. (Thomas 1967, 299)

Piri's conclusion in the final chapters seems to undermine the ethno-racial conflict that fuels the entire narrative by dismissing physical appearance. For Piri, one's identity is foremost based on the soul or spirit, which defies visual distinction because "nobody's seen them" (Thomas 1967, 299). Still, Piri does not disregard physical traits entirely. Instead, he reconfigures skin tones and phenotypes, social hierarchies and religious precepts, to create something new. Rather than describe a physical being in God's image, Piri suggests that God resembles the diversity of humankind. This divine and human spirit is also phenotypically white with blue eyes, of dark skin, and has wavy locks of hair that symbolically engulf all of humanity. Thus, Piri collapses Puerto Rican and U.S. racial hierarchies in favor of a racial utopia based on a belief system that offers little redress of social inequities. According to Lisa Sánchez-González (2001, 118), this appeal to Christianity is one of the many escapes of which Piri avails himself in trying to contend with an identity crisis he is unable to resolve. Marta Caminero-Santangelo, on the other hand, argues that Piri resolves his dilemma earlier in the narrative when he considers himself a "Puerto Rican black," thereby reconciling the two identities. Piri's self-identification in this instance not only discredits the Puerto Rican denial of blackness, it is also a step toward pan-ethnic solidarity between African-Americans and Puerto Ricans. According to Caminero-Santangelo, the scene, "less than one-third from the end of the book, for all practical purposes resolves this particular identity crisis" (2007, 67).

This study proposes that Piri's turn to religion is not an escape from his racial dilemma, nor is his final resolution the coalescence of black and Puerto Rican identities. Instead, Piri engages *la gran familia puertorriqueña* and the figure of the *jíbaro* to formulate his final articulation of race.[1] More specifically, Piri contests nationalist ideals that advocate the harmonious coexistence of Puerto Rico's racially diverse population while promoting racial and cultural whitening. Piri, thus, exposes the racial myth of Puerto Rican nationalist discourse and rewrites the gran familia puertorriqueña within the U.S. context. As such, *Down These Mean Streets* is an example of Puerto Rico's transinsular literature. This reading of the novel offers an alternate conception of race inclusive of black identity. It also evinces the integral role of Piri's mother in this process for she conveys Puerto Rico's national discourse. Despite her ostensibly marginal character, Piri's mother exerts significant influence on his views on race, which ultimately correspond to a form of *mestizaje*.[2]

The assertion that *Down These Mean Streets* belongs to a transinsular Puerto Rican literary tradition evokes an ongoing debate regarding literary genealogies. Given the socio-historical context of the civil rights era in which Thomas's autobiography emerged, as well as a conception of Puerto Rican identity that denies blackness, *Down These Mean Streets* was originally considered a black nationalist novel and not recognized by historians and sociologists as a Puerto Rican text until the 1980s (Sosa-Velasco 2009, 288). The novel has long since been considered a foundational work of the Nuyorican movement, yet its incorporation in the U.S. Latinx literary canon has also excluded it from the Puerto Rican literary tradition.[3] Puerto Rican literati on the Island tend to put forth a bifurcated conception of Puerto Rican letters that differentiates the literature produced on the Island from U.S. Puerto Rican literature based on linguistic, thematic, discursive, and formal differences (Acosta-Belén 1992, 980–1). The use of English rather than Spanish is but one of the criteria used to distinguish U.S. Puerto Rican literature from that of the Island. The argument for mutual exclusivity, however, goes beyond mere differences in attributes. For some Puerto Rican literati, the distinct features of Puerto Rican diasporic literature are indicative of a Nuyorican identity crisis or a deficiency in Puerto Rican culture, both of which "weaken" notions of Puerto Rican identity (Acosta-Belén 1992, 980–1). But *Down These Mean Streets* treats one of Puerto Rico's most prominent literary and political nationalist tropes and challenges the view that Puerto Rican letters are exclusive of U.S. Puerto Rican literary production, suggesting a more expansive, or transinsular,[4] approach. This study thus is aligned with the work of critics such as Jorge Duany, Edna Acosta-Belén, and Marisel Moreno, who assert that Puerto Rican identity and its literary and cultural production extend beyond geographical borders.

In Down These Mean Streets *the tenets of la gran familia are passed down through actions or conversations between family members, and either uphold or dismantle the paradigm.*

The schism between Puerto Rican and U.S. literatures has hindered scholarly study of subjects such as la gran familia puertorriqueña in diaspora literature (Moreno 2010, 85). In *Family Matters* (2012), Moreno examines the literature of Puerto Rican women writers on the Island and in the U.S. to demonstrate how they debunk the gran familia narrative (Moreno 2012, 19). She argues that since the notion of la gran familia circulated on the Island in the 1930s and during the Great Migration, the myth was not only prevalent in Puerto Rico but also "remained a cornerstone of Puerto Rican identity among the diaspora, as the narratives of U.S. Puerto Rican authors illustrate" (Moreno 2010, 86). In *Down These Mean Streets* the tenets of la gran familia are passed down through actions or conversations between family members, and either uphold or dismantle the paradigm. At the same time, Piri is confronted by the U.S. racial discourse as he navigates the social and geographic spaces of New York City, suburban Long Island, and the South. As such, Piri considers his experiences in- and outside of the home to formulate his ideas of race and, ultimately, transform the Puerto Rican nationalist trope.

La gran familia puertorriqueña, along with the figure of the jíbaro, were promoted by the *generación del treinta* as a strategy to assert Puerto Rican identity in response to encroaching U.S. imperialism (Moreno 2010, 77). The origins of the latter are traced to Manuel A. Alonso's *El jíbaro* (1845), a collection of *costumbrista* sketches that depict characteristics, customs, and manners of speech of the jíbaro, whose identity had been shaped by the creole elite since the end of the eighteenth century. This jíbaro peasant inhabited remote areas of the countryside with rather loose connections to a greater community, making his lifestyle nomadic and isolationist. To survive, the jíbaro depended on subsistence agriculture and was known for his bellicose nature, making him an exemplar of the "savage" native population subject to colonialism's civilizing mission (Scarano 1999, 66). By the start of the nineteenth century, Puerto Rico's creole elite advocated a liberal agenda in opposition to the political and economic interests of the Spanish crown. To signify their growing disillusionment with Spanish governance, the creole elite revalorized the jíbaro. The rural peasant was consequently elevated as a symbol of indigenous identity to assert Puerto Rican autonomy (Scarano 1999, 66). Alonso's novel is considered part of Puerto Rico's national literary tradition for its profile of the jíbaro, which was later appropriated in the twentieth century and embodied many of the values of la gran familia (Moreno 2012, 42). In addition to portraying a peaceful coexistence among Puerto Rico's racially and socio-economically diverse population, la gran familia romanticizes an agrarian Spanish past, and promotes patriarchy represented by a light-skinned benevolent father who requires the submissiveness of others to maintain his control (Moreno 2012, 17). La gran familia, thus, promotes the unity of national life, while simultaneously reinforcing hierarchies of race, culture, and gender.

Piri's is not the prototypical family of Puerto Rican lore or nationalist imagery. In fact, the multiracial profile of his parents and siblings, and their domestic life in the cold and gritty urban center, are at odds with the romanticized vision of the light-skinned jíbaro and his family who reside in the rural countryside. From the novel's opening pages, Piri's relations with both his father and his light-skinned brother, José, are particularly strained from racial tension. In the opening scene, for example, Piri is punished by his father for knocking over the toaster and a pot of coffee. In truth, his brother has caused the accident and Piri, in trying to prevent the appliance from falling from the table, spills the coffee. Piri's father, thus, unjustly beats Piri for an unintended and rather harmless blunder (Thomas 1967, 3-4).

Richard Perez (2007, 96) interprets the scene as exteriorization based on Slajov Žižek's hermeneutic emphasis on "material externality," whereby objects take on unconscious and ideological meaning. Read from this vantage, the toaster which darkens bread and the coffee pot filled with black liquid both represent the containment of blackness. To further restrict this blackness, the appliances are then carefully placed on the kitchen table and suggest the circumscription of blackness within society at large. The spilling of the coffee, Perez argues, represents displacement and an excess of blackness, which Piri's father seeks to redress by disciplining his son. In other words, punishment is meant to maintain the dominant narrative and suppress blackness. In keeping with Perez's argument, one might suggest that the father's decision to beat Piri alludes to the system of slavery established for those same ends.

The actions of Piri's father evince that he struggles with his own racial identity as an Afro-Puerto Rican. He chooses Piri as the target of reprimand not for what he has done but for his skin color, which is the same as his. This dynamic continuously plays out between Piri and his father since the former wonders why he and his father are always "on the outs," a condition which Piri attributes to his being the darkest skinned one in the family (Thomas 1967, 22). Piri's father, in this scene and others, is the antithesis of the benevolent patriarch of la gran familia for his discriminatory treatment of Piri. The proposed harmony of a multiracial society is further undermined since neither Piri nor his father can get along. As such, discord in the Thomas family not only arises between light- and dark-skinned family members, but also between those who share the same identity. That Piri claims he "hates" his father and light-skinned siblings on more than one occasion makes the lack of harmonious social relations even more disturbing since the animosity within the Thomas household signals the dissolution of the family itself (Thomas 1967, 2, 121, 146).

In a subsequent altercation between Piri and José the tenets of the gran familia are explicitly revealed and familial bonds are, indeed, tested. While in the bathroom,

José denies Piri's claims of blackness and insists on the family's Puerto Rican heritage, which extolls whiteness. Yet, this narrative only applies to Piri's brother who, in addition to having light skin, has nearly blonde hair, blue eyes, and a straight nose (Thomas 1967, 145). When questioned about the dark complexion of Piri and their father, José attributes these non-white features to their "Indian" lineage (Thomas 1967, 144). Thus, José conveys the sentiment of la gran familia by denying Puerto Rico's African ancestry and appealing to either phenotypical evidence of European descent, or to indigenous genealogy when white features are absent. In both cases, European and indigenous lineage are used to erase blackness.[5]

The intimacy of the setting, however, suggests that the problem of racial identity is also tied to gender. Given that the bathroom is typically a private space reserved for the individual, José's demand that Piri share the bathroom transforms the space into a communal one based on their mutual identification as men. Yet José's engagement in what is presumably a universal act among men complicates the notion of a shared masculine identity. As Piri watches José urinate, he is triggered by the uneasy confluence of race and gender. For Piri, their anatomical similarities are undermined by their epidermal differences: "I looked at my brother. *Even his peter's white,* I thought, *just like James's. Only ones got black peters is Poppa and me, and Poppa acts like his is white, too*" (Thomas 1967, 142).

The tension between brothers quickly escalates when Piri informs José of his plans to travel to the South. Piri explains the purpose is to witness the racism against blacks in an attempt to gain a deeper understanding of his own plight. Despite repeatedly asserting his (and his brother's) black identity, Piri fails to convince José and he starts a fist fight, evincing his frustration with the inability of words to resolve his dilemma. The physical altercation between the brothers suggests there are other facets of Piri's identity at stake in addition to race and gender. Piri's assertion of black identity, at this point, explicitly raises the question of his legitimacy as a family member:

"Like I said, man, you can be a nigger if you want to," he [José] said..." I don't know how you come to be my brother, but I love you like one. I've busted my ass, both me and James, trying to explain to people how come you so dark and how come your hair is so curly an'-... I said, "You and James had to make excuses for me? Like for me being un *Negrito*?" I looked at the paddy in front of me. "Who to?" I said. "Paddies?" (1967, 146)

José's acquiescence, dismissive as it is, may be the closest Piri gets to having his brother acknowledge his black identity. Yet, José's remark is quickly followed by his disassociation from Piri, whom he loves "like" a brother. The statement implies that José, and perhaps the other Thomas siblings, are not related to Piri at all, in which case they would not share Piri's racial profile. José's disavowal of Piri denies the notion of la gran familia, demonstrating that interracial fraternal ties are scrutinized and difficult to sustain in the U.S. That José "busted my [his] ass" defending Piri, however, demonstrates the utter ambivalence with which he looks upon his brother, for in this case José acknowledges and even protects his fraternal link to Piri. Metaphorically, José's comment foreshadows the physical violence between the brothers, which shifts the focus to masculinity.

Since Piri fails to convince José of his black identity, he turns to the other set of codes that he lives by: he is un hombre who must have—and maintain—corazón. In other words, for Piri, there are no words to resolve his contested racial identity.

For Piri, being *un hombre* means having *corazón* and *cara-palo*, both of which are performative measures he develops on the streets. Arnaldo Cruz-Malavé (2012, 8) argues that Piri utilizes these masculine codes as a way to compensate for his dispossessed state. Both corazón and cara-palo are rooted in machismo, an excessive or exaggerated display of masculinity in order to exert dominance. To have corazón is a show of courage when confronted with violence or pressure that often takes the form of physical aggression. Cara-palo is to have a "wooden face," a cara de palo, to control and obfuscate emotions that could indicate weakness. In addition to having corazón and cara-palo, Piri's masculinity also rests on other acts that establish his dominance. Thus, when José speaks of the altercations he endured on behalf of his brother's racial identity, Piri's masculinity is threatened on two counts. For one, Piri's absence from the scene precludes his ability to assert his masculinity through a show of corazón or cara-palo. Moreover, José's defense further emasculates Piri since he acts in lieu of his brother. José effectively displaces Piri and then subordinates him by a show of corazón in Piri's stead. That José defends Piri, presumably to whites, also reinforces racial hierarchies. As a white Puerto Rican, José acts as intermediary between the "paddies" and his black brother.

The arguments between Piri and his brother, as well as José's altercation with the "paddies," center on Piri's contested ethno-racial identity, but they ultimately play out within the conventions of masculinity. On the one hand, Piri's physical and violent response may function as a means to reassert his masculinity over his brother. But it also is a reaction to the frustration that results from an ineffectual argument. Since Piri fails to convince José of his black identity, he turns to the other set of codes that he lives by: he is un hombre who must have—and maintain—corazón. In other words, for Piri, there are no words to resolve his contested racial identity. Instead, the struggle for race is displaced in the reassertion of masculinity through traditional codes, particularly physical violence, to recover and secure his placement at the apex of the masculine hierarchy. In this scene, both racial and masculine identities are destabilized, with the latter becoming a secondary site of conflict. And while Piri can reaffirm his masculinity through performance, there is no performance, no language, to which he can appeal to articulate his racial identity without invoking other subjectivities, such as culture or nationality, which prove equally vexing.

This reading of the altercation between Piri and José Piri's speaks to discussions about the intersectionality of race and gender addressed by Marta E. Sánchez and Arnaldo Cruz-Malavé. Sánchez (2006, 48) proposes that anxieties produced by the destabilization of race are displaced in the reinforcement of traditional gender hierarchies. She focuses, however, on Piri's subjugation of women in sexual acts, rather than on the creation of hierarchies among men, and views masculinity as a more stable site than race. Cruz-Malavé (2018, 9) proposes a similar kind of displacement wherein abjection is mollified, or ostensibly resolved, through the creation of analogous conditions of abjection. As such, the victim projects their abject status onto a more vulnerable other (Cruz-Malavé 2018, 9).

Any productive discussions Piri appears to have about race transpire among peers outside of his family. They are, like Piri, young black or mulatto men. Take, for example, Brew, who represents the novel's "African-American male consciousness" (Sánchez-González 2001, 116). When Piri attempts to differentiate between Puerto Rican and African-American identities, Brew insists that culture is subordinate to race since identity is externally imposed and based foremost on skin color, regardless of ethnicity or nationality. Throughout their conversation, Piri maintains his claim to Puerto Rican identity, but slowly begins to acquiesce. He goes on to make an analogous argument that subordinates economic status to race and, as such, begins to consider skin color the primary determinant of one's identity. Piri, ultimately, disregards this line of thinking, but not before modifying it the way he sees fit and journeying down South to garner a deeper understanding of the U.S. racism that informs Brew's perception. Piri's critical perspective and his consideration of alternate modes of thinking characterize his encounters throughout his trip with Brew, including their discussion with Gerald Allen West, a man of mixed racial descent from Pennsylvania.

At this point in their travels, Piri and Brew are in Norfolk, where they meet Gerald Allen West, and initiate a conversation about biological conceptions of race. West's rejection of racial paradigms is ostensibly radical, yet his stance is quite conservative (Caminero-Santangelo 2007, 54). Whereas West asserts self-identification as opposed to social constructs that impose identity, he does so to obtain greater prominence within the existing racial hierarchy. Moreover, he validates the premise of the one-drop rule by suggesting its inversion such that one could also claim to be white if they had white ancestry. West's approach is a counter-narrative, yet Piri recognizes: "Gerald had problems something like mine. Except that he was a Negro trying to make Puerto Rican and I was Puerto Rican trying to make Negro" (Thomas 1967, 177). Piri sees West's approach as akin to his own and comes to realize its limitations. He recognizes that by "making it" Gerald seeks to achieve social mobility by manipulating the existing racial hierarchy. Gerald's claim to self-identify thus challenges social norms that subjugate him to biological categorization, but his appeal to agency only serves to deny his black lineage and ensure the privilege that comes with whiteness (Caminero-Santangelo 2007, 64-5). Despite identifying with Gerald, Piri is not entirely convinced, finding it "hard to hate a guy that was hung up on the two sticks that were so much like mine" (Thomas 1967, 178).[6]

When conversation fails to resolve his racial quandary, Piri turns to performative masculinity once again, and the heated debate with Gerald ends with Piri and Brew shifting their attention to having sex with the "broads" at the bar. Through this assertion of masculinity, Piri reaches a conclusion: "pussy's the same in every color" (Thomas 1967, 178). Piri's subordination of racial issues to gender, however, only serves to reveal that he continues to be caught between competing and incongruous racial paradigms. Although he collapses racial hierarchies in his sexual conquest at the bar, he later seeks to have sex with a white prostitute as an act of vengeance. Although Piri rails against U.S. racial discrimination by violating miscegenation laws, he simultaneously reinforces inequities of gender by exerting male dominance (Sánchez 2006, 48; Caminero-Santangelo 2007, 64). The scene also demonstrates the fluidity of identity since Piri gains entrance to the brothel by asserting his Puerto Rican heritage. The attendant generalizes Piri's ethnicity as Latin American, which he then distorts by calling him "Spanish," making Piri, consequently, not black and able to pass. In this case, ethnicity subverts the U.S. racial binary (Thomas 1967, 187–8).

Scholars have thoroughly analyzed the aforementioned episodes, attesting to their importance in Piri's exploration of race.[7] All of them, however, are intimately tied to masculinity. Piri either resorts to physical violence and conversations with men or sexual aggression in an attempt to resolve his racial conundrum. And yet, Piri engages in discussion with women, albeit sparingly, that are equally important in shaping his notion of race. In a brief interlude, and in one of the few exchanges between Piri and his mother, the latter recalls her youth on the Island. Her reminiscence is akin to the romanticized vision of the jíbaro who inhabits the countryside. She speaks of the "quiet of the greenlands and the golden color of the morning sky, the grass wet from the *lluvia*...the *coquís* and the *pajaritos* making all the *música*" (Thomas 1967, 9). Hers is almost a biblical paradise, Moses's veritable "land of milk and honey," as Piri comes to imagine it. While the Island landscape seems Edenic, Piri questions his mother about how everyone got along and "if everyone was worth something," to which she replies: "*Bueno hijo,* you have people everywhere who, because they have more, don't remember those who have very little. But in Puerto Rico those around you share *la pobreza* with you and they love you, because only poor people can understand poor people" (Thomas 1967, 10).

Although the conversation revolves around economic status, his mother's vision is a totalizing one that applies to all who are poor, subsuming potential racial distinctions. While one might argue that Puerto Rico, like other former Spanish colonies, employed a caste system where racial profiles corresponded to socio-economic status such that those "around you" were of the same race, Torres's study on the gran familia shows that Puerto Rico's settlement and agrarian development yielded racially diverse populations within this singular economic stratum throughout the island. Along with the white jíbaro that populated the interior, there also existed a mixed-race peasant population that inhabited these areas, as well as a black yeomanry (Torres 1998, 292–3). The literary depiction of the jíbaro was also equally diverse as authors represented the figure as either black, white, *mulato* or *mestizo* (Scarano 1999, 67). What Piri's mother underscores is a sense of unity surrounding a shared condition, in this case an economic one, that incorporates and supersedes racial distinctions. This notion of harmonious racial plurality that is subsumed and erased by another dominant social condition is at the heart of la gran familia puertorriqueña. Through his mother, Piri is presented with both tenets of the Puerto Rican nationalist trope. Unlike his brother José, who only advocates whiteness, Piri learns of the harmonizing aspect of la gran familia puertorriqueña as well.

The source of confusion is not the inability to communicate per se, but rather Marcia's preconceived notions about language, race, and ethnicity that precludes recognition of Afro-Puerto Ricans.

   Piri's mother promotes other precepts that are also pertinent to his understanding of race. On more than one occasion, she turns to religious principles to quell the violence that results from racial tension. And while his mother's insistence on Christian teachings yields a sense of a harmonious racial coexistence by attempting to prevent or mitigate racist acts, it does little to address racist ideology. Her response when Piri returns home after getting into a fight shortly after the family moves to Italian East Harlem is but one example: "*Bendito,* Piri, I raise this family in [a] Christian way. Not to fight. Christ says to turn the other cheek" (Thomas 1967, 27). His mother's call for peace seeks to deter violence, but fails to acknowledge the racism Piri experiences. Piri, for his part, makes no mention that the fight was racially motivated, nor that he was attacked by a gang of Italian kids who instigated the scuffle because of his skin color. Instead, Piri claims the fight was with some kids in school because he is "new." Moreover, Piri paints himself as having the upper hand, having "whipped the living—outta two guys" (Thomas 1967, 27). His mother's adage to "turn the other cheek" is problematic for she evokes it under false pretenses, ignoring any possible racial discrimination her son has endured. She also directs Piri to restrain himself from self-defense. From her vantage, Piri is the more violent of the lot having beat up those who are seemingly weaker than him. Piri's role as the target of racial discrimination is, thus, essentially transformed into that of an aggressor.

   Nevertheless, Piri lends credence to his mother's faith to resolve racial conflict. He avoids physical altercations by ignoring provocations or running away, but learns the strategy is ineffective. Neither Rocky nor the members of his Italian gang are dissuaded from persecuting him. Unable to endure the taunting, Piri confronts his tormentors, but not before reflecting upon his mother's faith once again: "I didn't like the sounds coming out of Rocky's fat mouth. And I didn't like the sameness of the shitty grins spreading all over the boys' faces. But I thought, *No more! No more! I ain't gonna run no more.* Even so, I looked around, like for some kind of Jesus miracle to happen. I was always looking for miracles to happen" (Thomas 1967, 30). Although Piri is tempted to have corazón, he is reluctant to abandon his mother's advice and continues to long for a "Jesus miracle."

Piri's sustained interest in religion as a means to resolve his racial dilemma is expressed by the actions and dialog of the protagonist as well as by the narrative voice, which often describes events in biblical terms. Piri's fight with José, for instance, is referred to as the clash between Cain and Abel. The chapter "Babylon for the Babylonians," similar to the biblical story, intimates how a lack of communication results in dispersion. In this case, a series of misunderstandings arise between Piri and Marcia, a white girl Piri meets when he moves to Long Island. The source of confusion is not the inability to communicate *per se,* but rather Marcia's preconceived notions about language, race, and ethnicity that precludes recognition of Afro-Puerto Ricans. For Marcia, Piri's accent and skin color mark him as African-American, regardless of Piri's attempts to assert his ethnicity. In either case, Marcia's decision to politely reject Piri's advances are due to his race. Piri is unaware of Marcia's prejudice until he overhears her dehumanize him when speaking with friends. In describing Piri's invitation for her to dance, she becomes indignant: "imagine the nerve of that black thing" (Thomas 1967, 85). The town of Babylon, Long Island, eventually comes to resemble its biblical counterpart in more than just name for Piri abandons his family and returns to *El barrio* as a result of the interracial "misunderstandings" he suffers.

Piri's ongoing quest to articulate his racial identity thus is accompanied by an ongoing treatment of religion. According to William Luis, this focus on religion may be attributed to the author's rehabilitation and spiritual conversion, which was completed before he penned his autobiography. For Luis, Thomas writes *Down These Mean Streets* from a "rehabilitated point of view" (Luis 1997, 142–3). Piri's spiritual rebirth also signals the resolution of his racial dilemma, and is articulated in the narrative when he arrives at the phenotypically divine spirit representative of all humankind described earlier.

Piri's representation displays the disparate physical attributes of blue eyes, dark skin, and spirituality. These three attributes are also defining characteristics of José, Piri and his father, and his mother, respectively. The figure, thus, suggests not only the interconnectedness of humanity, but also the restoration of his own family. In this way, Piri's symbolic deity serves as a corrective to the gran familia that denies blackness; it acknowledges both black and white races and casts features of each as constituent parts of a whole, whether these parts be members of his family, fellow Puerto Ricans, or individuals that transcend the boundaries of nation yet form a community. The divine being discredits the nationalist narrative that would erase Afro-Puerto Rican identity. Despite its function in recuperating blackness, the image elides non-white identities. The dark skin of the figure may well be representative of African ancestry as Piri refers to himself as being the "darkest" in the family (Thomas 1967, 22). This reading either dismisses or conflates that "other" dark-skinned iden-tity—the indigenous—making the image less than totalizing. The omission of indig-enous referents is even more notable given that Puerto Rican conceptions of racial mixing utilize indigenous ancestry to disavow blackness (Sánchez 2006, 47–8). Thus, José is only reiterating a well-rehearsed narrative when he explains the dark skin of Piri's father as attributable to "the Indian blood in him" (Thomas 1967, 144). If there is a definitive connection between the symbolic image and indigeneity, it may not be in the representation of physical traits, but rather in Piri's act of conceptualiza-tion. As Marta E. Sánchez notes, what Piri needs to make sense of his Puerto Rican mulatto identity is "something akin to Mexican or Chicano and Chicana models of mestizaje, not U.S. constructions of racial apartheid" (Sánchez 2006, 48). Piri's sym-bolic figure is just that: a model of mestizaje.[8]

The ideology of mestizaje is principally elaborated in the work of Mexican intellectual and statesman José Vasconcelos. His *La raza cósmica: misión de la raza iberoamericana* (1925) and *Indología: una interpretación de la cultura ibero-americana* (1926) propose the convergence of races would simultaneously engender the con-solidated identities of the Mexican nation as well as Latin America (Miller 2004, 27). He envisions that a fifth race—*la raza cósmica*—would emerge over time from the coalescence of white, black, indigenous, and Asian races to yield a "super" race made up of only the desirable traits of each. At its most advanced stage, the cosmic race would then initiate a spiritual or esthetic era. Vasconcelos, thus, foregrounds his theory of race in Christianity and promotes racial mixing as a means to a spiritual end as well as the "divine mission" of Latin Americans (Miller 2004, 30).

Piri's symbolic representation, though borne of a different context, displays many of the hallmarks of Vasconcelos's raza cósmica. It is an example of interracial mixing that aims to dismantle racial disparity and appeal to spirituality, all in the name of inclusion and universality. To speak of *Down These Mean Streets* in terms of mestizaje may appear incongruous given that Vasconcelos's theory is not neces-sarily applicable to the Caribbean or to a U.S.-Puerto Rican context. In contempo-rary discourse, mestizaje is most closely associated with Mexico or the Chicano/a movement, which appropriated Vasconcelos's term in order to assert indigenous lineage. Caribbean intellectuals in the first half of the twentieth century also deemed *La raza cósmica* as ill-suited since the indigenous population of the islands had been eradicated shortly after the start of colonization and blacks made up a greater portion of non-white residents. Nonetheless, as a concept, racial mixing was of interest to Cuban and Puerto Rican intellectuals at the time of *La raza cós-mica*'s publication and subsequent circulation.[9] Consequently, Vasconcelos's work initiated an esthetic movement in the Caribbean known as *mulatez* or *mulataje* that explored distinct modes of contact between blacks and whites, and portrayed the *mulata* as the embodiment of interracial identity (Miller 2004, 46–7).[10] Cuban ethnographer Fernando Ortiz also responded to Vasconcelos's theory, calling it a "complete paradox" (Ortiz 1940, 7). In *Cuban Counterpoint: Tobacco and Sugar* (1947), Ortiz sees culture as a more appropriate approach to understanding the Cuban condition. He coined the term "transculturation" to describe a process of cultural intermingling such that each culture, when in contact, undergoes both loss and acquisition to yield a new one (Ortiz 1947, 98, 101–3). Ortiz, thus, shifts the discourse from race to culture and emphasizes process. In his well-known metaphor of the *ajiaco,* Ortiz identifies the stew's ingredients as representative of the cultures that contributed to this Cuban dish: the indigenous, Spanish, African, French, and Asian (Ortiz 1940, 5). He then describes in detail how the stew is in a continuous state of change with new ingredients constantly being added as previous ones dissolve into the broth (Ortiz 1940, 5–6). For Ortiz, there is no culminating moment of development, only continued transformation.

Piri's spiritual figure depicts miscegenation, yet its cultural significance and the process by which it was formulated is deserving of further attention. Of equal interest are the doubts and limitations scholars have expressed about Piri's spiritual rehabilitation as a solution to his racial dilemma, and about mestizaje as a viable theory to dispute racial hierarchies and exclusion. Sanchez-González, as we saw, considers Thomas's turn to spirituality an escape, and in *Hybrid Cultures* (1995), Néstor Canclini points out that hybridity, of which mestizaje is a form, may erroneously contest and reinforce notions of purity upon which racial hierarchies are based[11] (Sánchez-González 2001, 116). He argues that while the conjoining of white and indigenous races subverts hierarchical systems that would maintain them as separate and disparate groups, it also implicitly assumes that each race is pure and that they exist within a prescribed social order. Rather than conceive of *mestizaje* as the conflation of pure and disparate races or cultures, Canclini suggests that the previously existing constituent parts may themselves be considered products of hybridization, thereby undermining the premise of originary and distinct races upon which hierarchies are established (Canclini 1995, xxv, xxviii).

In keeping with Canclini's criticism, Piri's symbolic figure is informed by a syncretic belief system and la gran familia, both of which are themselves hybrid concepts. Piri's symbolic figure thus is a palimpsest of hybridity. It serves to destabilize the exclusionary practices of Puerto Rican nationalist discourse beyond the conflation of races. In addition to revising la gran familia such that it recognizes black and white identities, symbolized by dark skin and blue eyes, the figure, when mapped to Piri's family reveals the hybridity of these very features. When Piri's brother asserts that his blue eyes are proof of his exclusive white lineage, for example, Piri insists that he, José, and the other Thomas siblings are the children of an interracial union (Thomas 1967, 144). Consequently, blue eyes are not limited to nor indicative of the white race. Instead, they lose their racial specificity and represent a mixed racial ancestry, thereby emphasizing mestizaje while denying the notion of a pure race.

There is, however, one idea Muhammad shares that does resonate with Piri: "No matter a man's color or race, he has a need of dignity and he'll go anywhere, become anything, or do anything to get it – anything…"

To the extent that a process can be gleaned in the development of Piri's symbolic figure, I explore the syncretic belief system that informs it. In the chapter preceding Piri's epiphany of the mestizo figure, he recounts his experience with Islam. Along with the teaching of Muslim rituals, such as Ablution or Wudzu, Piri's mentor Muhammad also shares his racialized religious ideology. Muhammad considers Christianity the "white devil's religion" and proclaims the superiority of the Muslim people to overcome a Christianity that has been used to oppress dark-skinned people: "White man—for two thousand years you've been on us—and now we're going to be on you. We want a piece of this world and we're going to get it, even if we have to take it all away from you" (Thomas 1967, 291, 294). Muhammad thus seeks not to eradicate the system of oppression based on racial superiority by way of religion, but rather to invert it, much like Gerald West. Rather than White-Christian, he advocates for Black-Islamic dominance. Piri discontinues his brief practice of Islam, suggesting that he does not believe in its teachings or Muhammad's point of view. There is, however, one idea Muhammad shares that does resonate with Piri: "No matter a man's color or race, he has a need of dignity and he'll go anywhere, become anything, or do anything to get it – anything…" (Thomas 1967, 297). Muhammad admits certain universalities among men, regardless of race. For Piri, this universality is the spirituality of humankind; it is also the interracial solidarity among Puerto Rico's socio-economic classes his mother mentions, both of which are embodied by the symbolic figure. Piri's encounter with Islam demonstrates how he engages with distinct religious practices—first Christianity, then Islam—and selects teachings from multiple sources—his mother, Muhammad—to articulate a syncretic belief system that reflects its constituent parts.

Piri's turn to spirituality in resolving his racial dilemma may seem a contradiction in terms as the symbolic figure is both invisible and visible. It is an imperceptible soul that also underscores racial distinctions through the configuration of certain phenotypical attributes. Yet, this articulation captures the incongruities of racial discourse within and between cultures that Piri confronts throughout his journey, and exposes them. It reveals a U.S. binary confounded by ethnicity; the symbolic and harmonious coexistence of the gran familia undermined by the racial tension of the Thomas household; and the U.S. one-drop rule that does not square with mestizaje. Piri's response to his racial dilemma is the process by which he engages these racial discourses and then modifies them as he sees fit. In cultivating a Nuyorican model of mestizaje, Piri lays bare the various components or influences that informed his conception of identity. Many of these are highly reminiscent of his mother.

In an interview with Ilan Stavans, Piri speaks of how he was greatly disturbed when traveling south on a bus with his close friend, Billy. The driver, upon crossing the Mason-Dixon line, instructed all black passengers to move to the back of the bus. Despite Piri's insistence that he was Puerto Rican, and hence not black, the driver refused to recognize the distinction and demanded that Piri comply. He looked to his mother to make sense of the rage he felt and credits her for this wisdom: "There is no one in this world better than you, only maybe better off with money and so forth" (Stavans and Thomas 1996, 351). The saying is simple, yet it is strikingly similar to how Piri describes his Nuyorican model of mestizaje: "God looks like all of us... We're all the same in our souls and spirits and there's nobody better than anybody else, only just maybe better off" (Thomas 1967, 299). Rather than advocate for the inversion of racial hierarchies, Piri recognizes difference as sameness. In so doing, he undermines the discourse of racial disparity and exclusion to stress the mestizaje of humankind.

Piri's universalizing approach, rooted in mestizaje and represented by the spiritual being, would appear to be aligned with critics who see Piri's time in jail as a catalyst and conduit for his transformation into a law-abiding citizen and a "new harmonious rehabilitated and unfractured diasporic U.S. Puerto Rican and Latino ethnic subject" (Cruz-Malavé 2012, 15; Viego 2007, 3). For some, reading *Down These Mean Streets* as a novel about rehabilitation conforms to the precepts of ego psychology prevalent at the time of the novel's writing (Cruz-Malavé 2012, 14; Viego 2007, 3). Indeed, in the passage just before Piri articulates the divine figure of inclusivity, he speaks about psychology, leading him to ponder: "Maybe God is psychology, or psychology is God" (Thomas 1967, 299). In *Dead Subjects,* Antonio Viego proposes that Piri conforms to ego psychology, which advocates strategies to strengthen the subject's ego, thereby allowing the person "to adapt to the demands of some predetermined notion of 'reality'" (2007, 3). Within this framework, Piri's appeal to *mestizaje* can be seen as a strategy for responding to the imperatives of reality, which require him to define himself in preexisting cultural and ethnic terms lest he be rendered "illegible" (Viego 2007, 3). Since Piri cannot lay claim to Puerto Rican, African American, or black identity without conflict, he utilizes *mestizaje* to propose a profile that is inclusive and unifying. For Viego (2007, 4, 6), the ethnic subject's claim to wholeness and transparency, however, ultimately functions within racist discourse since it denies the subject its claim to illegibility. Since Piri's appeal to mestizaje conforms to a sense of wholeness, his articulation of the multiracial figure does not correspond to preexisting ethnic or racial terms. The image Piri describes defies U.S. racial binary paradigms and challenges Puerto Rico's racial discourse of la gran familia that erases black identity. Thus, Piri asserts a different kind of racial mixing, one that is not easily legible and might be called *Nuyorican mestizaje.*

For Cruz-Malavé, *Down These Mean Streets* articulates the instability of U.S. Puerto Rican identity as predicated on loss rather than the continued process of aggregation typical of mestizaje (Cruz-Malavé 2012, 15–6). Cruz-Malavé reminds us that change is intimately tied to loss, as well as the incorporation of the new and disparate. Ortiz's metaphor of the ajiaco recognizes the continued addition of diverse ingredients, as well as their disintegration into the broth. For Cruz-

Malavé (2012, 15–6), the sense of loss at the end of the novel is particularly acute. I propose that Piri willfully accepts this loss in the search for an alternative conceptualization of the self.

In the final chapters, Piri returns to the "mean streets" of *El Barrio* after being released from prison. While the streets may have remained the same, Piri begins to abandon cara-palo and having corazón in the creation of new measures of masculine performativity. Piri's response to his probation officer upon arriving late to his first appointment marks the departure:

> He looked at his watch and told me "You're thirty minutes late." I nodded in agreement. "It's a good way to start off, eh?" He was pretty insistent, but I wasn't gonna get mad, no matter what. I made my face stay the same, relaxed and soft. "You got a job?" he finally asked me. "No sir, not yet." "Get one fast." "Yes sir." (Thomas 1967, 320)

At this point, Piri begins to transform masculine performance through loss. Rather than putting on his cara-palo to abscond his emotions, Piri decides to maintain the same countenance as if the officer's instigations had no impact. In effect, Piri's consistent facial expression hides his disturbance at the officer's insistence. Yet Piri does not claim to evoke cara-palo as he has on previous occasions. Cara palo, whether translated literally as "wooden face" or rendered in English as "stone face" or "straight face," equates lack of emotional expression with physical hardness and linearity, but here Piri keeps his face "relaxed and soft." Piri's cara-palo, thus, seems to be undergoing a process of mestizaje, in which the wood becomes softened or the stone more porous, such that the materials disintegrate. Piri's more malleable and disintegrating cara-palo is accompanied by an internal struggle that allows for him to maintain a "soft and relaxed" expression and makes the traditional cara-palo unnecessary. In other words, instead of using cara-palo to control the expression of emotion, Piri seeks to control emotion itself. As such, Piri also disregards that other masculine performance, "having corazón," as the officer's provocations go uncontested.

Piri's response to the probation officer demonstrates loss since Piri is, in fact, giving up the masculine codes by which he lived. As a result, Piri retaliates against the system that seeks to control his decisions and invalidate his masculinity by entering into his old life of drugs, alcohol, and partying until he sees his reflection in the mirror and decides not only to abandon cara-palo, but also the street life that preceded his landing in prison:

> Then, one morning, after a wild, all-night pot party, I crept into Tia's apartment and dug myself in the mirror. What I saw shook me up. My eyes were red from smoke and my face was strained from the effort of trying to be cool...I pulled away from the mirror and sat on the edge of my bed. My head

still full of pot, and I felt scared...I felt as though I had found a hole in my
face and out of it were pouring all the different masks that my *cara-palo* face
had fought so hard to keep hidden. I thought, *I ain't goin' back to what I was.*
(Thomas 1967, 321—emphasis added)

Piri's initial appeal to loss—the softening and disintegration of the cara-palo, discarding corazón—becomes a resounding desire to relinquish his previous life and the masculine codes he followed in order to embrace change. In so doing, Piri risks losing neither his masculinity nor his ethnic identity, though they are articulated differently: "Everything was the same; only I had changed. I wasn't the grubby-faced Puerto Rican kid any more; I was a grubby-faced Puerto Rican man. I am an *hombre* that wants to be better. Man! I don't want to be nuttin'. I want to be somebody. I want to laugh clean" (1967, 322).

It is notable that in this moment of literal self-reflection there is no mention of his skin color or his racial identity.[12] Instead, Piri is troubled by the redness of his eyes and his altered state of mind. In the opening scene of the novel, Piri wonders if he and his father are on the outs because "it's something I done, or something I am" (Thomas 1967, 22). Now, at the close of the novel Piri seems more concerned with the former than the latter. And yet his characterization as a "grubby-faced Puerto Rican" brings his appearance to the fore again, while alluding to a similar description from his younger years. One day, Piri arrives home, and his mother chases him from the kitchen because he is dirty after being out in the streets. She conflates dirtiness with blackness, seeing it as undesirable, yet inflects her speech with the Spanish diminutive to convey affection: "I have to love you because only your mother could love you, *un negrito* and ugly. And to make it badder, you're dirty and smelly from your sweat!" (Thomas 1967, 19).

The cleanliness of which Piri speaks at the end is not about physical hygiene or skin color, but rather his state of being. In his desire to change, Piri begins to consistently turn away from his earlier ways. After accepting an invitation to visit his former girlfriend, Trina, for example, Piri imagines getting into a physical altercation with Trina's husband, Georgie. Yet, when he arrives at the apartment, the visit is nothing short of anticlimactic, and Piri opts to leave early. Likewise, Piri runs into an old friend, Carlito, who offers him drugs, which Piri declines. Piri seeks to be "clean" not only from drugs, cara-palo, and having corazón. He appeals to God for help in his quest to be "nice, all the way," to be clean inside and out (1967, 323). Yet Piri's spirituality is not based on orthodox religion. His is a product of religious syncretism that encourages a complete reconceptualization. Rather than "something I done, or something I am," Piri now engages what he does *and* who he is, evincing that the two are interconnected. For Piri, inside and out are interconnected, comprising the soul and the spirit of Nuyorican mestizaje.

NOTES

[1] See Santiago-Díaz and Rodríguez (2012-2013) for an analysis of Piri's crisis within the context of the Hispanic-American racial consciousness. They note Piri challenges the trope of *la gran familia,* but that the protagonist concludes he is a "young black Puerto Rican man from Harlem" (Thomas 1967, 18, 20).

[2] Mohr, a contemporary of Thomas, criticizes publishers for their promotion of the misogynist depiction of women offered in works like *Down These Mean Streets*: "The major problem for me has been exposure of my books. Recognition is given more to those books that are great escapades: a little bit of robbing, shooting, swearing; men going around like Puerto Rican John Waynes, and women who are either morons or prostitutes devoid of any real depth or substance. Those books for some reason get an enormous amount of play and recognition" (Stavans 2011, 1051).

[3] See Sosa-Velasco (2003) for a discussion of how *Down These Mean Streets* has been situated in multiple literary traditions, including the process for its inclusion as foundational text of Latinx literature.

[4] I have adopted the term transinsular also used by Moreno, rather than transnational, to stress a reciprocal literary exchange between Puerto Rican authors on the Island and those in the U.S. (Moreno 2012, 26).

[5] See Ileana M. Rodríguez-Silva's *Silencing Race* (2012) for an in-depth study of racial discourse in Puerto Rico from the 1870s to the 1910s. Through an exploration of literary sources as well as periodicals and census data, she demonstrates that questions of racial discrimination were rearticulated as issues of class and nationality (2012, 6-7). The chapter "Liberal Elites' writing" explores texts such as Salvador Brau's *Disquisiciones sociales,* which advocates erasure. Considered one of the "main architects" of Puerto Rican racial harmony, Brau acknowledges Puerto Rico's indigenous ancestry—stance not adopted by his contemporaries—but erases indigenous and African racial identity in favor of class (2012, 76-9).

[6] See Sosa-Velasco (2009) for a discussion of how Gerald serves as the other with which Piri identifies, allowing him to differentiate in the conception of the self.

[7] In addition to Caminero-Santangelo (2007) and Sánchez-González (2001), see Martínez San-Miguel (2015) for an analysis of the brothel scene.

[8] For a reading of mestizaje in *Down These Mean Streets,* see Rodríguez (1984), who assesses the concept as it relates to survival narrative.

[9] *La raza cósmica* circulated in the Caribbean since a review of the work appeared in Cuba's *El diario de la marina* shortly after its publication (Miller 2004, 47).

[10] See Miller for an analysis of *mulatez* in the works of Cuban poet Nicolás Guillén, and Puerto Rico's Luis Palés Matos (2004, 45-78).

[11] Canclini defines hybridity—a term he prefers over mestizaje—as "socio-cultural processes in which discreet structures or practices, previously existing in separate form, are combined to generate new structures" (Canclini 1995, xxv). Hybridity, thus, not only refers to racial or cultural fusion, but encompasses other forms of social synthesis as well (Lund 2006, 28).

[12] See Yolanda Martínez-San Miguel (2015) for a discussion on Lacan's "mirror stage."

REFERENCES

Acosta-Belén, Edna. 1992. Beyond Island Boundaries. *Callaloo* 15(4), 979–98.

Caminero-Santangelo, Marta. 2007. *On Latinidad: U.S. Latino Literature and the Construction of Ethnicity*. Gainesville: University Press of Florida.

Canclini, Néstor. 1995. *Hybrid Cultures: Strategies for Entering and Leaving Modernity*. Minneapolis: University of Minnesota Press.

Cruz-Malavé, Arnaldo M. 2012. The Antifoundational Fiction of Piri Thomas (1928-2011). *CENTRO: Journal of the Center for Puerto Rican Studies* 24(1), 4–19.

_____.2018. The Latino Fiction of Piri Thomas. *Oxford Research Encyclopedia of Literature*. 1–26. New York: Oxford University Press.

Duany, Jorge. 2003. *Puerto Rican Nation on the Move: Identities on the Island and in the United States*. Chapel Hill: University of North Carolina Press.

Luis, William. 1997. *Dance Between Two Cultures: Latino Caribbean Literature Written in the United States*. Nashville: Vanderbilt University Press.

Lund, Joshua. 2006. *The Impure Imagination: Toward a Critical Hybridity in Latin American Writing*. Minneapolis: University of Minnesota Press.

Martínez San-Miguel, Yolanda. 2015. Ethnic Specularities. Exploring the Caribbean and Latino Dimensions of *Down These Mean Streets*. *Latino Studies* 13(3), 358–75.

Miller, Marilyn Grace. 2004. *Rise and Fall of the Cosmic Race: The Cult of Mestizaje in Latin America*. Austin: University of Texas Press.

Moreno, Marisel. 2010. Family Matters: Revisiting *La Gran Familia Puertorriqueña* in the works of Rosario Ferré and Judith Ortiz Coffer. *CENTRO: Journal of the Center for Puerto Rican Studies* 22(2), 76–105.

_____. 2012. *Family Matters. Puerto Rican Women Authors on the Island and Mainland*. Charlottesville: University of Virginia Press.

Ortiz, Fernando. 1940. Los factores humanos de la cubanidad. *Revista Bimestre Cubana* 45, 161–86.

_____. 1947. *Cuban Counterpoint: Tobacco and Sugar*. New York: Alfred A. Knoff.

Perez, Richard. 2007. Racial Spills and Disfigured Faces in Piri Thomas' *Down These Mean Streets* and Junot Díaz's "Ysrael." In *Contemporary U.S. Latino/a Literary Criticism,* eds. Lyn Di Iorio Sandín and Richard Perez. 93–114. New York: Palgrave Macmillan.

Rodriguez, Joe. 1984. The Sense of *Mestizaje* in Two Latino Novels. *Revista Chicano-Riqueña* 12(1), 57–63.

Rodríguez-Silva, Ileana M. 2012. *Silencing Race: Disentangling Blackness, Colonialism and National Identities in Puerto Rico*. New York: Palgrave Macmillian.

Sánchez, Marta E. 2006. *Shakin' Up Race and Gender: Intercultural Connections in Puerto Rican, African American and Chicano Narratives and Culture (1965-1995)*. Austin: University of Texas Press.

_____. 2019. *The Translational Turn: Latinx Literature into the Mainstream.* Pittsburgh: University of Pittsburgh Press.

Sánchez-González, Lisa. 2001. *Boricua Literature: A Literary History of the Puerto Rican Diaspora.* New York: New York University Press.

Santiago-Díaz, Eluterio and Ilia Rodríguez. 2012-2013. The Afro-Puerto Rican Outcry of Piri Thomas. *Bilingual Review. La revista bilingüe* 13(1), 12–29.

Scarano, Francisco A. 1999. Desear el jíbaro: Metáforas de la identidad puertorriqueña en la transición imperial. *Iles i Imperis* 2, 65–76.

Sosa-Velasco, Alfredo J. 2009. Gerald and Thomas: The Subtext Within the Text in *Down These Mean Streets. Romance Notes* 49(3), 287–99.

Stavans, Ilan. 2011. Nicholasa Mohr. In *The Norton Anthology of Latino Literature,* eds., Ilan Stavans, Edna Acosta-Belén, Harold Augenbraum, María Herrera-Sobek, Rolando Hinojosa, and Gustavo Pérez Firmat. 1050–2. New York: W.W. Norton and Company.

Stavans, Ilan and Piri Thomas. 1996. Race and Mercy: A Conversation with Piri Thomas. *The Massachusetts Review* 37(3), 344–54.

Thomas, Piri. 1967. *Down These Mean Streets.* New York: Alfred A. Knopf.

Torres, Arlene. 1998. La gran familia puertorriqueña e' prieta de'belda. In *Blackness in Latin America and the Caribbean: Social Dynamics and Cultural Transformations,* eds. Arlene Torres and Norman E. Whitten Jr. 287–306. Bloomington: Indiana University Press.

Vasconcelos, José. 1997. *The Cosmic Race/ La raza cósmica.* Translated by Didier T. Jaén. Baltimore: Johns Hopkins University Press.

Viego, Antonio. 2007. *Dead Subjects: Toward a Politics of Loss in Latino Studies.* Durham, NC: Duke University Press.

VOLUME XXXIII • NUMBER II • SUMMER 2021

Reinvigorating Puerto Rico's Pharmaceutical Industry: A U.S. Security Imperative

LYNNE CHANDLER GARCIA AND MICHAEL BEVERLEY

ABSTRACT

In the wake of COVID-19, U.S. policymakers have come to the realization that overreliance on foreign manufacture of medical devices, pharmaceuticals, and active pharmaceutical ingredients is a danger to U.S. security. Countries such as China, upon which the U.S. is dependent for pharmaceuticals, could use this dependency to its advantage in a time of conflict by withholding supplies or producing medicines that are laced with contaminants. The U.S. must take action to reshore its pharmaceutical industry and bolster American made products. Historically, Puerto Rico has led the U.S.'s pharmaceutical production, and with the current crisis, Puerto Rico has an opportunity to bolster manufacturing on the Island. This paper explores whether Puerto Rico can reinvigorate its pharmaceutical industry, thereby not only bolstering the island's crippled economy but also helping the U.S. meet a national security imperative. [Key Words: COVID, pharmaceuticals, national security, reshore, Hurricane Maria, Puerto Rico]

Lynne Chandler Garcia (lynne.chandlergarcia@afacademy.af.edu), PhD, is an Associate Professor of Political Science at the U.S. Air Force Academy. Her areas of research include civil discourse, empathy and efficacy in political behavior, foreign policy, military operations, and the art of pedagogy for underprivileged learners.

Michael Beverley (Michael.Beverley@afacademy.af.edu) is a Cadet First Class at the U.S. Air Force Academy. He is majoring in political science and economics. Upon graduation, he will attend New York University for his Master's degree in economics.

The COVID-19 pandemic served as a wakeup call to U.S. policymakers who have come to the grim realization that overreliance on foreign manufacture of medical devices, pharmaceuticals, and active pharmaceutical ingredients (API) is a danger to U.S. security.[1] Whereas it was once the world's leader in producing drugs and medical equipment, the U.S. is now dependent on foreign nations, especially China and India, for many pharmaceutical products, most notably APIs (the core ingredients used to manufacture finished pharmaceuticals) and generic drugs. With overreliance on foreign production of drugs and medical products both a national health problem and a national security issue, the U.S. must take action to reshore the manufacturing of pharmaceutical products. Puerto Rico leads the U.S. in pharmaceutical manufacture, although production in the territory is down after the economic downturn on the Island that began with the repeal of favorable tax laws and continued through Hurricane Maria. This paper explores whether Puerto Rico can reinvigorate its pharmaceutical industry, thereby not only bolstering the Island's crippled economy but also helping the U.S. meet national health and security imperatives.

The Security Challenge of Pharmaceuticals

While the U.S. maintains 47 percent of the facilities to make finished dosage form (FDF) pharmaceuticals, other nations are racing to take over this market share (Woodcock 2019). This is especially true for generic drugs. Due to the exorbitant costs of name-brand products, 90 percent of prescriptions in the U.S. are for generic drugs (U.S. FDA 2019). While the exact percentage of foreign produced generic drugs is not certain, U.S. manufacture of generics is extremely low as U.S. firms prefer to develop patented drugs rather than manufacture generics (Hicks 2019). India is the world's largest producer of generic and over-the-counter drugs. Chinese companies have cornered much of the U.S. market for common pharmaceuticals, including producing 97 percent of antibiotics, 90 percent of vitamin C, 95 percent of ibuprofen, and 70 percent of acetaminophen (Hang 2020). Each of these items is critical during both a pandemic and during a time of war. For the global market, China is the world's largest producer of APIs with India taking the number two position. Even the supply of APIs to U.S. markets are increasingly produced in foreign locations. As of August 2019, only 28 percent of the facilities supplying the U.S. market were located on American soil, while 72 percent

Figure 1. Percentage of API Manufacturing Facilities for All Drugs by Country or Region, August 2019

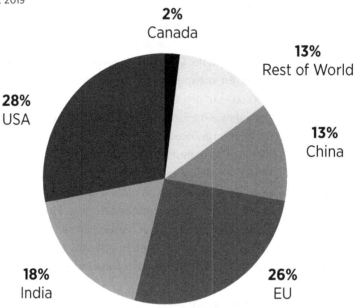

Source: U.S. Food and Drug Administration, Safeguarding Pharmaceutical Supply Chains in a Global Economy, October 29, 2019. <https://www.fda.gov/news-events/congressional-testimony/safeguarding-pharmaceutical-supply-chains-global-economy-10302019/>.

of manufacturing facilities producing APIs for U.S. markets were located outside of the U.S. (Woodcock 2019). The table demonstrates the number of registered facilities supplying APIs for the U.S. market.

The COVID pandemic spotlights concerns over foreign dominance of pharmaceuticals. As COVID moved through China, a number of manufacturing sites halted production, creating concern over U.S. imports. Further, government officials in India limited exports of 26 drugs and APIs in order to ensure supply for the Indian people (Goel 2020). With COVID affecting the entire world simultaneously, it was in India's self-interest to prioritize its own population and therefore unsurprising. However, the move created uneasiness around the globe as to the availability of needed drugs in times of crisis. Given China's and India's dominance in the pharmaceutical industry, COVID highlights the fragility of the global supply chain for essential medications. Ensuring the supply of medications was thrust to the forefront of U.S. security concerns.

Xinhua hinted at the fact that withholding pharmaceutical products could be a tactic used by Chinese officials in foreign policy disputes.

After the SARS outbreak in 2005, China focused on producing face masks, and quickly became the largest supplier of the product. In 2017, the Chinese Ministry of Science and Technology targeted production of nucleic acid tests, which can be used to detect COVID (Bradsher 2020). China's strategy is to achieve dominance for essential items in sectors such as health and technology. As China gains a near monopoly on certain products, fears arise that Chinese companies could raise the price of medicines or require concessions from the U.S. government as an exchange for low prices. These fears are well founded, as demonstrated when China monopolized production of vitamin C and fixed the prices and quantities. When challenged, the Chinese companies did not deny their actions, but instead argued that the Chinese government requires them to fix prices and quantities of the vitamin.[2]

As a war of words escalated between Washington and Beijing over responsibility for COVID, an article from the official Chinese news agency Xinhua stated that if China halted the export of pharmaceutical products, "the United States would sink into the hell of a novel coronavirus epidemic" (Spetalnick, Brunnstrom and Shalal 2020). Xinhua hinted at the fact that withholding pharmaceutical products could be a tactic used by Chinese officials in foreign policy disputes. During a 2010 standoff with Japan, China blocked the export of rare earth metals which Japan uses in a number of key industries, including the production of some pharmaceuticals. China also holds that card against the U.S. The possibility of China halting shipments of drugs or medical equipment gives pause not only to economic trade discussions, but also to defense operations in areas such as the South China Sea. Thinly veiled threats such as these demonstrate the security issues raised by drug shortages.

In his statement to the U.S.-China Economic and Security Review Commission, Christopher Priest, a deputy at the Defense Health Agency, referred to pharmaceuticals as "critical war-fighting material" and stated:

The issues raised by the increased Chinese dominance in the global API market cannot be overstated. There is risk that existing regulations, programs, and funding are insufficient to guarantee U.S. independence from unreliable foreign suppliers. Our concern is the ability of the domestic manufacturing capability to adjust to that risk, alternate sources, if any, and how long the solutions would take to produce results. (Priest 2019)

Not only were experts such as Priest weighing in, but elected officials began to call for a return to U.S. manufacturing of medicines. In a letter to the Government Accountability Office (GAO), Senate Minority Leader Chuck Schumer wrote, "I am greatly concerned by the strategic vulnerability created by our reliance on China, a strategic adversary, for the APIs used to manufacture a very wide range of life-saving drugs that are vital to our healthcare system." He requested that the GAO look into the matter (Schumer 2019). In the wake of the COVID pandemic, members of Congress introduced a number of bills to reshore pharmaceutical production while the Trump Administration issued an executive order calling for increased domestic production of essential medicines.

Why the U.S. Lost the Strategic Advantage

The U.S. was once the largest producer of APIs, generics, and brand-name prescription drugs, but over the last several decades other nations are challenging this position. India and China have lower manufacturing costs due to a labor cost advantage ranging from 30 to 40 percent compared to labor costs in the U.S. and Europe (U.S. FDA 2019). China enjoys lower electricity, coal, and water costs, which brings down production expenses. Further, Chinese firms have built up their network of raw materials and have lower shipping and transaction costs for these raw materials (Woodcock 2019).

Finally, both India and China have fewer environmental regulations concerning toxic chemicals, which lead to lower production costs. While loose environmental regulations have allowed India and China to produce at rock bottom prices, there are significant drawbacks. In both countries, numerous problems have been associated with large pharmaceutical companies not property containing and treating waste products. Toxins and antibiotic wastewater is often dumped into nearby rivers or soil, causing widespread contamination (Litovsky 2016; IPEN 2014).

While lower costs create significant savings for these nations, China's greatest advantage is government intervention, which prioritizes production of medical products. The Chinese government views dependency for medical supplies as a security hazard, and thus intervenes to promote the industry. The Chinese government offers tax breaks to pharmaceutical companies to encourage production. Companies producing generic drugs benefit from low corporate tax rates. Pharmaceutical manufacturers are included within China's New and High Technology Enterprises (HNTE) program, which provides lower tax structures and deductions to eight technological areas. Pharmaceuticals and medical devices are included within the "Made in China 2025" industrial strategy (Bradsher 2020). The strategy centers on producing high value products within China in order to alleviate dependence on foreign supplies and rocket China as the world's producer of key high-tech products. The strategy calls for massive government investment in key technology sectors. Pharmaceuticals are listed within the strategy, and the Chinese government pledged to streamline regulation of the industry in addition to investing in research and development of drug manufacture through tax incentives and grants.

In addition to these government subsidies, China instituted the Thousand Talents Program to coax scholars and industry experts to Chinese universities and industries. Pharmaceuticals is a key area for recruitment for this program, as China heavily recruits American researchers to work in Chinese universities and laboratories. In exchange for generous research funding, China expects that scientific discoveries will be shared with the Chinese government. The program also aims to recruit Chinese professionals after an exodus of young, talented Chinese students who sought educational opportunities abroad and then stayed overseas, leaving China with a shortage of professional workers.

Regaining the Strategic Advantage

COVID has demonstrated that pandemics and medical crises are national security concerns for which the U.S. must be prepared. The U.S. must regain its ability to independently manufacture enough pharmaceuticals to meet U.S.

domestic needs and break its reliance on other nations. In doing so, the U.S. will need to follow China's lead and create incentives for pharmaceutical companies to return to American soil. Tax breaks, grants, and creating special economic zones are possible methods to support the U.S.-based pharmaceutical industry.

In April 2020, President Donald Trump signed an executive order requiring federal agencies to buy essential drugs and medical products from U.S.-based manufacturers rather than from overseas. Additionally, Congress passed the CARES Act, an omnibus bill that includes provisions to secure the American supply chain of pharmaceuticals and empowers the Biomedical Advanced Research and Development Authority (BARDA) to work with private firms to produce COVID-related treatments. Through Operation Warp Speed, BARDA is already providing funding to companies researching COVID treatments that have a U.S. base or extensive American operations. While this is a step in the right direction, it is not enough to return manufacturing to American soil. The U.S. must jump start manufacturing in locations that have a history of pharmaceutical production and many of the resources in place—Puerto Rico might fit this requirement.

Puerto Rico—A U.S. Pharmaceutical Hub

From the 1970s through the 1990s, a vibrant pharmaceutical industry arose on the Island thanks to tax incentives that lured manufacturers. However, the repeal of the tax incentives coupled with enticements to move the industry overseas to China, Ireland, and India caused many of these companies to leave the Island. Consolidation of operations and the loss of patent protection for blockbuster products produced in Puerto Rico were also factors leading to reduced investment by multinational pharmaceutical companies. In recent years, economic downturn from the loss of industry, coupled with failing infrastructure and the damage of Hurricanes Irma and Maria, have devastated the Puerto Rican economy. Revitalizing the Puerto Rican pharmaceutical industry would not only allow the U.S to shore up domestic production of drugs, it would also support the territory's economy.

The Legacy of Section 936

Puerto Rico's legacy as the U.S. pharmaceutical hub began in 1976, when the U.S. government enacted Section 936 of the Internal Revenue Code. The Code treated Puerto Rico as a foreign entity and thus U.S. investments on the Island as foreign investments. The code allowed U.S. corporations operating in Puerto Rico to claim a credit against their U.S. income tax liability equal to the U.S. income taxes attributable to income derived from the active conduct of a trade or business in Puerto Rico and from certain investments in Puerto Rico. In addition, the tax code allowed the U.S. parent companies to deduct 100 percent of dividends received from their Puerto Rican subsidiaries, effectively eliminating U.S. corporate taxes as long as profits were distributed through dividends. It is estimated that companies received $2.67 in tax breaks for every dollar invested in Puerto Rico. Puerto Rico, in turn, taxed income from the manufacturing operations at significantly reduced rates. This was particularly attractive to pharmaceutical firms, and the industry on the Island soared. By 1982, pharmaceutical corporations were 46 percent of total manufacturing net assets (President's Task Force 2011). An additional benefit of 936 was that it required companies to make a 5 percent deposit in local banks, which led to a flourishing banking industry. At the same time, the Puerto Rican economy became dependent on these foreign investments with few domestic corporations to supplement the economic base.

Pharmaceutical companies were taking advantage of the code by developing a drug in a U.S. mainland facility and then transferring the patent to its subsidiary in Puerto Rico.

By the 1990s, the pitfalls of Section 936 were apparent. On the mainland, policymakers from the various states resented the advantages given to firms operating in Puerto Rico. Further, Section 936 was viewed as a way for corporations to avoid taxes. Pharmaceutical companies were taking advantage of the code by developing a drug in a U.S. mainland facility and then transferring the patent to its subsidiary in Puerto Rico. The subsidiary would then produce the drug and claim tax-free income (U.S. GAO 1992). While some of the production did happen on the Island, many companies simply transferred their patents to Puerto Rico but did most of their manufacturing elsewhere, thereby not creating many jobs (Puerto Rico Report 2018). An additional problem was that Puerto Rico's tax code, which reduced tax rates on such operations, did not support the provincial government's tax base, ultimately depriving the government of tax revenue. Of the tax funds that were generated, the Puerto Rican government often failed to reinvest this money in infrastructure projects.

In 1996 President Clinton signed a law phasing out Section 936 over ten years with full repeal in 2006. With repeal, firms were subject to the same corporate income tax as all foreign subsidiaries, and many foreign companies left the Island and relocated to other countries such as China and Ireland. Puerto Rico not only lost factory positions but also high-paying management and skilled positions. Ripple effects were felt as companies that serviced the pharmaceutical firms, such as maintenance, shipping, and even landscapers, were forced to lay off workers. Unemployment on the Island skyrocketed, leading to a deep depression.

In retrospect, Section 936 had both benefits and failings. Many companies did take advantage of the loopholes to shelter income from taxes. At the same time, the tax breaks supported the Puerto Rican economy, providing jobs in the pharmaceutical industry, as well as myriad supporting industries. Furthermore, due to 936, Puerto Rico established the most significant and

Figure 2. Top Exporters of Pharmaceutical Products by State/Territory

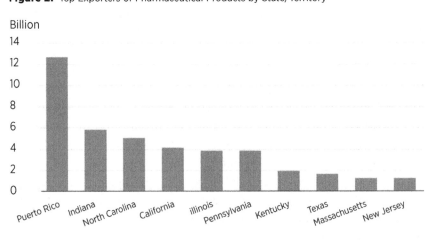

Source U.S. Census Bureau, 2019, <usatrade.census.gov/>.

robust pharmaceutical hub within American jurisdiction and placed Puerto Rico on the global stage for pharmaceutical production.

Although the pharmaceutical industry contracted on the Island with the repeal of Section 936, Puerto Rico remains the U.S. hub of pharmaceutical production. Puerto Rico is a well-developed ecosystem of concentrated pharmaceutical production, supply chains, logistics networks, associated manufacturing such as bottles and vials, and expertise in the industry. At the same time, this ecosystem has fallen into disrepair and needs to be strengthened in order to regain a dominant foothold in the pharmaceutical industry. If Puerto Rico can strengthen the ecosystem, the territory is poised as the U.S. base for production that is needed for national security. Puerto Rico has distinct industrial advantages, including status as part of the United States, a lower cost yet well-trained labor force, facilities for production, and a strong logistical and direct service backbone. At the same time, Puerto Rico faces challenges with infrastructure, utilities, and complex regulation policies that hinder new development. Each of these arenas is addressed in turn.

Advantages Associated with Territorial Status
As a U.S. territory, Puerto Rico falls under U.S. intellectual property protection laws, which is an advantage when outsourcing production to countries like China with very lax intellectual property protection. Puerto Rico falls under U.S. custom regulations, which facilitate imports and exports. Because Puerto Rico is part of the U.S., it is much easier for the Food and Drug Administration (FDA) to conduct regular inspections of facilities compared to conducting inspections in foreign nations, where access can be denied or appointments must be set so far in advance that factories have time to cover up any negligence in standards. Problems with quality of products and a lack of FDA-enforced standards, especially with generic drugs, has been a persistent issue with Chinese-made products, resulting in numerous American deaths (Gibson and Singh 2018). In 2019 alone, an estimated 60 percent of inspections performed by the FDA in the Asia Pacific region prompted Form 483s, which are issued when an inspector observes conditions that may constitute violations of FDA standards. Only 15 percent of domestic inspections, to include the mainland and Puerto Rico, resulted in FDA Form 483s (U.S. FDA 2020; Plaza 2020a). Thus, easy FDA access is a significant advantage for Puerto Rico.

A 2011 study comparing quality of products produced in Puerto Rico with products made on the mainland found that Puerto Rican products were of a lower quality (Gray, Aleda and Leiblein 2011). However, the results of this study have been questioned by industry experts, who point to constant FDA oversight and inspection of facilities and the large pool of compliance experts based on the Island. Compared to the quality of products in China, Puerto Rican facilities are far superior. The FDA often struggles to gain inspection access to Chinese facilities, whereas a regular FDA presence in Puerto Rico helps ensure that the industry is continuously investing in compliance and quality initiatives and personnel training to ensure products meet the highest U.S. standards.

Assessing the Labor Pool
In terms of the labor pool, Puerto Rico is challenged by a significant migration of residents to the contiguous U.S. Before Hurricane Maria, net migration from the Island was about half a million or 10 percent of Puerto Rico's population. After Maria, it was estimated that Puerto Rico would experience an exodus of nearly 14 percent more of the population (Meléndez and Hinojosa 2017). Because younger cohorts were more likely to leave the Island compared to older cohorts, the migration resulted in a much older demographic left on the Island, many of whom were past working age. Multinationals based in countries such as Switzerland, Ireland, and Singapore heavily recruit Puerto Rican talent and thus contribute to the exodus.

...throughout their decades on the Island, the pharmaceutical companies invested in rigorous training programs that produced expert engineers and managers to lead the industry.

Due to its history in pharmaceuticals, Puerto Rico has a well-educated labor force available to support the industry. Although plants laid off workers during the economic downturn of 2006, plants increased productivity and automation to make up the difference and now are among the most labor efficient in the world. According to an internal study conducted by Pharma-Bio-

Serv, the Puerto Rican worker, on average, generates $1,859 worth of exports of life sciences products, which is almost double that of Switzerland, the second largest with $966 generated in exports per employee, and more than five times that of Indiana, the most productive state in the United States, with $351 of exports being generated by one employee on average (Comerford 2020).

Figure 3. Estimates for NAICS 325400—Pharmaceutical and Medicine Manufacturing, May 2019

Occupational Group	% Total Employment	U.S. States	Puerto Rico
Production Occupations 51-000	30.33	$19.23	9.41
Life, Physical and Social Science 19-000	15.07	53.61	18.9
Management Occupations 11-0000	10	67.14	29.86
Business and Financial Operations 13-0000	7.89	37.66	16.61
Sales and related occupations 41-0000	6.1	38.55	9.19
Architectural and Engineering operations 17-0000	5.72	42.02	23.89
Installation, Maintenance, Repair 49-0000	4.22	28.64	10.67
Transport and Material Moving 53-0000	4.01	16.72	9.16
Computer and Mathematical 15-0000	3.14	45.95	18.12
Healthcare Practitioners &Tech Oper 29-0000	1.18	27.68	14.2
Art, Design...Media 27-0000	0.76	33.33	13.95
Building and Grounds Keeping 37-0000	0.6	14.91	8.99
Legal operations 23-0000	0.37	60.48	26.88
Construction and Extraction 47-0000	0.3	27.2	9.17
Protective Service 33-0000	0.12	17.4	9.64
Farming Fishing Forestry 45-0000	0.07	17.09	8.93
Healthcare Support 31-0000	0.06	19.13	9.01
Personal Care and Service 39-0000	--	18.65	9.1

Source: Bureau of Labor Statistics, National Industry Specific Occupational Employment and Wage Estimates.

According to Invest Puerto Rico, the Island ranks sixth in the world in terms of scientists and engineers for the industry (Invest Puerto Rico 2020). This is primarily because throughout their decades on the Island, the pharmaceutical companies invested in rigorous training programs that produced expert engineers and managers to lead the industry. In addition, Puerto Rico's three major university systems provide a continuous stream of educated professionals for the labor force, oftentimes in close cooperation with pharmaceutical corporations (such as Amgen) on the Island (Miller 2020).[3]

Puerto Ricans are U.S. citizens governed by the same labor laws as stateside facilities. Puerto Rico has a labor cost advantage compared to the mainland. As demonstrated in Table 1, in the primary labor sectors involved in the pharmaceutical industry, Puerto Rico's hourly wage is much lower, in most cases about half, the salary requirements of the U.S. as a whole. On average, wages in Puerto Rico are 40 percent less than the stateside industry average.

Although Puerto Rico boasts a less expensive labor force when compared to the mainland United States, wages in many countries are lower still, making Puerto Rico more expensive by comparison. In the wake of the security crisis created by dependency on Chinese pharmaceuticals, a number of Latin American countries, including Colombia, Mexico, and Costa Rica, began marketing campaigns advocating for "near-shoring" rather than on-shoring. Touting their proximity to the U.S. as well as their allied status, these nations are potential competitors for Puerto Rico.

Facilities for Production

Currently, twelve of the world's top twenty pharmaceutical companies and seven out of the top ten medical device companies have operations in Puerto Rico. Puerto Rico has 49 FDA-approved pharmaceutical plants to produce both medical devices and pharmaceuticals (Puerto Rico Report 2020). Additionally, Puerto Rico boasts several continuous manufacturing facilities that are faster and more reliable compared to batch production. Continuous production has additional benefits in that the process cuts down waste and is friendlier to the environment (ERC 2015). Currently, Puerto Rico has a small inventory of plants that are idle or are able to expand for further production. And while some plants were damaged during Hurricanes Irma and Maria, many of these plants are in good repair or can be renovated.

At the same time, Puerto Rico faces a real estate problem. Repair of existing facilities will only take the industry so far, and new construction is required. And while Puerto Rico also has a robust construction industry that is capable of erecting new facilities, finding the land for these facilities might prove more problematic. If the real estate can be secured, then preliminary construction can be started to ready the sites and cut down on the time needed to build a new site from the ground up.

Infrastructure Concerns

In 2017, Hurricanes Irma and Maria caused widespread destruction across the Island, wiping out much of the infrastructure. After the storm, many Puerto Rican-based plants relied on generators and ingenuity to work around the crisis. Some companies worked together to share nitrogen and oxygen—gasses essential to the industry. Stories abound of plants utilizing low security inmates to repair facilities to flying in plane loads of cash to pay workers (Langhauser and Parrish 2018).

Despite these heroic efforts, infrastructure remains a critical problem for the island. The 2019 Report Card for Puerto Rico's Infrastructure, rated by the American Society of Civil Engineers (ASCE), gave the Island a grade of D- after assessing water, energy, ports, roads, and other components of critical infrastructure (ASCE 2019).

The report notes that investment in infrastructure was well below the ASCE-recommended 3.5 percent of gross domestic product. Public investment declined after 2008, which roughly coincides with the end of Section 936 and the tax incentives to support manufacturing including the pharmaceutical industry. Puerto Rico's depression meant less tax revenue generated, which impacted the government's ability to invest in infrastructure. Because up-to-date and functional utilities are essential in attracting investment, the economic downturn created a downward spiral of decreased tax revenue and infrastructure investment.

The ASCE found that much of Puerto Rico's infrastructure is aging, while rebuilding after Hurricane Maria is still in progress. Water supply, a critical resource in the pharmaceutical industry, is a particular concern with more than 4.38 breaks or leaks per mile of line. Additionally, reservoirs were functioning at 40 to 60 percent of storage capacity due to sedimentation.

While the report concluded that Puerto Rico's water system could meet current demands, the ASCE recommended significant investment in capital projects such as new supply facilities, water filtration plans, distribution systems, and increased maintenance. The report found that compliance with water health regulations was very high, with very few health-based water quality violations (ASCE 2019).

The ASCE gave Puerto Rico an F for its energy grid, noting that even before Hurricanes Maria and Irma, the infrastructure was in poor condition, but after the hurricanes the grid was exceedingly fragile and prone to frequent blackouts. In the immediate aftermath of the hurricanes, authorities focused on restoring power as quickly as possible, but long-term needs were overlooked. The power grid is antiqued and in poor repair, with modest winds taking down the system. The report cites poor maintenance, insufficient capacity, and inadequate restoration following the hurricanes, as well as a lack of investment in the energy sector (ASCE 2019).

The government-owned Puerto Rico Electric Power Authority (PREPA), which controls power production and distribution, has been riddled with corruption problems, and constant shifts in upper administration have created instability. The electric system is largely reliant on fossil fuels, with petroleum providing 40 percent of electricity generation, natural gas 39 percent, coal 18 percent, and renewables just 2.3 percent. Further, energy costs in Puerto Rico are much higher than those in the mainland: electricity in Puerto Rico is 18.38 cents per kilowatt hour compared to 6.4 cents on the mainland (U.S. EIA 2020). The lack of a reliable energy infrastructure, combined with expensive rates, is a deterrent for firms trying to establish large-scale manufacturing and contributes to Puerto Rico's economic crisis.

While power generation is a significant issue, Puerto Rico is trying to improve both generation and distribution. The Island put in place a plan to convert entirely to renewable energy by 2025, and contracted Luma Energy to assess and revamp the energy infrastructure in the Island. Luma Energy, a joint venture between the Quanta Services and Canadian Utilities Limited, signed a 15-year contract valued between $70 million and $105 million to diversify power generation in the Island by using natural gas, solar, and wind energy. While the contract with Luma Energy seems promising, a recent report from the Institute for Energy Economics and Financial

Figure 4. Report card for Puerto Rico's infrastructure

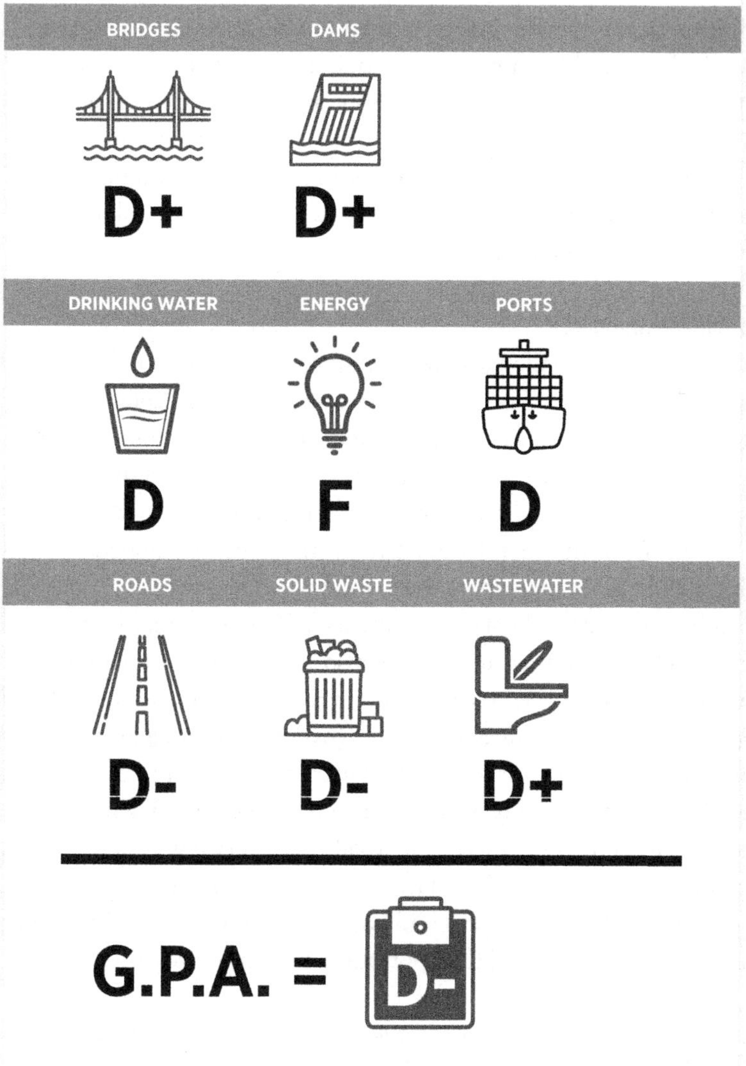

Source: American Society for Civil Engineers, Puerto Rico Section, (2019), "Report Card for Puerto Rico's Infrastructure." <https://www.infrastructurereportcard.org/wp-content/uploads/2019/11/2019-Puerto-Rico-Report-Card-Final.pdf/>, page 6.

Analysis (IEEFA) criticizes the contract, arguing that Luma Energy will drive up the price of electricity, does not have the capacity to meet Puerto Rico's needs, is not incentivized to convert to renewable energy, and does not have proper oversight to protect the public interest (Sanzillo 2020).

In addition to government efforts to upgrade the Island's electrical grid, pharmaceutical plants have invested in their own power generation and have ventured into solar, wind, biodigestion, and ocean geothermal capabilities. These micro-grids, coupled with disaster and accountability plans, have allowed the industry to continue operating through earthquakes, hurricanes, and other natural disasters, in many cases making the plants more resilient than they were before.

Transportation and Shipping

Puerto Rico faces both challenges and advantages when it comes to transporting and shipping products. As an island, there are no ground lines of transportation to mainland and international destinations, and the roadways crossing the Island are in poor repair, making transportation of raw materials difficult and costly. The Jones Act drives up the cost of shipping products to and from the mainland. At the same time, developed air and ocean shipping ports aid the export of goods across the globe.

The economic crisis and corresponding lack of tax revenues that devastated energy and water infrastructure has also taken a toll on maintenance for roadways and seaports. Hurricanes Maria and Irma destroyed much of the transportation infrastructure, while the government struggles to repair and maintain the remaining road network. Further, the government does not always require municipal roads to be constructed with high quality control standards and allows heavy trucks on the roads with very few weigh stations to monitor stress on the roads. These circumstances cause much faster degradation of pavement. The government will need several billion dollars to repair and maintain its existing ground transportation infrastructure (ASCE 2019).

Shipping ports are essential for importing supplies and exporting finished products. Puerto Rico has a number of large seaports for passengers and cargo. Although the hurricanes did considerable damage, repair remains a top priority as these ports are essential for commerce and the import of necessities. Considerable federal funding continues to be devoted to restoration efforts.

The Merchant Marine Act of 1920, commonly known as the Jones Act, drives up shipping prices for Puerto Rico.

The Merchant Marine Act of 1920, commonly known as the Jones Act, drives up shipping prices for Puerto Rico. The regulation requires that goods shipped between American ports be transported on vessels that are American-built, American-owned, and crewed by U.S. citizens or permanent residents. This requirement bars shipping to the mainland on less expensive foreign vessels with lower labor costs and thus significantly drives up the cost of transporting goods. Not only is it about twice the cost to transport cargo on a Jones Act—compliant ship, bringing in raw materials such as oil is also much more expensive. Due to this regulation, imports to Puerto Rico are more expensive, and it costs more to export goods to the mainland (Grennes 2017). In the wake of Hurricane Maria, the Jones Act was temporarily suspended, but efforts to permanently overturn the regulations have been unsuccessful.

Augmenting shipping lines has been a focus for Puerto Rican planners, who have recently made advances in aviation capacity to transport cargo and personnel. In addition to having the largest non-contiguous Foreign Trade Zone, the Department of Transportation recently designated Puerto Rico as an air cargo hub for a two-year term. Air transportation is particularly important for perishable pharmaceutical products, as well as medical supplies that are part of a "just in time" supply chain.

The air cargo hub designation means that shipments can go straight to international destinations without having to process at a mainland port first. It also allows planes from international destinations to pick up cargo in Puerto Rico and then continue on to another international destination, thereby shortening transportation time. For instance, a plane from Europe could land in Puerto Rico, pick up pharmaceutical products, and then continue on to Asia for delivery. The hub also has potential for synergies in other industries as inbound planes could drop off products before picking up their pharmaceutical shipments. Puerto Rico exports pharmaceuticals to more than eighty nations around the world, making the hub a valuable asset (JLL 2020). This classification could benefit the pharmaceutical industry operating on the

Island since it expands the cargo capacity moving in and out of the territory, improves travel time of products, and lowers the supply chain cost of transporting goods to costs that rival those of the shipping industry.

While the hub designation is a boon for Puerto Rico's economy, the designation is for a limited 2-year term with no promise of extension. The fixed term limits its effectiveness in attracting new business to the Island because firms cannot count on the benefit to be in place for future years. Thus while the air hub is a major benefit for Puerto Rico, the duration limits its effectiveness. Nonetheless, coupled with the Foreign Trade Zone benefits, the pharmaceutical companies in Puerto Rico enjoy an expanded reach to markets all over the world. These transportation costs provide a considerable advantage for companies aiming to access multiple markets with low cost barriers.

Bureaucratic Issues

Red tape and inefficient bureaucratic processes are obstacles to doing business on the Island. According to World Bank's Doing Business report, Puerto Rico (considered separately from the U.S.) ranks 65th out of 190 economies analyzed. The U.S. ranks 6th. Complex regulatory procedures and wait times brought down the territory's scores across the board. For instance, although Puerto Rico does not require a minimum paid-in capital, which eases the cost of starting a new business, six different registrations are required, thus bringing down Puerto Rico's rank to 59th (World Bank Group 2020).

Alarmingly, Puerto Rico ranks 143rd in dealing with construction permits due to the 22 procedures required and the average of 165 days it takes to obtain a permit (World Bank Group 2020). Reforms enacted in late 2019 consolidated various permits, certifications, and licenses into one package and streamlined the online application system. Public Affairs Secretary Anthony Maceira boasted that the reforms would cut construction permit time to just 20 days (Caribbean Business 2019). Equally alarming is Puerto Rico's 161st ranking on the registering property index, which measures the time, cost, and procedural steps involved as well as the quality of the land administration system. Again, wait times, which average 190 days, and bureaucratic procedures are problematic (World Bank Group 2020). Pharmaceutical companies cite a lack of stability in the local tax structure as a drawback compared to doing business in the States (Boston Consulting Group 2020).

Operational Risk and Stability

In its study commissioned for the Puerto Rico Financial Oversight and Management Board, the Boston Consulting Group pointed to the perceived operational risk and potential instability in tax incentives as key detractors in attracting investment to the Island. Since Hurricane Maria, political and economic instability have crippled the Island. The economic crisis created by COVID hit the Island particularly hard as the economy relies on tourism and the cruise industry.

Puerto Rico's economy has been in shambles for decades with a significant depression, increasing public debt and the largest municipal declaration of bankruptcy in the United States. Since 2010, the unemployment rate has hovered between a high of 17 percent to current lows of around 8.5 percent (Bureau of Labor Statistic 2020). In 2019, the poverty rate was 43.5 percent, which was significantly higher than the national rate of 10.5 percent, and more than double that of Mississippi's 19.6 percent, which was the highest poverty rate on the mainland (U.S Census Bureau 2019).

Economic instability, fueled in part by changes in the Internal Revenue Code in the treatment of the territory, created a precarious situation for investors. Moreover, frequent changes in the territorial tax laws create uncertainty for businesses looking to relocate in Puerto Rico. Tax advantages might be fleeting and therefore not worth the cost of relocating.

Corruption problems are another issue that dissuades corporations from locating in Puerto Rico. Allegations of corruption concerning the distribution of federal assistance led to massive protests against the territorial government and Governor Ricardo Rosselló in the summer months of 2019. As mentioned earlier, the government-owned Puerto Rico Electric Power Authority (PREPA) has been implicated in a number of corruption issues. In 2009, the Department of Homeland Security's audit of PREPA's use of Federal Emergency Management Agency (FEMA) funds found a number of questionable accounting practices including undocumented charges, duplicate charges, and accounting errors (Kimble 2009). Allegations of corruption continued throughout the next decades as PREPA faced 9 billion dollars of debt. PREPA's management of reconstruction after Hurricane Maria prompted charges of mishandling of contracts, as well as bribery among PREPA and FEMA officials. In an effort to mend the beleaguered utility,

PREPA's board began efforts to privatize the company in the hopes that private entities, driven by profits, would be motivated to maintain assets and improve efficiency. While some observers lauded privatization as a step forward, others argued that the move would do little to curb corruption within the organization (Holz-Eakin 2019; Morales 2020).

Political instability also deters investors from the Island. The eruption of protest against corruption allegations for Governor Rosselló came just days after the FBI arrested two high- ranking Puerto Rican officials on charges of providing lucrative government contracts to their friends. The government also struggles with dysfunction in its operational capabilities. The August 2020 primary elections had to be partially postponed after ballots failed to reach polling places on time, causing confusion and a bevy of lawsuits claiming the election was unfair.

Instability and dysfunction within the territorial government discourages investors who see the Island as too risky for development. Speaking of the political upheaval on the Island, economist Santos Negrón explains:

Failures of the sort foster mistrust and insecurity to foreign capital investors, who first examine the political system, conflicts with protests and institutions, which are as important as tax benefits. These failings are intangible, but business owners don't go to a country where there are changes and conflicts all the time because it doesn't ensure the investment. (Vázquez Colón 2020)

Businesses considering locating their operations in Puerto Rico have to take into the account the credibility and capacity of the government to handle economic affairs. For some investors, the political and economic risks are too high. To attract investment, the government will need to demonstrate stability and capability.

Reinvigorating the Puerto Rican Pharmaceutical Industry

With the national security crisis created in the wake of COVID and U.S. reliance on foreign suppliers of medicine, Puerto Rico has an opportunity to expand its manufacturing capability. Currently, approximately 25 percent of the U.S.'s pharmaceutical and medicine exports come from Puerto Rico, and the Island has a leading edge in manufacturing brand-name drugs;

Figure 5. Global Pharma Companies Puerto Rico Manufacturing

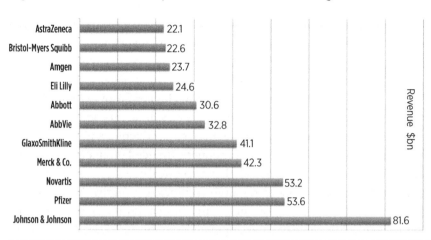

Source: Dina Spencer, (2019), Pharma Boardroom, "Did you know? Puerto Rican Pharma Manufacturing," <https://pharmaboardroom.com/articles/did-you-know-puerto-rican-pharma-manufacturing/#:~:text=Included%20in%20the%20list%20of,Myers%20Squibb's%20Opdivo%20(%234)%2C/>.

five of the top ten drugs of 2018 are produced on the Island. In the wake of Hurricane Maria, certain products such as insulin pumps and pacemakers, which are predominantly manufactured in Puerto Rico, were in critical supply, demonstrating the importance of Puerto Rico's contribution to the U.S.-based supply chain. While these statistics indicate the importance of Puerto Rico to the industry, these numbers are lower than they have been in the past because patents for several branded drugs have expired, prompting the production of the generic variants for a fraction of the cost abroad (Plaza 2020b). As Puerto Rico revitalizes its footing in the medical supply industry, the manufacture of brand-name drugs, generic drugs, and APIs are all attractive options. Leaders must consider the types of manufacturing best suited for the Island's capabilities, the effects of each type on the economy, and the national security needs of the nation as a whole.

Historically, pharmaceutical companies have prioritized the production of brand-name drugs for a number of reasons. Under now revoked provisions of the U.S. tax code, corporations could transfer intangibles associated with new drugs to their Puerto Rico manufacturing affiliates on a tax-free basis, while sheltering all or a significant portion of the income derived from the sale of manufactured products from U.S. income taxation (U.S. GAO 1993). The profit margins of branded products are higher, which means that the companies could shelter more income, as well as pay higher wages to employees. Companies could also deduct expenses related to research and development of new products. Because of the higher profit margins, Puerto Rico has pursued branded pharmaceuticals, even at very low-income tax rates. Puerto Rico needs to continue branded production and take steps to increase production of blockbuster products. Branded products rely heavily on research and development, and pharmaceutical companies seek to locate in areas with ready access to research facilities. Currently, the U.S. mainland with a robust network of universities has an advantage in supporting pharmaceutical research and development (Brandwein 2003). While Puerto Rico's universities have STEM programs, more investment is needed in technology as well as research and development to sustain innovation and new products (Vélez 2020). Continuing relationships between Puerto Rico's universities and pharmaceutical companies, such as exist with Amgen, are a step in the right direction, but more must be done. Beyond the university level, augmenting the standards of public education at all levels, from elementary to graduate levels, is necessary to attract all types of high-tech industry to include biomedicine.

While branded drugs are a lucrative field, markets for branded products often collapse when patents expire. At this point the generic drug market tends to explode. Although Puerto Rico emphasized branded production, the Island

Figure 6. Number of FDA API Facilities By FDA Region Annually

FDA Region	2013	2014	2015	2016	2017	2018	2019
San Juan	6	5	5	4	2	3	1

Source: Neriman Beste Kaygisiz et. al. Working Paper, "The Geography of Prescription Pharmaceuticals Supplied to the U.S.: Levels, Trends, and Implications," Working Paper 26524; National Bureau of Economic Research.

does have experience in generics and APIs. In respect to APIs, the number of sites producing these materials has decreased in recent years (see chart). In order to wrest control of this industry from China, API production in Puerto Rico would need to be restored and augmented. The Boston Consulting Group found Puerto Rico has a strong value proposition for APIs, compared to other U.S. options, due to the robust pharma ecosystem, skilled workforce, and ability to quickly retrofit existing sites (Boston Consulting Group 2020).

Due to lower profit margins, income from generic drugs and API is made through high volumes. China and India excel in the manufacture of these products in large part due to weak environmental regulations that allow manufacturers to dump toxic byproducts of production. While weak regulations help keep costs down, the toll on the environment is extremely high. When considering increasing production of these products, threats to the environment must be factored into the cost-benefit equation. Because profit margins are the determining factor of production, labor and production costs as well as expenses related to regulation and high-quality standards are all key factors, as are government incentives and environmental regulation policies.

Currently, China and India provide the most favorable conditions for generics and APIs. However, with a national security imperative, the U.S. government and Puerto Rican government should consider creating more favorable conditions for these products. A "China Plus One" strategy recognizes that an existing company is not likely to move its factory from China, but new investments would be planned for U.S.-based facilities. Political pressure from U.S. policymakers, combined with a new U.S. demand, creates an incentive to set up parallel factories in the U.S. Because generics and APIs exist on such a thin profit margin, ultimately it may require a government security mandate backed with lucrative incentives to encourage production of these products in Puerto Rico and the U.S. at large.

Lower wages in Puerto Rico compared to the mainland help bring down production costs, but it bears repeating that wage rates in Puerto Rico are still not low enough to compete internationally with China, India, and the host of Latin American countries now bidding for a stake in the pharmaceutical business.

Whereas branded products can often absorb higher production expenses, the cost of electricity and transportation are important factors for generic and API production. Incentives for real estate, as well as building and refurbishing facilities, are critical. While improvements in Puerto Rico's power generation and the new transshipment hub are helpful, further incentives may be required to help with these expenses. Lower wages in Puerto Rico compared to the mainland help bring down production costs, but it bears repeating that wage rates in Puerto Rico are still not low enough to compete internationally with China, India, and the host of Latin American countries now bidding for a stake in the pharmaceutical business. Singapore and Ireland offer significant tax incentives to help compensate for the higher labor costs in their countries. The U.S. will likely need similar policies to bring down overall costs to compensate for labor expenses.

Tax Incentives to Lure Pharmaceutical Corporations
With China's domination of APIs and generic drugs creating a significant security threat to the U.S., numerous plans have been proposed to bring back domestic production of drugs and reinvigorate Puerto Rico's pharmaceutical sector. One method to incentivize pharmaceutical companies to locate on the Island is through tax incentives.

Although Section 936 had numerous pitfalls, it did create a vibrant pharmaceutical industry and supporting ecosystem. Enacting tax incentives similar to Section 936 is a possibility to revive the industry. Drawing on the lessons learned of Section 936, new tax incentives must avoid measures that simply allow firms to transfer their intellectual property and shift profits in order to achieve a tax break. Instead, locating production and creating jobs on the Island must be part of the tax incentive package through measures such as wage tax credits. In addition, firms must be incentivized to invest in the infrastructure and development of the Island rather than pocketing tax breaks to maximize profits. The Puerto Rican government also plays an important role in ensuring investment in infrastructure and would need to use a portion of revenues to correct the myriad infrastructure concerns specified earlier in the paper.

Unwieldly territorial tax codes are problematic for business development due to their complexity and high costs. Tax reforms have generally made the system more complex while doing little to stimulate economic activity (Economic Advisory Taskforce 2020). Despite the Island's troubles with tax incentives and code, tax reform is still a valid strategy to reinvigorate investment. At the territorial level, Act 20 and Act 22, which were then consolidated under Act 60 (collectively known as the Incentives Code) streamlined the tax code and made the process more transparent. The Incentives Code offers corporations a 4 percent corporate income tax, a 75 percent exemption on both property and construction taxes, and a number of other municipal incentives (JLL 2020).

Another method to reinvigorate the industry is by altering Puerto Rico's status as a foreign jurisdiction for tax purposes. Such a move would release Puerto Rico from deleterious policies such as those imposed by the Tax Cut and Jobs Act of 2017. The goal of this law is to cut corporate tax rates for American companies and increase taxes on foreign corporations. Because Puerto Rico is a foreign jurisdiction, corporations operating on the Island are considered foreign and subject to higher taxes. The law created a new tax on Global Intangible Low-Taxed Income (GILTI); it targets intangible assets such as patents, trademarks, and copyrights from U.S. firms whose operations are based abroad. GILTI was designed to discourage U.S. companies from shifting high-yielding assets to foreign nations. This law particularly hit pharmaceutical companies, whose profits are largely derived from intellectual property. Companies with operations in Puerto Rico found themselves subject to this much higher rate on income derived from their worldwide operations. Instead of maintaining the same tax status as New Jersey or North Carolina, Puerto Rico is classified with Ireland and Singapore, which are among its biggest competitors for brand-name pharmaceuticals. Also included in the tax law is a clause called the base erosion and anti-abuse tax (BEAT), which adds back taxable income to otherwise deductible payments to foreign subsidiaries. The tax cuts for stateside-based operations, combined with penalties for foreign-based operations make Puerto Rico much less attractive for investment. Altering Puerto Rico's status as a foreign jurisdiction would alleviate many of these tax-related issues. At the federal level, revising Puerto Rico's status from foreign to domestic would help Puerto Rico compete on a level playing field.

Both tax incentives and changing Puerto Rico's status as a foreign jurisdiction have been considered by Puerto Rican lawmakers. Under the 2017

Tax Cuts and Jobs Act, most of Puerto Rico was declared an Opportunity Zone, which is an impoverished area that qualifies for special tax provisions. An investor in an Opportunity Zone can take capital gains from asset sales to invest in the zones. The investor can then defer taxes until 2026, which in effect reduces the amount owed. If the investor keeps the asset for at least ten years, he can avoid paying capital gains tax on the appreciation (Light 2018). A 2019 amendment granted further tax exemptions to investors. However, there has not been a considerable increase in investment in manufacturing facilities that come with the classification of Opportunity Zones because the funds are overwhelmingly invested in real estate due to lower risk and the ability to realize gains more quickly.

Legislation to Reshore Pharmaceuticals
 In the wake of the COVID pandemic, legislators in Washington, D.C., introduced a number of House and Senate resolutions to strengthen domestic pharmaceutical manufacturing. Resident Commissioner Jenniffer González Colón proposed House Resolution 6443, "Securing the National Supply Chain Act of 2020," followed by House Resolution 7527, "The Medical Manufacturing, Economic Development, and Sustainability (MMEDS) Act of 2020." In the Senate, Florida Senator Marco Rubio filed a companion bill, S. 4467, "A bill to rescue domestic medical product manufacturing activity by providing incentives in economically distressed areas of the United States and its possessions," to match HR 7527. Both bills are designed to reshore pharmaceuticals by providing incentives to pharmaceutical and medical device manufacturing firms investing in economically depressed areas, including Puerto Rico. Resolution 7527 includes increased incentives for firms producing products required for the national supply chain or supporting population health products such as diabetic supplies or heart disease medications (HR 7527 2020).

The bills propose a dollar-for-dollar federal tax credit for 50 percent of wages, investments, and purchases to U.S. companies, making medical supplies for the strategic national stockpile. They also provide tax credits for payments and purchases made in an economically distressed zone, as well as a credit for depreciation and amortization of property within the zone (HR 6443). Resolution 7527 allows either a credit or an expense deduction for capital investment in order to appeal to both startups and large companies. The goal of the legislation is to increase investment in economically distressed zones by requiring companies receiving incentives to hire locally and make enduring capital investments in the economically depressed areas.

Both bills are designed to work under the CARES Act, which is a 2.2 trillion economic stimulus bill in response to the economic disaster caused by the COVID pandemic (Public Law 116-136 2020). While the bills are not specifically designed to help Puerto Rico, most of the Island qualifies as an economically depressed area and thus would benefit from the legislation. Because the bills would benefit states like Georgia, which are vying for industry and also have economically depressed areas, there may be more support in Congress from other state legislators. Although controlled foreign corporations (CFCs) do not receive the same incentives as companies based in Puerto Rico, business-to-business credits are available to companies who are doing business with their state-side branches.

At the same time, Delegate Stacey Plaskett of the U.S. Virgin Islands pressed forward with House Resolution 6648, the "Territorial Economic Recovery Act," which seeks exemption from GILTI for U.S. territories. This bill is popular with CFCs and foreign-owned companies doing business and Puerto Rico and other territories. Plaskett stated, "This bill will place the territories on par with other states here in America," and underscores how "the Virgin Islands is NOT a foreign country" (O'Brien 2020). Former governor of Puerto Rico and candidate for resident commissioner Aníbal Acevedo Vilá also endorsed the resolution: "The measure would revitalize the advanced Puerto Rican manufacturing sector through a competitive differential between Puerto Rico and foreign low-tax countries such as China, India, Ireland and Singapore, our main competitors for vital supply lines for pharmaceutical, biotechnology and manufacturing of medical devices" (O'Brien 2020).

A drawback of 6648 for large branded corporations is the cap on foreign tax credits, which limits the value of the tax exemptions. At the same time, lower margin firms such as those specializing in generics, and small molecules and biologics, and medical device companies would not likely be able to take full advantage of the GILTI exemptions offered under 6648. Compared to González Colón's bill, Resolution 6648 has significantly lower tax credits for wage and depreciation expenses, leading a report contracted by the Financial Oversight Management Board to conclude that González Colón's "Securing the National

Supply Chain Act of 2020" would have a higher aggregate effect on the production of pharmaceutical products. The report estimated a potential to in-shore manufacturing of approximately $1.5-4.5 billion by the year 2026. The elimination of the GILTI Tax, on the other hand, would result in an estimated $0.5-2.5 billion in manufacturing by 2026 (Boston Consulting Group 2020).

House Resolution 6648 is also unpopular among Puerto Rican leaders who seek statehood for the Island because the bill is based on territorial status. If Puerto Rico becomes a state, Resolution 6648 will no longer apply. Thus, statehood advocates tend to favor legislation that does not apply specifically to territories. Since its introduction to the House of Representatives in May 2020, the bill has not moved out of the Ways and Means Committee.

While these bills seem to be steps forward, there are a number of other steps that will be critical. First, the government will need to provide long-term price and volume guaranteed contracts so that manufacturers are assured that they will be able to sell their product at a profitable price, thereby taking out some of the risk in reshoring to Puerto Rico (Comerford 2020). The executive order requiring government agencies to buy American-made products is a step in the right direction in providing a guaranteed market for U.S. firms. Funding from BARDA is also a forward step in offsetting the costs of investment and higher wages required compared to companies operating abroad.

Legislation that favors either statehood or territorial status is immediately mired in this political quagmire before the economic components of the legislation are even considered.

It is also imperative that the local and federal government grant opportunities to small and medium enterprises (SMEs). Puerto Rico's Economic Task Force argues that COVID hit SMEs on the Island especially hard; SMEs experienced insecure supply chains and an inadequate amount of saved capital to survive (Economic Advisory Task Force 2020). While the report referred to all SMEs, this argument readily applies to SMEs in the bioscience industry. Development of new products, such as a vaccine for COVID or targeted therapies for certain strains of a disease, are often led by SMEs before large-scale production is turned over to the large companies. However, more often than not, contracts involving a research and manufactory intensive industry such as the pharmaceutical industry are beyond the reach for small- and medium-size companies, whose risk tolerance is hindered by the size of the contract. SMEs often struggle to compete for large Department of Defense contracts unless there are small business set-asides in the contract.

Finally, if the U.S. wants to effectively compete with Chinese firms, government officials must fast track approvals. The FDA needs to streamline approval processes for new products, while Puerto Rican officials must look at fast tracking bureaucratic procedures such as building permits (Comerford 2020). Relaxing environmental standards to those of India and China would lower costs; thus the harm it could cause to the Island would likely outweigh any advantages. Instead, government incentives must be offered to help reduce this cost burden.

The Issue of Status

As the U.S. looks to reshore pharmaceutical production, Puerto Rico is a logical location for the industry. Not only does Puerto Rico have the ecosystem to support reshoring the industry, revitalizing this sector would help solve Puerto Rico's economic woes. The various proposals circulating through Congress are a step in the right direction, although gaining enough political support among legislators might prove difficult.

One of the obstacles facing any type of legislation involving Puerto Rico is its status as a territory rather than a state because status has become a political hot button issue. Legislation that favors either statehood or territorial status is immediately mired in this political quagmire before the economic components of the legislation are even considered.

Although U.S. citizens, Puerto Ricans have very little say in the enactment of federal regulations. The Island's territorial status means that Puerto Ricans cannot vote in federal presidential elections, thus greatly diminishing its political voice within the executive branch. The territory has no representative in the Senate and only one representative in the House of Representatives. Further, the House delegate is a non-voting member who can sponsor legislation but is denied a vote on legislation on the House floor. The Resident Commissioner, as Puerto Rico's member is called, therefore does not have the constituency or voting power equal to Representatives from the States. Informal vote trading within the House is difficult for the Commissioner because she doesn't hold that bargaining power.

With many states competing for federal funding in the pharmaceutical sector, Puerto Rico's lack of representation in Congress is a distinct disadvantage.

Many state legislators are also seeking federal programs, such as new tax policies, to revitalize the pharmaceutical industry in their home states. Thus, Puerto Rico is competing against other stateside locations for re-shoring opportunities. With many states competing for federal funding in the pharmaceutical sector, Puerto Rico's lack of representation in Congress is a distinct disadvantage. State legislators may not support programs such as more favorable tax treatment through the repeal of GILTI if it has a nega-tive impact on their own constituents.

Puerto Rico's unequal representation means that the territory must rely on the diaspora of Puerto Ricans living on the mainland. Approximately 5.4 mil-lion Puerto Ricans live on the mainland, with the largest concentrations in New York, Florida, and New Jersey. Harnessing the political capital of these citizens may be critical in swaying Congressional members to vote for legislation that favors the territory. For this reason, the recent collaboration between Resident Commissioner Jenniffer González Colón and Florida Senator Marco Rubio is sound strategy. Rubio can harness the strong Puerto Rican constituency in Florida while solving a broader U.S. security concern. Further, seeking support for eco-nomically distressed zones in general has a wider appeal than legislation aimed just at Puerto Rico. Thus, this type of legislation may have a stronger chance of being supported in Congress than bills aimed at eliminating the GILTI tax.

Because solutions to the U.S.'s security issue involving dependency upon foreign pharmaceuticals and solutions to Puerto Rico's economic crisis ultimately rest on political solutions, Puerto Rico will need to har-ness enough political capital to secure legislation that puts the Island at the center of reshoring efforts. At the same time, because Puerto Rico is ready to increase pharmaceutical production, almost any legislation to reshore production will benefit the Island. Thus, Puerto Rico stands to benefit from any number of legislative initiatives currently in Congress.

Concluding Thoughts

Although this national security issue had been growing for decades, the COVID pandemic exposed the U.S's critical dependency on foreign nations for prescription drugs and medical devices. White House Office of Trade and Manufacturing Director Peter Navarro commented, "If this crisis has taught us anything across party lines is that we do indeed need to bring home the pharmaceutical supply chain, that it is not just a public health issue, but a national security issue and an economic security issue" (Doyle 2020).

Heading into the 2020 presidential elections, the fate of legislation and presidential plans for reshoring was precarious. On the campaign trail, President Trump boasted of his executive order to import less expensive pharmaceuticals from Canada. This was a step in the wrong direction because although it might reduce prices, it does not alleviate U.S. dependency on foreign countries. Candidate Joe Biden's campaign promises included efforts to bring supply chains back from China, but his plan for Puerto Rico did not include a strong effort to bolster manufacturing. In recent months neither President Trump nor President-elect Biden has publically discussed the need to reshore the pharmaceutical industry. Further, the legislation discussed has stalled within Congress, and there is little indication that any movement on these bills is forthcoming. With COVID vaccinations rolling out to the public, a sense of complacency could set in, and there is a danger that the issue might fall off the political agenda as new security challenges take center stage. It remains to be seen if President-Elect Biden and the Democrat-controlled Congress will prioritize the security problems caused by foreign manufacture of pharmaceuticals and medical devices.

The other unknown is if the citizens of the United States will be willing to bear the costs of reshoring in order to secure supply lines. Despite the urgency of this issue, the cost of reshoring will be extremely expensive. Higher wages, more expensive land, stricter quality and environmental standards, and increased government incentives all add up to much higher costs of production for American-made pharmaceutical products. These costs will likely be passed on to consumers in the form of higher prices. At the height of the

COVID pandemic, consumers may be willing to pay more for American-made products. However, memories are short, and once fervor over the pandemic quiets down, consumers may be reticent to pay higher prices.

The national security crisis caused by U.S. dependency on foreign pharmaceuticals must be solved, and Puerto Rico's capacity to help solve this problem should be capitalized. Legislators must act while public sentiment is in favor of new solutions.

NOTES

[1] The views expressed are those of the authors and do not reflect the official policy or position of the US Air Force, Department of Defense or the US Government. PA#: USAFA-DF-2020-354.

[2] A court challenge rose to the U.S. Supreme Court where the Court ruled that although a foreign company may have different antitrust laws that should be given consideration, U.S. courts are not bound to reach conclusions based on the law in a foreign country. The decision was important in upholding U.S. antitrust regulations as applied to foreign countries.

[3] At the same time, it should be noted that Puerto Rico's public education system is suffering overall. The population exodus combined with the economic depression led to a sharp enrollment decline and the closing of many elementary and secondary schools (Hinojosa, Meléndez and Pietri 2019). Recent reports from the National Assessment of Education and Progress reveal that achievement scores across a range of studies are lower in Puerto Rico compared to the mainland, and high school dropout rates are highest in Puerto Rico (National Center for Education Statistics).

REFERENCES

American Society of Civil Engineers (ASCE) Puerto Rico Section. 2019. 2019 Report Card for Puerto Rico's Infrastructure. Accessed 16 August 2020. <https://www.infrastructurereportcard.org/wp-content/uploads/2019/11/2019-Puerto-Rico-Report-Card-Final.pdf/>.

Bradsher, Keith. 2020. China Dominates Medical Supplies, In this Outbreak and in the Next. *The New York Times* 5 July. <https://www.nytimes.com/2020/07/05/business/china-medical-supplies.html?action=click&module=Top%20Stories&pgtype=Homepage/>.

Brandwein, Scott. 2003. Site Selection for Pharmaceutical and Bio Industries. *Trade and Industry Development* 30 June. Accessed 17 December 2020. <https://www.tradeandindustrydev.com/industry/bio-pharma/site-selection-pharmaceutical-and-bio-industries-444/>.

Boston Consulting Group. 2020. Manufacturing Opportunities for Puerto Rico: Pharmaceuticals and Medical Devices. Report by the Boston Consulting Group, Inc. for the Puerto Rico Financial Oversight and Management Board, 4 August.

Bureau of Labor Statistics Data Tools, Data extracted on 5 October 2020. Accessed 15 July 2020. <https://data.bls.gov/timeseries/LASST720000000000004?amp%253bdata_tool=XGtable&output_view=data&include_graphs=true/>.

Comerford, Michelle. 2020. Preparing for Global Volatility: Reshoring & Securing your Supply Chain. Videoconference 18 June. Accessed 30 September 2020. <https://vimeo.com/430480061/>.

Congress. House, MMEDS Act of 2020. HR 7527, 116th Cong, Introduced July 9, 2020. Accessed 30 September 2020. <https://www.congress.gov/bill/116th-congress/house-bill/7527/titles?r=1&s=1/>.

Congress. House, Securing the National Supply Chain Act of 2020. HR 6443, 116th Cong, Introduced 3 April 2020. Accessed 30 September 2020. <https://www.congress.gov/bill/116th-congress/house-bill/7527/titles?r=1&s=1/>.

Congress. The Coronavirus Aid, Relief, and Economic Security Act, Public Law No: 116-136 116th Congress, Passed 27 March 2002. Accessed 30 September 2020. <https://www.congress.gov/bill/116th-congress/house-bill/748/text?overview=closed/>.

Corporate Tax Reform and Puerto Rico. 2018. *Puerto Rico Report* 7 January. Accessed 30 September 2020. <https://www.puertoricoreport.com/corporate-tax-reform-puerto-rico/#.Xs5v32hKi70/>.

Doyle, Katherine. 2020. Peter Navarro calls on Congress to 'bring home' manufacturing to Puerto Rico. *The Washington Examiner* 28 May. <https://www.washingtonexaminer.com/news/peter-navarro-calls-on-congress-to-bring-home-manufacturing-to-puerto-rico/>.

Economic Advisory Taskforce. 2020. Workstream #3 Group Report: Mid and Long Term Strategic Initiatives. 8 July.

ERC for Structured Organize Particulate Systems. 2015. FDA Approves Tablet Production on Continuous Manufacturing Line. Accessed 10 September 2020. <https://erc-assoc.org/content/fda-approves-tablet-production-continuous-manufacturing-line-0#:~:text=On%20April%208%2C%20 2016%2C%20the,facility%20in%20Gurabo%2C%20Puerto%20Rico/>.

Gibson, Rosemary and Janardan Prasad Singh. 2018. *China Rx: Exposing the Risks of America's Dependence on China for Medicine.* Amherst, NY: Prometheus Press.

Goel, Vindu. 2020. As Coronavirus Disrupts Factors, India Curbs Exports of Key Drugs. *The New York Times* 3 March. <https://www.nytimes.com/2020/03/03/business/coronavirus-india-drugs.html/>.

Gray, John V., Aleda V. Roth and Michael J. Leiblein. 2011. Quality Risk in Offshore Manufacturing: Evidence from the Pharmaceutical Industry. *Journal of Operations Management* 29, 737–52.

Grennes, Thomas. 2017. An Economic Analysis of the Jones Act. Mercatus Research, George Mason University. Accessed 10 January 2021. <https://www.mercatus.org/publications/trade-and-immigration/economic-analysis-jones-act/>.

Hang, Yanzhong. 2020. The Coronavirus Outbreak Could Disrupt the U.S. Drug Supply. *The Council on Foreign Relations* 5 March. Accessed 10 September 2020. <https://www.cfr.org/in-brief/coronavirus-disrupt-us-drug-supply-shortages-fda/>.

Hicks, Tony. 2019. China has More Control Over Your Prescription Drugs than You May Think. *Healthline* 19 September. Accessed 15 September 2020. <https://www.healthline.com/health-news/china-control-over-your-prescription-drugs#Controlling-the-supply/>.

Hinojosa, Jennifer, Edwin Meléndez and Kathya Severino Pietri. 2019. Population Decline and School Closure in Puerto Rico. Centro Center for Puerto Rican Studies, Centro RB2019-01. Accessed 17 December 2020. <https://centropr.hunter.cuny.

edu/sites/default/files/PDF_Publications/centro_rb2019-01_cor.pdf/>.

Holz-Eakin, Douglas. 2019. The Rebuilding and Privatization of the Puerto Rico Electric Power Authority (PREPA). Testimony to the United States House of Representatives Committee on Natural Resources. Accessed 16 December 2020. <https://www.americanactionforum.org/testimony/the-rebuilding-and-privatization-of-the-puerto-rico-electric-power-authority-prepa/>

Invest Puerto Rico. n.d. BioScience Brochure. Accessed 2 September 2020. <https://assets.website-files.com/5daf5d8a5d7dc953af9ee0a7/5ee7dc15d287bf4134825a92_BioScience-Invest-Puerto-Rico.pdf/>.

IPEN Project. 2014. China chemical safety case study: Industrial dumping at the Tuoketuo Pharmaceutical Industrial Park. September. Accessed 15 September 2020. <https://ipen.org/sites/default/files/documents/Case%20Study%20Report%20Tuoketuo%202014r.pdf/>.

JLL. 2020. Puerto Rico Life Sciences Report. Accessed 5 September 2020. <https://www.us.jll.com/en/trends-and-insights/research/puerto-rico-life-sciences-manufacturing-report/>.

Kimble, C. David. 2009. Hurricane Georges Activities for Puerto Rico Electric and Power Authority. Department of Homeland Security. 11 August. Accessed 17 December 2020. <https://www.oig.dhs.gov/assets/GrantReports/OIG_DA-09-21_Aug09.pdf/>.

Langhauser, Karen and Meagan Parrish. 2018. Puerto Rico's Pharma: Battered but Unbroken. *Pharma Manufacturing* 12 September. Accessed 30 September 2020. <https://www.pharmamanufacturing.com/articles/2018/puerto-rico-pharma-battered-but-unbroken/>.

Light, Joe. 2018. Puerto Rico's New Tax Break Lures Money as Expiration Date Looms. *Bloombergnews,* 11 December. <https://www.bloomberg.com/news/articles/2018-12-11/billion-dollar-tax-break-could-give-puerto-rico-false-hope-again/>.

Litovsky, Alejandro. 2016. Antibiotic Waste is Polluting India and China's Rivers; Big Pharma Just Act. *The Guardian* 25 October. <https://www.theguardian.com/sustainable-business/2016/oct/25/antibiotic-waste-pollution-india-china-rivers-big-pharma-superbugs-resistance/>.

Meléndez Edwin and Jennifer Hinojosa. 2017. Estimates of Post Hurricane Maria Exodus from Puerto Rico. Center for Puerto Rican Studies, Centro RB2017-01. Accessed 15 August 2020. <https://caribbeanmigration.org/sites/default/files/repository/disaster_puerto_rico_rb2017-01-post-maria_exodus_v3_centropr.hunter.cuny_.edu_2017.pdf/>._

Miller, Rodrick T. 2020. Puerto Rico's Big Pharma Push. *IndustryWeek* 1 June. Accessed 16 December 2020. <https://www.industryweek.com/the-economy/article/21132824/puerto-ricos-pharma-push#:~:text=As%20mentioned%2C%20Puerto%20Rico's%20life,Opdivo%2C%20Enbrel%20and%20Xarelto/>.

Morales, Ed. 2020. Privatizing Puerto Rico. *The Nation* 1 December. <https://www.

thenation.com/article/world/puerto-rico-privatization-prepa/>.

National Center for Education Statistics. n.d. Accessed 16 December 2020. <https://
     nces.ed.gov/>.

Obrien, Garret. 2020. Territorial Economic Recovery Act Could Lessen the
     United States' Reliance on Foreign Import. *Pasquines* 29 May. <https://
     pasquines.us/2020/05/29/territorial-economic-recovery-act-could-
     lessen-the-united-states-/>.

Plaza, Elizabeth 2020a. Discussion with author.

_____. 2020b. Puerto Rico as a Prime Location for Reshoring, Presentation.

President's Task Force on Puerto Rico's Status. 2011. Report. March. Accessed 15
     July 2020. <https://obamawhitehouse.archives.gov/sites/default/files/
     uploads/Puerto_Rico_Task_Force_Report.pdf/>.

Priest, Christopher. 2019. Prepared Statement of Mr. Christopher Priest, Principal
     Deputy, Deputy Assistant Director, Healthcare Operations, Defense
     Health Agency, Regarding The Military Health System, Before the U.S.-
     China Economic and Security Review Commission. 31 July. Accessed
     10 August 2020. <https://www.uscc.gov/sites/default/files/Priest%20
     US-China%20Commission%20Statement.pdf/>.

Puerto Rico Govt: Doing Business on the Island 'Now Easier than Ever.' 2019.
     Caribbean Business 8 May. <https://caribbeanbusiness.com/puerto-rico-
     govt-doing-business-on-the-island-now-easier-than-ever/>.

Sanzillo, Tom. 2020. Contract Between Puerto Rico, LUMA Energy Sets up Full
     Privatization, Higher Rates for Island Grid, Report from the Institute for
     Energy Economics and Financial Analysis (IEEFA). October.

Schumer, Senator Charles. 2019. Letter to The Honorable Gene L. Dodaro. 12
     December. Accessed 15 July 2020. <https://www.schumer.senate.gov/imo/
     media/doc/CES%20to%20GAO%2012-12-191.pdf/>.

Spetalnick, Matt, David Brunnstrom, and Andrea Shalal. 2020. Trump Risks
     Blowback from War of Words with China over Coronavirus *Reuters* 25
     March. <https://www.reuters.com/article/us-health-coronavirus-usa-
     china/trump-risks-blowback-from-war-of-words-with-china-over-coro-
     navirus-idUSKBN21C3KS/>.

U.S. Census Bureau Quick Facts. 2019. 1 July. <https://www.census.gov/quickfacts/
     fact/table/US/PST045219/>.

U.S. Energy Information Administration. 2020. Puerto Rico Territory Energy
     Profile. Accessed 15 September 2020. <https://www.eia.gov/state/print.
     php?sid=RQ/>.

U.S. General Accounting Office (GAO). 1992. Pharmaceutical Industry: Tax Benefits
     of Operating in Puerto Rico. May. Accessed 30 September 2020. <https://
     www.gao.gov/assets/80/78407.pdf/>.

_____. 1993. Tax Policy: Puerto Rico and the 936 Tax Credit. June. Accessed 10
     July 2020. <https://www.gao.gov/assets/220/218131.pdf/>.

U.S. Food and Drug Administration (FDA). 2019. Generic Drugs. 21 November. Accessed 30 September 2020. <https://www.fda.gov/drugs/buying-using-medicine-safely/generic-drugs/>.

_____. 2020. Form 483, Accessed 30 September 2020. <https://www.fda.gov/inspections-compliance-enforcement-and-criminal-investigations/inspection-references/fda-form-483-frequently-asked-questions/>._

Vázquez Colón, Brenda A. 2020. Chaos at Puerto Rico Primaries Transcends Politics. *The Weekly Journal* 11 August. <https://www.theweeklyjournal.com/business/chaos-at-puerto-rico-primaries-transcends-politics/article_9c5f60fc-dbe3-11ea-9c3d-6b22a41e6cd3.html/>.

Vélez, Xenia. 2020. Conversation with author.

Woodcock, Janet. 2019. Securing the U.S. Drug Supply Chain: Oversight of FDA's Foreign Inspection Program, Testimony before the House Committee on Energy and Commerce, Subcommittee on Oversight and Investigations. 10 December. Accessed 15 September 2020. <https://www.fda.gov/news-events/congressional-testimony/securing-us-drug-supply-chain-oversight-fdas-foreign-inspection-program-12102019/>.

World Bank Group.2020. Doing Business 2020, Economy Profile Puerto Rico. Accessed 30 September 2020. <https://www.doingbusiness.org/content/dam/doingBusiness/country/p/puerto-rico/PRI.pdf/>.

Puerto Rico's Outmigration and the Deterioration of Economic Conditions As Identified With National Debt

IVIS GARCÍA

ABSTRACT

Scholars of migration have focused on economic conditions but mostly unemployment as the main driving force behind outmigration. However, the literature has rarely concerned itself with how declining economic conditions linked to national debt affects the perception of people and their decision-making related to migration. By employing a case study of Puerto Rico, this article attempts to examine how economic conditions driven by a growing debt might be related to outmigration. A regression analysis shows that there is a moderate relationship between migration flows and debt, while a weak relationship exists between outmigration and unemployment. To further understand the relationship between debt and outmigration, this article relies on personal interviews with 15 individuals who moved to Florida between 2013 and 2017. Interviews show that economic concerns related to the debt crisis in various shapes and forms have become a dominant narrative explaining why people leave. I employ a political economy framework discussing concepts such as neoliberalism, deindustrialization, financialization, austerity, and colonialism to understand the fiscal and migration crisis of the Island. [Keywords: Economic crisis, emigration, neoliberalism, austerity, and Puerto Ricans]

Introduction

Previous research suggests that there are many drivers of outmigration (Hear, Bakewell and Long 2018). Researchers often use the push-pull migration framework to understand these drivers. These drivers could be divided into two categories: economic and non-economic. On the non-economic side, migrants might be pushed by environmental degradation (Ezra and Kiros 2001; Gray 2009), food insecurity (García-Barrios et al. 2009), natural disasters (Gray and Mueller 2012), or escaping war, guerrilla warfare, or political turmoil (Hatton and Williamson 2003; Menjívar 1993). Meanwhile, emigrants might be pulled by employment opportunities (Katz, Creighton, Amsterdam and Chowkwanyun 2010; Kline 2003), educational opportunities (Findlay, McCollum, Coulter and Gayle 2015), family reunification (King 2015), and geographic amenities (Gabriel, Shack-Marquez and Wascher 1992; Partridge, Rickman, Olfert and Kamar 2012).

Although the literature recognizes that there are many drivers of outmigration, most scholars of migration have focused on economic as opposed to social and political conditions (Clark and Robey 1981). What is more, most studies concentrate on unemployment (Beaudry, Green and Sand 2013; Glaeser and Gottlieb 2009; Moretti 2011, 2013; C. Pissarides 2000; C. Pissarides and Wadsworth 1989). However, the literature has rarely concerned itself with how the deterioration of economic conditions, due to growing national debt, affects the perceptions of people and influences their decision-making related to emigration. In an era of globalization, neoliberalism, privatization, deindustrialization, and financialization, it becomes imperative that scholars pay more attention to how these processes affect global and regional migration. Put simply: finance and, thus, debt, have taken over. This article departs from the premise that deindustrialization, along with financialization, one of the driving forces of neoliberalism, has been linked to increasing private and public debts that end up in economic crisis (Brenner, Peck and Theodore 2010;

The author (ivis.garcia@utah.edu) is an Assistant Professor in City & Metropolitan Planning at the University of Utah. She chairs Planners for Puerto Rico and it is involved with the National Puerto Rican Agenda, the Disaster Housing Recovery Coalition of the National Low-income Housing Coalition, and Centro's IDEAComún—all of which promote Puerto Rico's recovery. Dr. García has a Ph.D. in Urban Planning and Policy from the University of Illinois at Chicago.

Harvey 2007a; Koser 2010; Krippner 2012). Thus, we can expect that financial shocks will increase migration well into the future. By using evidence from Puerto Rico, this article attempts to examine how a collapsing economy resulting from a growing national debt relates to outmigration.

As of May 2017, Puerto Rico had $74 billions of bond debt and $49 billions of unfunded pension liabilities (Kobre & Kim LLC 2018). Credit Rating Agencies became concerned in particular with government-owned public utilities' (electricity, transportation, water, and sewage) reliance on funding from Puerto Rico's Government Development Bank. These amounts were excluded from calculations related to the Constitutional Debt Limit (Kobre & Kim LLC 2018). Starting in 2012, Moody's downgraded the Island's bond rating to "junk" status (Moody's downgrades Puerto Rico general obligation and related bonds to Baa3 from Baa1 and certain notched bonds to Ba1 2012).

The Puerto Rican economy has been in recession since 2006, right after the possession tax-credit (section 936 of the Internal Revenue System) ended. Between 2002 and 2006 a total of 27,000 manufacturing jobs were lost; from 1996 to 2006 the economy contracted by 10 percent and employment declined by 14 percent (U.S. Department of Treasury 2018). According to Decennial Census data and the American Community Survey (ACS) 1-year estimates, Puerto Rico has been experiencing significant population losses since 2000, from 3.8 million to 3.3 million by 2016. Based on ACS data, from April 1, 2010, to July 1, 2017, net migration accounted for -431,942 individuals. In 2010, unemployment in Puerto Rico hit a peak at 19.0 percent compared to 9.3 percent in the U.S., according to the U.S. Bureau of Labor Statistics.

News of the recession and outmigration demoralize citizens and engender a negative outlook for the future of the Island. Puerto Rico's largest newspaper, *El Nuevo Día*, echoes such lethargy with headlines such as: "Population Decline Continues in the Island," "Mass Migration Limits Economic Recovery in Puerto Rico," "Unstoppable Emigration," and so forth (Continúa la baja en la población de la isla 2014; Emigración masiva limita la recuperación económica de Puerto Rico 2015; Cortés Chico 2013). Given these narratives linking migration to dire economic conditions as they relate to the debt crisis, I seek to understand the question, How are economic conditions driven by a growing debt tied to outmigration?

This article is organized as follows. In the first section, I outline a literature review on how economic hardship, emigration, and social networks are related. The second section will examine the historical processes that led to Puerto Rico's fiscal crisis. The third section will serve as a theoretical framework by outlining the global and structural changes that triggered the collapse of Keynesianism and the rise of the neoliberal paradigm along with its austerity measures and the preservation of colonialism. The fourth section will discuss the methods employed: quantitative and qualitative methods through a regression analysis and interviews of 15 individuals who emigrated to Florida where most Puerto Ricans are moving. The fifth section will present findings from the above methods. The sixth and final section will be dedicated to our discussion and conclusions.

Economic hardship, emigration, and social networks

Most studies have tried to understand which push-pull factors related to economic conditions affect migration. Economic conditions are also varied; they tend to be understood in terms of government spending (Barro 1979), Gross Domestic Product (GDP) (Milne 1993), housing prices (Gabriel et al. 1992; Glaeser and Gottlieb 2009; Jackman and Savouri 1992), and differential wages (Kennan and Walker 2011; C. Pissarides 2000; C. Pissarides and Wadsworth 1989). Unemployment is understood as the most critical push factor affecting outmigration (Beaudry et al. 2013; Glaeser and Gottlieb 2009; Moretti 2011, 2013; C. Pissarides 2000; C. Pissarides and Wadsworth 1989). Some studies have demonstrated that economic crisis can be a significant determinant of outmigration (Bertoli, Brücker and Moraga 2013; Chalamwong 1998; Koser 2010). Moreover, these studies have shown that expectations on future economic conditions create an incentive to move (Bertoli, Brücker and Fernández-Huertas Moraga 2016; Cebula and Vedder 1973; Schultz and Sjöström 2001).

This article is concerned with how deteriorating economic circumstances driven by national debt might be associated with outmigration. To date, few studies analyze the relationship between financial crisis, recessions, and migration, but they have not concentrated on growing national debt (Beets and Willekens 2009; Caraveli and Tsionas 2012; Martin 2009). Still, it might be useful to understand how migration is affected during economic crises. It has been noted that when economic conditions are good, potential emigrants tend to stay in their home countries or regions (Beaudry et al. 2013; Glaeser and Gottlieb 2009; Moretti 2011, 2013; Pissarides 2000;

Pissarides and Wadsworth 1989). On the contrary, if the home country or region economic conditions are bad, then people are more likely to migrate (Bertoli et al. 2013; Bertoli, Brücker and Fernández-Huertas Moraga 2016).

Not surprisingly, the 2008 recession resulted in less demand for labor and thus, migration declined, generally speaking. For example, the U.S. saw a significant slowdown in immigration (including illegal crossings) paired with a massive outflow of immigrants, mainly from Mexico (Ghosh 2013). As the debt crisis deepened in Greece, unemployment rose to 27.5 percent in 2013, according to Eurostat. Fiscal austerity measures in Greece resulted in wage reductions and spending cuts were implemented with no obvious impact of these reforms on labor market outcomes (Pissarides 2013). During the recession there were significant declines in immigration paired with the emigration of Greek nationals (Caraveli and Tsionas 2012). Similarly, in the 1980s the Latin American debt crisis accelerated migration to the U.S., most notably from Mexico (Davis 1991).

Puerto Rican men and women have relied historically on their cultural networks, community organizations, and transnational cultural ties, to move to new destinations.

Even during times of economic crisis, at the international, national, and regional levels, economic conditions vary from one geography to another. Thus, individuals move to geographies that might offer them better opportunities (Overman 2008). During the financial crisis in the U.S. people move from one state to another. Demographer William Frey from the Brookings Institution found that Florida, Arizona, Nevada, and California saw more households moving out than coming in (Frey 2001). The years before the recession these states experienced more growth in the housing market than other regions. Thus, many Mexicans, who mostly worked in construction, left in record numbers cities like Las Vegas and Phoenix (Frey 2009). As demonstrated above, individuals and households move because they perceived other states, towns, or regions to be relatively better.

Migrants also move where they have social networks (Massey et al. 1993). Network theory helps us explain the interpersonal ties connect migrants from the country of origin and destination. Migrants simply move to where they have family or friends; and they usually have a shared origin most times based on geography or kinship. In other words, migrants mobilize their social capital to find employment and other opportunities (Portes 1998). Puerto Rican men and women have relied historically on their cultural networks, community organizations, and transnational cultural ties, to move to new destinations. Among Puerto Ricans there are no visa restrictions because they are American Citizens. That being said, moving is relatively easy. However, for migrants, not knowing the language is one of the most important reasons for choosing to live near their kinship in communities of Puerto Rican nationals (Portes 1998; Portes and Böröcz 1989; White and Kaufman 1997).

It is evident today that Puerto Ricans are moving to the U.S., particularly Florida, to find employment, improve their lives and provide a better future for their families. In the case of Puerto Rico, the root cause of the economic crisis is the loss of manufacturing jobs. Based on a review of the literature, we can assume that deteriorating economic conditions tied to national debt relates to outmigration. Understanding perceptions of weak economic conditions driven by the debt crisis concerning emigration is essential—not just in the context of Puerto Rico, but also to the U.S. mainland and internationally. The following historical background presents economic and political factors that contributed to Puerto Rico's fiscal crisis.

Historical Background

When Luis Muñoz Marín was elected governor in 1952, he implemented his economic policy structure, Operation Bootstrap. His feeling was that, given the inability for the impoverished Island to create the capital necessary for economic growth, he would leverage the Island's only real asset (i.e., cheap, abundant, and expendable labor) and offer enormous incentives to U.S. capitalists to jumpstart the Island's failing economy (United States Congress 1950). The framework to offer these tax incentives already existed, but Muñoz Marín was able to convince Congress to ratify it through the 936 of the Internal Revenue Code (United States Congress 1950). Also known as the possession tax-credit, it allowed mainland companies willing to locate on the Island to "repatriate income generated from their investments in Puerto Rico to their parent companies on the mainland free of federal taxes" (Rivera-Batiz and Santiago 1998, 11). Many U.S. manufacturing companies moved to

Puerto Rico including apparel, food processing, ceramics, tobacco, and, later, electronic and pharmaceutical products (Pantojas-García 1985; Rivera-Batiz and Santiago 1998). Operation Bootstrap worked, to some degree, at least for a time. From the 1950s to the 1960s, life expectancy rose, education rates tripled, and Puerto Rico's per capita GDP became the highest in Latin America (Rivera-Batiz and Santiago 1998). Before long, the Island would go from the "Poorhouse of the Caribbean" to the "Caribbean Showcase" for development in the third world (LaCossitt 1958; Roman 1997b).

The industrial sector started to decline in the late-1970s in the U.S. after the oil crisis, and revenues kept falling through the 1980s (Brenner et al. 2010; Harvey 2007a). Given that salaries in Puerto Rico were higher than in foreign markets, more and more American industries set up shops outside of the U.S. possession (Rivera-Batiz and Santiago 1998). By the 1990s, the Puerto Rican government privatized some state-run companies—including hotels, hospitals, telecommunications, and transportation (Ayala and Bernabe 2009). With the decline in manufacturing, the tax-shelters under the possession tax-credit

Figure 1. Manufacturing Employees In Puerto Rico

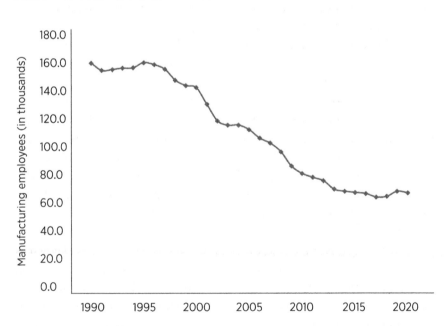

Source: Bureau of Labor of Statistics, State and Area Employment, Hours, and Earnings.

were allowed to expire as part of the Small Business Job Protection Act of 1996 (Abel and Deitz 2014; Dietz 1987; Roman 1997). A 10-year phased-out period was given to companies grandfathered under the program (Kobre & Kim LLC 2018). Between 1996 and 2002 about 27,000 industrial jobs were lost (U.S. Department of Treasury 2018). Figure 1 "Manufacturing Employees In Puerto Rico," paints a clear picture of deindustrialization.

From 1996 to 2006 the Puerto Rican economy contracted by 10 percent and employment declined by 14 percent (U.S. Department of Treasury 2018). After the possession tax-credit, section 936 of the Internal Revenue System, phase-out period ended in 2006 ended, Puerto Rico entered a recession. In 2010 the unemployment reached its peak at 19 percent (see Figure 2). And in 2012 the financial crisis erupted, causing the deteriora-

Figure 2. Puerto Rico Statistics

Year	Population in Puerto Rico	Moved to the U.S.	Percent out-migration	Unemploy-ment rate %	Debt (Billions)	Per capita debt
2005	3,668,730	47,208	1.3%	15.2	$40.2	$10,976
2006	3,745,007	67,110	1.8%	15.7	$43.1	$11,518
2007	3,765,840	60,388	1.6%	16.0	$46.1	$12,264
2008	3,781,815	67,862	1.8%	14.8	$53.3	$14,118
2009	3,784,396	62,074	1.6%	18.9	$58.4	$15,436
2010	3,554,642	59,885	1.7%	19.0	$62.2	$17,500
2011	3,542,571	76,218	2.2%	18.5	$64.2	$18,145
2012	3,515,844	74,500	2.1%	17.3	$69.9	$19,895
2013	3,466,804	73,846	2.1%	18.1	$70.0	$20,204
2014	3,404,122	83,844	2.5%	18.5	$72.2	$21,229
2015	3,329,046	89,000	2.7%	18.9	$72.2	$21,689
2016	3,411,307	88,676	2.6%	16.2	$70.0	$20,520
2017	3,468,963	142,000	4.1%	16.4	$66.9	$19,314

Source: Puerto Rican Community Survey, Bureau of Labor Statistics, and Center for a New Economy.

tion of the tax base due to population loss. In 2015 the debt was its highest at 72 billion—$21,628 per capita.

The percent of people who left Puerto Rico was much higher than in Greece. From 2014 to 2015, the population in Puerto Rico shrank by 2.7 percent. In comparison, in Greece the maximum was 0.6 percent from 2011 to 2012 (see figure 3). However, the unemployment rate in Greece was much higher than Puerto Rico—reaching 27.5 percent in 2013. The per capita debt peaked in 2011 at $32,014.

As happened in Greece, in Puerto Rico, instead of developing another economic development strategy, the government relied in short-term fixes such as 1) creating the Sales and Use Tax (SUT), 2) creating COFINA, a public corporation dedicated to issuing bonds secured by SUT, 3) insurer's use of interest-rate swapping arrangements to generate cash and close budget gaps, 4) increasing debt financing, and 5) insuring Puerto Rico related bonds purportedly secured with Employees Retirement System contributions (Kobre & Kim LLC 2018).

Figure 3. Greece Statistics

Year	Population in Greece	Moved to another E.U. country	Percent out-migration	Unemploy-ment rate (percent)	Debt (Billions)	Per capita debt
2007	11,040,000	22,898	0.2%	8.0	$240	$21,739
2008	11,060,000	23,485	0.2%	7.8	$265	$23,924
2009	11,090,000	14,927	0.1%	9.6	$301	$27,142
2010	11,120,000	11,579	0.1%	12.7	$330	$29,676
2011	11,120,000	32,315	0.3%	17.9	$356	$32,014
2012	11,090,000	66,494	0.6%	24.4	$305	$27,412
2013	11,000,000	59,148	0.5%	27.5	$319	$29,000
2014	10,040,000	47,198	0.5%	26.5	$317	$29,003
2015	10,860,000	44,934	0.4%	24.9	$320	$29,466
2016	10,780,000	10,332	0.1%	23.5	$320	$29,592

Source: Eurostat.

Puerto Rico owned-entities such as the Puerto Rico Electric Power Authority ($10 billion in debt), Puerto Rico Aqueduct and Sewer Authority ($5 billion), and Puerto Rico Highways and Transportation Authority ($5 billion) incurred more than $20 billion in liabilities; the rest, $54 billion, went to primary government obligations (Government Accountability Office 2017). These entities used appropriations from the General Fund, bond proceeds, and short-term cash influxes from the Government Development Bank of Puerto Rico, instead of finding additional revenues or cutting cost (Diaz 2013; González 2012; Kobre & Kim LLC 2018).

When Puerto Rico-owned entities did not have access to credit markets, they sought bankruptcy. The island-government enacted the Recovery Act of 2014, which was contested by a host of investment groups including California Tax-Free Trust. They argued that Puerto Rico, like a U.S. state, was prohibited from creating any scheme of their own that resembled formal bankruptcy laws (*Puerto Rico v. Franklin California Tax-Free Trust* 2016). The U.S. Supreme Court concluded that, for this purpose, Puerto Rico is more similar to a "State" and therefore cannot enact or enforce their Recovery Act. The Supreme Court reaffirmed the First Circuit court's declaration that "it was up to Congress, not Puerto Rico, to decide when the government-owned companies could seek bankruptcy" (*Puerto Rico v. Franklin California Tax-Free Trust* 2016, 4).

On June 28, 2014, Puerto Rico started to take steps to restructure its debt by enacting the Recovery Act (*Act of June 17, No. 71, 2014 P.R. Laws 273* 2014). Bondholders challenged it. On February 6, 2015, the U.S. District Court of Puerto Rico sided in favor of the bondholders (*Puerto Rico v. Franklin California Tax-Free Trust* 2016). On June 15, 2015, the Governor of Puerto Rico declared that the debt was unpayable, and by August, the Puerto Rico Public Finance Corporation defaulted (*Act of June 17, No. 71, 2014 P.R. Laws 273* 2014). In April, 2016, the Puerto Rico Legislative Assembly enacted a moratorium and presented to the U.S. House of Representatives a bill constituting the first version of the Puerto Rico Oversight, Management, and Economic Stability Act (PROMESA). The proposal was approved in June 2016. Through PROMESA, an Oversight Board, with seven members appointed by the U.S. President and one member selected by the Government of Puerto Rico, was created to "provide a method to achieve fiscal responsibility and access to the capital markets and, among other things, improve fiscal governance, accountability, and internal controls" (U.S. Supreme Court 2016). It has been argued that the Oversight Board is anti-democratic and exacerbates colonialism (Atiles-Osoria 2018; Cabán 2017).

According to the ACS 1-year estimates for 2017, 43.5 percent of the Puerto Rican people live in poverty with a per capita income of $11,688—lower than that of any state of the union.

Puerto Rico's ability to pay for health, education, infrastructure, and other essential services has diminished since PROMESA has forced the Puerto Rican Government to pay its creditors by imposing fiscal discipline and profound structural adjustments (Cabán 2017). The University of Puerto Rico, which relied upon bond issuances, owed $551 million in 2017, and has to pay by increasing tuition and reducing staff (U.S. Supreme Court 2016). One-third of all public schools have been closed across the Island (El Departamento de Educación anuncia el cierre de 283 escuelas 2018). Municipalities have not been able to pay Medicaid, traditionally funded with bonds. As a result, many healthcare providers have either left to the U.S. or stopped accepting Medicaid; this has created a long waitlist for treatment by healthcare providers who still accept it (Johnston and Merling 2017).

Everyday people have been affected deeply by the fiscal crisis. According to the ACS 1-year estimates for 2017, 43.5 percent of the Puerto Rican people live in poverty with a per capita income of $11,688—lower than that of any state of the union. The debt of Puerto Rico as a percentage of aggregate income was 101 percent, compared to 29 percent for the State of New York and 59 percent for the City of Detroit (Kobre & Kim LLC 2018). The burden on people has been of massive proportions—to the point that the debt has been called a humanitarian crisis (Cabán 2017; Kobre & Kim LLC 2018). Many have argued that the debt crisis is not a Puerto Rico only phenomenon but part of broader global processes: neo-liberalization and the perpetuation of colonialism (Cabán 2017; CLACLS 2017). The following section is an effort to outline the changes from Keynesianism to Neoliberalism and from an industrial to a financial economic development model. I hope that the theoretical framework presented below can help us understand outmigration surrounding declining economic conditions tied to debt and followed by austerity measures with contemporary links to colonialism.

Theoretical Framework

From the Great Depression to Reagan's tenure, Keynesian economics ruled, advocating for a strong state to quell the radical impulses and the terrors of the business cycle under capitalism (Brenner, Marcuse and Mayer 2011; Brenner et al. 2010; Peck, Theodore and Brenner 2013). Welfare systems were set up, and the state intervened in industrial practices. A system of "embedded liberalism" was born and brought significant prosperity and a reasonable amount of equality to the U.S. and Puerto Rico. In Puerto Rico, social change in the mid-20th century took place in two major waves: the New Deal and Operation Bootstrap. The New Deal moved quickly from extending democracy and relief to the poor masses to the idea of reconstruction and long-term economic development. From the mid-1930s to the mid-1950s, there was more investment in Puerto Rico than during the entire course of the Island's history (Burrows 2014; Mathews 1960).

By the 1960s, stagflation—the combination of high inflation and increasing unemployment—began to disrupt the Keynesian structures that had been put in place, and, once again, capital began to accumulate into fewer and fewer hands (Gaffikin and Warf 1993; Harvey 2007b). By the 1970s, the gold standard had broken down, and currencies were floated (Quiggin 1999). This led to a deepening of state control, while popular movements and the organization of labor became targets of capitalist antagonism: corporations urged that they needed a higher capacity for the accumulation of wealth—ostensibly because this allowed them to hire more workers (Brenner et al. 2010; Harvey 2007b; Krippner 2012). By the 1980s, inflation and debt became the sole enemy of the financial, city and state apparatuses. Austerity measures were implemented along with the privatization of public assets resulting in the subordination of the poor (Pohlmann 1982). This started a long and deep global recession as well as a period of structural readjustment.

In the case of Puerto Rico, after the departure of manufacturing companies, the government borrowed hundreds of millions of dollars to pay its bills: pay pensions, workers, everyday necessities as well as their debt obligations and not on activities that would jumpstart the economy (Abel and Deitz 2014; Cortés Chico 2013a; Diaz 2013; González 2012). The Puerto Rican government hoped that the economy was going to recover eventually. Given that, under PROMESA, the Government of Puerto Rican needed to pay bondholders, they started to implement austerity measures—increasing

taxes and cutting government spending. The imposition of austerity pro-
ceeds a process of "accumulation by dispossession," which can be witnessed
most egregiously in the Great Recession and the foreclosure crisis of 2008
in the United States (Harvey 2007a).

Krippner (2011) and others have come to see finance as the emergent
driver of accumulation because it is designed to protect financers from
catastrophic losses. The economic shift from industrial work to service
work mostly in the FIRE sector—finance, insurance, and real estate has
been recognized by Harvey (2007a) and a whole host of other scholars as a
characteristic of the neoliberal era. Scholars have noted how globalization
through the internationalization of capital and finance (also a characteristic of neoliberalism) has restructured labor markets and caused massive
migration (Katz et al. 2010; Sassen 2001). What is more, migration has been
closely tied to colonialism through history (Sánchez Korrol 2006). As many
see it, PROMESA has reaffirmed colonial relationships between Puerto Rico
and the United States (Cabán 2017; CLACLS 2017).

This article tries to understand if the compulsion for outmigration might
come from the economic conditions surrounding debt and subsequently a
degradation of economic opportunities. An overarching question is if and how
degrading economic conditions driven by debt has affected migration. In the
rest of the article, I seek to understand if there is a relationship between deteriorating economic conditions induced by the debt crisis and outmigration.
The next section explains the methods employed in the article.

Methods

I use Puerto Rico as a case study to understand how discourses surrounding debt affect migration patterns. Case studies are used to understand
a problem at hand and to answer how questions such as, What are the
relationships between debt and outmigration?, come into discussion.
In regards to time and space, attributes of interest to those who pursue
case study methodology, we are studying the outmigration in Puerto Rico
before and after the debt crisis took place in 2006 (Creswell 2008; Yin
2008). Case studies usually employ multiple sources of evidence—thus,
methodologies like interviews, descriptive statistics, and other quantitative techniques are used to triangulate data and offer an interpretation of
the phenomenon (Marshall and Rossman 2010; Yin 2008). In this case, I

am trying to explain and determine whether there are links between debt and outmigration. Even though case studies are trying to understand cause and effect relationships, the boundaries between the phenomenon and context are not clearly evident—meaning that the phenomenon is context-based and could be perceived differently (Yin 2008). This study takes an interpretative/constructivism approach to tell a story related to the relationship between outmigration and debt (Mertens 1997).

For this article, I conducted interviews in the Summer 2018 and Fall 2019. The sample was selected using a snowball sample developed by Goodman (1961), I first rely on friends and family who knew of someone who had emigrated. Then, I rely on the networks of the participants. In the snowball sample methodology, each respondent was asked if he or she could refer another person and so on (Goodman 1961). The target population only included people who had migrated to Florida because this is where most Puerto Ricans are moving to—as demonstrated in Figure 4.

Figure 4. Geographical Ability in the Past Year for Current Resident-State, County and Place Level in the United States

Geography	Year ago: Puerto Rico
Wisconsin	528
Rhode Island	692
Virginia	901
Illinois	942
North Carolina	1,044
Georgia	1,245
Ohio	1,639
Texas	2,605
New Jersey	3,059
Connecticut	3,117
Massachusetts	4,040
New York	4,269
Pennsylvania	5,287
Florida	13,258

Source: 2006-2010 American Community Survey Selected Population Tables.

Figure 5. Characteristics of Interview Participants

ID	Name	Gender	Age	Profession	Marital Status	Year of Migration	City they move from	Migration Destination
1	Mateo	M	36	Landscaper	Married	2021	Comerio	Palatka
2	Valeria	F	36	Pharmacologist	Married	2015	Bayamon	Orlando
3	Eduardo	M	27	Construction worker	Divorced	2012	Carolina	Kissimmee
4	Emilia	F	25	Nurse	Single	2014	San Juan	Miami
5	Karina	F	24	Student, part-time work	Single	2012	Rincon	Tallahasse
6	Julio	M	48	Professor	Single	2014	San Juan	Orlando
7	Alejando	M	24	Student, part-time work	Single	2012	Guaynabo	Tampa
8	Belinda	F	40	Self-employed	Divorced	2018	Lares	Jacksonville
9	Victor	M	53	Electrician	Divorced	2014	Carolina	Kissimmee
10	Manuel	M	20	Cashier	Single	2017	Juana Diaz	Wesley Chapel
11	Nellie	F	34	Engineer	Married	2016	Guayama	Largo
12	Martha	M	26	Human resoruces	Married	2015	Dorado	Apopka
13	Erika	F	37	Homemaker	Married	2018	San German	Orlando
14	Maribel	F	42	Teacher	Divorced	2013	Barceloneta	Immokalee
15	Oscar	M	77	Retired	Married	2017	Humacao	Orlando

I interviewed only people who made the move to Florida between December 13, 2012 (when Moody's downgraded Puerto Rico) and September 20, 2018 (before Hurricanes Irma and Maria). A total of 15 individuals participated. Eight were women, and seven were men, between ages 20 and 77. The participants move to Florida from different municipalities (see Figure 5).

I used a semi-structured interview, and I asked only two questions: 1) What motivated you to leave Puerto Rico?, and 2) Would you come back to Puerto Rico? The first question intended to see if people would bring up the issue of the unemployment, debt crisis, or related matters as the reason to migrate. The second question was designed to understand interviewees perceptions of the overall situation in Puerto Rico.

Interviews were conducted using Zoom video conference. They took between 20 to 53 minutes. Participants were given a pseudonym. The interviews were conducted in Spanish. I listened to the data collected carefully and identified theme coding in the audio using Atlas.ti. I only transcribed and translated the most insightful quotes chosen for the article. The analytical approached utilized in this research was grounded theory (Corbin and Strauss 2007).

In addition to using interviews and macro data to paint a demographic portrait, this article employed a linear regression model to investigate the relationship between three variables debt, unemployment, and outmigration. Debt was used as the independent variable (or predictor), while outmigration and unemployment were used as dependent variables. Before running a linear regression, a histogram and a scatter plot were used to determine if the data from 2005-2016—concerning debt in billions from the Government Bank of Puerto Rico, the unemployment rate, and Puerto Rican migration to the U.S. from the American Community Survey—were normal and linear, which it was. In addition, the variance inflation factor (VIF) was used to detect multicollinearity; the VIF was closer to one which does not signal multicollinearity. Therefore, the assumption of independence between the two variables was not violated. Taken together, the assumptions of normality, linear relations, and independence between variables means that we could perform a linear regression analysis.

The validity of the model was determined using the R-square and the adjusted R-square—measuring the extent of variation in the response variable that is being accounted for by the independent or predictor variable. A 5 percent level of significance, which corresponds to 95 percent confidence interval, was used throughout the analysis. The correlation co-efficient ranges from $-1 < r < +1$. The closer it is to one, the stronger the relationship, so that the following may be surmised: in: (1) $0.7 < |r| \leq 1$ there is a strong correlation, in (2) $0.4 < |r| < 0.7$ there is moderate correlation, in (3) $0.2 < |r| < 0.4$ there is a weak correlation, and in (4) $0 \leq |r| < 0.2$ there is no correlation.

Findings

The Relationship between Unemployment, Debt and Outmigration

The null hypothesis (H_0) is that debt is not related to outmigration and unemployment, while the alternative hypothesis (H_1) would be that there is a relationship. Figure 6 shows that there is a moderate positive correlation for model 1 and 2. In model 1, 64.7 percent of the variability in migration can be accounted for by the amount of debt according to the R-square (coefficient determination), while about 60.8 percent of the variation is accounted for by the adjusted R-square (adjusted coefficient of determination). Similarly, model 2 shows that about 61.2 percent of the variation of the unemployment rate in Puerto Rico accounted for the amount of national debt in billions by the R-square, while about 56.9 percent of the variation is accounted for by the adjusted R-square. As shown in Figure 3, the correlation of model 1 and 2 is statistically significant at 0.001 and 0.002, respectively.

Since p-value is $0.000 < 5$ percent, we can reject H_0 and conclude that there are statistically moderately effect perceptions of debt on migration. According to figure 7, for every 8 billion dollars in the increase in debt, there are approximately 21,848 people who out-migrate. Similarly, there is a moderate effect of debt on unemployment. For every one billion increase in debt there is a 0.11 points increase on the unemployment rate. It is important to note, however, that correlation does not imply causation. There are a number of limitations on this analysis. First, there is a limited number of observations. Second, the percentage of variation explained by the predictor variables are low. This means there are still some extraneous variables that determine the predictor. Usually a R-square of greater than 85 percent is expected and not however met. When we used outmigration as the dependent variable, R-square explained 64.7 percent, and when we used the unemployment rate as the dependent variable it was 61.2 percent, respectively. Further research should take place to identify other parsimonious independent variables.

Figure 6. Model Summary

Model	R	R Square	Adjusted R Square	Std. Error of the Estimate
1	.805a	0.647	0.608	7434.455
2	.782a	0.612	0.569	1.0666

Model 1
a. Predictors: (Constant), Debt in Billions
b. Dependent Variable: Outmigration
Model 2

Figure 7. ANOVA

Model		Sum of Squares	df	Mean Square	F	Sig.
1	Regression	912932033.7	1	912932033.7	16.517	.003b
	Residual	497440084	9	55271120.44		
	Total	1410372118	10			
2	Regression	16.169	1	16.169	14.214	.004b
	Residual	10.238	9	1.138		
	Total	26.407	10			

Model 1
a. Dependent Variable: Outmigration
b. Predictors: (Constant), Debt in Billions

Model 2
a. Predictors: (Constant), Debt in Billions
b. Dependent Variable: Unemployment rate in Puerto Rico

As described above, unemployment only has a weak relationship to debt, but debt has a moderate relationship with outmigration. What I seek to explain in the sections below is that because of the debt narratives people start having a negative outlook about the future (e.g., more austerity measures lead to loss of basic services such as public schools in their neighborhoods, fears of experiencing future unemployment, and so on). Service cuts, increased taxation, etc. act as push factors for migrants who are seeking for better opportunities elsewhere. The next section explores why people move using interviews.

Narratives of Puerto Rico's Dire Economic Conditions
Interviewees were mostly young and of working age; and the majority

Figure 8. Coefficients[a]

Model	Unstandardized Coefficients		Standardized Coefficients	t
	B	Std. Error	Beta	
1	21847.539	11881.062		1.839
	8.00E-07	0	0.805	4.064
	11.044	1.704		6.479
2	1.07E-10	0	0.782	3.77
	Residual	10.238	9	9
	Total	26.407	10	10

Model	Sig.	95.0% Confidence Interval for B		VIF
		Lower Bound	Upper Bound	
1	0.099	5029.29	48724.367	1
	0.003	0	0	
2	0	7.188	14.9	1
	0.004	0	0	

Model 1. Dependent Variable: Outmigration
Model 2. Dependent Variable: Unemployment rate in Puerto Rico

left for Florida to work or study. They offered different reasons to the question of why they migrated among them: aspirations of doing better, improving their quality of life, better schools for their children, seeking higher education, healthcare, higher wages, employment, better career prospects, promise for remunerative labor, opportunities for professional self-fulfillment, running away from austerity measures, heavy taxation, poverty, and following family members, partners, and friends, among others. Three economic push and pull forces at work emerged from these interviews: 1) unemployment and underemployment, 2) seeking better opportunities, and 3) austerity public policy measures related to debt. Their stories show how they used their social (networks) and human capital (current skills).

Pushed by Unemployment and Underemployment

The stories of interviewees described how the deteriorating economic conditions linked to the debt exacerbated the problems of unemployment and underemployment. Mateo identified unemployment as the primary factor for migrating, "Because of the crisis in Puerto Rico, there is no employment creation. I lost my job. I got tired of searching. My debt was increasing. I was very discouraged." Mateo speaks of unemployment but in the context of the debt crisis. Two of the interviewees discussed underemployment in connection with the economic situation. Valeria shared her story,

I left with my husband and children to go and find a job here. I studied pharmacology, and those companies left. After being laid-off, I was working part-time at a consulting firm for $10 an hour. In Puerto Rico, opportunities are minimal. Because of the economic recession, people leave with no options. I did not have to go, but I wanted to. We had income, but it was not enough.

Similarly, Eduardo, who doesn't have a bachelor's degree and worked two jobs, explained, "I could not do it anymore, the situation was unsustainable. The jobs I had did not allow me to pay child support." Others who were unemployed wanted to work. Manuel explained:

I was living with my mom, just doing odd jobs. I did not have a real job, you know. A Florida company recruited my friend and I, to do manual labor. We stayed for a couple of months with the company, but the work conditions were bad, 10 hour days and hard labor. My friend and I ended up leaving. I work as a cashier now, the pay is low, but I am much more relaxed and I keep my eyes open for better opportunities. I just do not want to go back home, so I can sit with my mom and do nothing. I know I am better off here. I just want to make it work.

Nellie, an engineer, said, "My husband, who is a mechanical engineer like me, found a better job in Largo. He got me an interview too. We left because we both got better jobs, not only better pay, but simply better positions that further develop our skills and with more mobility." Interviewees identified unemployment and underemployment as closely related to the debt crisis. Looking for employment and better employment opportunities seem to be a compelling reason that propels people to leave the Island.

Pulled By Better Opportunities

There are pull factors related to better opportunities in the U.S. that explain outmigration. Ideas about the U.S. vary from person to person, but a historical belief among Puerto Ricans is that life is better in the United States. Nellie expressed this general feeling in her own words: "For me it was a choice for something better. We were doing it for our future and the future of our daughter. We are happy here, and I keep telling my mom, she should move here with us." Martha married a Puerto Rican gentleman who lived in Apopka and the plan from day one was to move to Florida. When I asked why she responded:

Moving to Florida was the right decision. He was already there with a job and an apartment, and the job prospects here were bad for me. I worked part-time in human resources. I wanted to do my master's, find a real job, one that made me feel good about myself. I just wanted to build a new life, fulfill my dreams. I felt I could not do that in Puerto Rico.

Emilia, 25, just graduated as a nurse. Like many other graduates, she did not look for employment in Puerto Rico. She explained:

Since I entered the program, I saw that many of those who graduated were leaving, looking for a better life. There is a demand for trained people who know Spanish in Miami and other places as well. When I was close to graduating, I took English classes, I started studying for the exam, and applied to do my internship in places where I knew someone. I had an offer there in Puerto Rico, but here the salaries and working conditions are better.

I asked Emilia if she would return. To that question, she replied:

If there was a change in the economy I would. But things there are difficult, from bad to worse. Government cuts are causing the quality of life to deteriorate. The public healthcare system is in crisis. There is a lot of people with chronic illness that can't get services. It is very sad and depressing. I prefer to work in a better resourced healthcare system where I can actually do my job.

Oscar moved because of his wife: "My wife needs dialysis treatment for kidney disease and I cannot really drive anymore and it is hard to get nurses to come home. My kids and grandkids are in Orlando. The health care system is so much better and faster. It made sense for us to move."

Erika who is a mother of two and a homemaker explained that she moved because of healthcare and education,

My son is autistic. He went to a special Christian school in Puerto Rico with individualized attention, it was not a school for kids for autism, but they had many students because this one teacher was so good with them. The teacher moved to Florida, she was telling me how there are nice schools in Orlando and how health therapy was part of the autism school. I told my husband, and we visited to go to Disney World and see the school. He did not tell me this at the time, but he had asked his company to transfer him Orlando, and they did!

Karina, a recent high school graduate, had a similar experience to Emilia: "As soon as young people graduate high school they leave [...] I was bothered by the economic situation of the country, the debt, all that. For nobody is easy." Those who graduate either high school or with a university degree leave for a wide range of reasons, but usually they report leaving because they can earn more, have more significant economic opportunities, better work conditions, and enjoy a higher quality of life in the United States—including better schools and health care. The effect of the debt seems to contribute to people wanting to leave.

Pushed By Public Policy Measures

The logic of neoliberal economic policies have been implemented with vigor as a way of being able to pay the debt—selling public assets, privatization, regressive tax increases, and other austerity measures—and as a result, many have left as a consequence. Take Julio, who was a Professor at the University of Puerto Rico (UPR). He explained why someone with tenure would be so eager to move,

There is something important to say about the debt and UPR. There have been countless budget cuts in the last ten years. We are freezing positions when people retire. They are threatening us to teach four classes a semester instead of two [...] Every time we are fewer and fewer, and all the work has to be distributed to those that remain. I was three years in the market until something came up at UCF.

Students at UPR, the public university, have suffered in other ways the consequences of national debt, Alejandro an undergraduate student commented,

The students have been protesting because they increased tuition costs. As a result
of the debt, they cut more than $500 million to UPR. The strike lasted like months. I
decided to go to Tampa. My idea was to get there and be with my friend for a short
time. I ended up transferring [...] The truth is that if the strike had not happened, I
would not have left. The debt, but what is more trying to pay it, by cutting government
expenses, put the country in total crisis.

The state has stopped spending money on higher education and also
schools. Belinda, a mother of two, moved to Florida:

They are closing hundreds of schools in Puerto Rico. They closed the little school where
my two children went. They wanted them to travel to a school that is about 30 minutes
from here. I have a sister who lives in Jacksonville. I was telling her this. She said,
"Look, why you don't move with me?"

Maribel, a teacher, was also affected by the school closures:

I lost my job at the local school. I guess I could have move to another school,
but it was impossible, too far and too cumbersome. I left and went to the
Immokalee Technical College just to learn, or I should say practice English. Meanwhile
I studied for the Florida department of Education Certification. I passed. I would not
have left if I did not have to. Migration was not a choice at all, I feel I was forced by the
cuts in school funding after the debt crisis.

To the question of whether to come back, Victor, an electrician who
moved as soon as he had the opportunity to find employment and rented an
apartment near his brother in Kissimmee, FL, responded:

Going back, for now, is not possible: unemployment, protests, austerity, poverty, [...]
PROMESA measures in response to the debt are punishing people, robbing them!
When you add up what everything costs...and on top of that, more taxes! The situation
will last, is not going to get better. We are getting poorer and poorer every time. The
government takes a massive debt on your behalf and then tells you that you have to
pay? If there is no government to work for us, we have to do something by ourselves,
and that's why we migrate!

Similarly, Eduardo mentioned that "Things are not like before. Since the government-debt crisis, I do not see much joy in people. That is why the massive escape." Austerity measures have been a significant push factor; underfunding public education and closing campuses, is just one example of many. Other interviewees discussed increasing taxes and cutting pensions, but these factors did not seem as closely tied to making someone move. Taken together, all of these stories have the same understanding of structural migration: people are moving from Puerto Rico, a place in deep economic trouble, into the U.S., a place where they have more financial stability. Interviewees also share a view of how government officials took decisions that affect them to a personal level. But they also recognized that their experiences were not only personal but shared by the Puerto Rican people.

Discussion and Conclusions

To return to the initial question at the introduction of the article: How are economic conditions driven by a growing debt linked to outmigration? Although the statistical analysis demonstrated the relationship is moderate, interviews showed that the debt crisis has become a powerful narrative that has made people think that the economy and the quality of life was not going to get better, and that outmigration represented a way of seeking out a better life. From this research we can conclude that in the case of Puerto Rico people are presumably inclined to migrate because of the deteriorating economic conditions, debt being one indicator. In comparison, other studies show unemployment as a significant factor, and increasing debt is not something that has been explored in the literature. In other words, this case shows that in Puerto Rico, the debt crisis has magnified the push and pull factors.

To assess economic conditions linked to the debt crisis I relied on conversations with recent emigrants. I discovered that the reasons why people move are complicated. It is not as simple as losing one's employment; there are many reasons tied to economic conditions that made for these individuals and households' emigration an obvious option. Some people, like Manuel left because they were unemployed to begin with. Others have lost their jobs, like Mateo, but many others, like Valeria and Eduardo, have been attracted because they are underemployed. Similarly, students that graduate like Emilia and Karina left without looking much at all for employment in Puerto Rico, even if they have been offered a job on the Island. For them leaving means to pursue opportunities they do not think are available in Puerto Rico because of the economic crisis.

I discovered that the reasons why people move are complicated.

These interviews were also telling on the role of social capital. Martha, Emilia, Alejandro, and Victor discussed how they use their networks before migrating, how they found employment, and how they moved in with their relatives or found out about opportunities from their friends and family. Kinship was an important reason for many of those who chose to move to Florida.

Similarly, austerity measures have been driving people out. Julio, the UPR professor, was burdened by the extra work placed on him as people retired and there were no new openings. His institution did not provide him with immunity from further potential changes such as doubling his workload. Closing the UPR due to protest was yet another debt-related disturbance that caused Alejandro to leave after classes were canceled for months. Belinda was affected by school closures, one of the measures taken to restructuring the excessive debt.

What lessons can we learn from these personal experiences? Clearly, migrants made connections between debt and their migration stories at the individual level. But telling their stories was also a way of assessing the economic condition of Puerto Rico as a whole. These stories show that migration is rooted in an individual migrant's advantage. Is fair to assume that when it gets to the personal level public debt becomes a problem for the individual. But rational choice at the individual level doesn't explain the whole story here because some emigrants were not pushed to leave because of the debt (which resulted in unemployment, closing public schools, etc.).

Leaving is not strictly about economic reasons. It is also related to overall and future prospects. Some seem to perceive their move as forced because of the economic crisis. At the same time migrants perceived the outcome as positive because they feel they have an opportunity for a better future. Some emigrants, like Nelly, Emilia, Martha, Oscar, Erika, and Karina, moved because of the perception of better opportunities being schooling, health care, quality of life, etc. Deteriorating economic conditions linked to the debt crisis have been the cause of insecurity; this pushes people away from Puerto Rico and pulls them into the U.S. in search of a better life. The debt crisis has caused a severe threat to future stability. But perhaps most important, public policies have magnified the adverse effects of these shocks by implementing neoliberal measures. Globally, austerity has been one of the mechanisms of paying national debts. Puerto Rico is no exception.

The consequences of growing debt distinguish this group of emigrants as a cohort, dividing them from previous emigrants. While Puerto Ricans have historically migrated from their homeland to the U.S. in mass because they have felt the compulsion of escaping their economic conditions, something is different this time. Puerto Rico entered a financial crisis in 2006 at the end period of the possession tax-credit, a time characterized by population decline, a rise in unemployment, and rising pension liabilities. The people of Puerto Rico have led grassroots movements as exemplified by the student struggle, in which many have argued the country's debt cannot be paid. But according to neoliberal and colonial thought, they cannot walk out from the deficit. The attempt to pay the debt by implementing austerity measures has disrupted social life in Puerto Rico to the extent that it has forced people to migrate. The Island is going through a neoliberal economic transformation that has resulted in an increase of migrant workers from all ages, social classes, educational backgrounds, and professions.

A critique of neoliberalism helps us to understand how the capitalist world-economy is a system that has resulted in accumulation by dispossession. The global implementation of neoliberalism seems to be pushing toward the continuing establishment and preservation of empire and colonial power, as well as the reinvigoration and exacerbation of class inequalities. The commonsense ideas of neoliberalism spread in a colonial manner from the global North to South have led many, regardless of party affiliation, toward a belief that market mechanisms are the most efficient and effective means of governing society. As a justification for undermining the state's ability to participate or intervene in the marketplace, the ideals of neoliberalism urge that state intervention in the market cannot be as effective as, and can only undermine the effectiveness of, market mechanisms. Decapitalization of the state follows, and as the state's capacity to effectively intervene in the economy is impaired, proponents of neoliberal and colonial ideals point at the dysfunction of the country as proof of governmental inefficiency. Austerity is presented as the only option.

In interviews, the proposition of returning to Puerto Rico became an invitation to describe debt, austerity, and severe economic conditions as the main reason why they would not return. The situation from past years is seen as unchanged and perhaps unchangeable even in the near future. The status of the Puerto Ricans vis-à-vis the Puerto Rican government and PROMESA following a broader trend of increasing debts and responding with neoliberal and austerity policies is an integral component of understanding outmigration. Discussions concerning the increasing sentiments that the federal and local government has relied on austerity measures as a way of paying the debt have indicated to people that the only thing they can do to exercise their agency is to leave. More research has to be done to explore these relationships further. I hope this article has contributed to the recognition that economic conditions tied to debt and the implementation of neoliberal as well as colonial policies have resulted in a new form of Puerto Rican migration.

REFERENCES

Abel, J. R. and R. Deitz. 2014. The Causes and Consequences of Puerto Rico's Declining Population. *Current Issues in Economics & Finance* 20(4), 1–8.

Act of June 17, No. 71, 2014 P.R. Laws 273. 2014.

Atiles-Osoria, J. 2018. State of Exception as Economic Policy: A Socio-Legal Analysis of the Puerto Rican Colonial Case. SSRN Scholarly Paper No. ID 3183309. <https://papers.ssrn.com/abstract=3183309/>.

Ayala, C. J. and R. Bernabe. 2009. *Puerto Rico in the American Century: A History Since 1898.* Chapel Hill: The University of North Carolina Press.

Barro, R. J. 1979. On the Determination of the Public Debt. *Journal of Political Economy* 87(5, Part 1), 940–71. <https://doi.org/10.1086/260807/>.

Beaudry, P., D. A. Green and B. M. Sand 2013. Spatial Equilibrium with Unemployment and Wage Bargaining: Theory and Estimation. Working Paper No. 19118. <https://doi.org/10.3386/w19118/>.

Beets, G. and F. Willekens 2009. The Global Economic Crisis and International Migration: An Uncertain Outlook. *Vienna Yearbook of Population Research* 7, 19–37.

Bertoli, S., H. Brücker and J. F.-H. Moraga. 2013. The European Crisis and Migration to Germany: Expectations and the Diversion of Migration Flows. SSRN Scholarly Paper No. ID 2210830. <https://papers.ssrn.com/abstract=2210830/>.

Bertoli, S., H. Brücker and J. Fernández-Huertas Moraga 2016. The European Crisis and Migration to Germany. *Regional Science and Urban Economics* 60(Supplement C), 61–72. <https://doi.org/10.1016/j.regsciurbe-co.2016.06.012/>.

Brenner, N., P. Marcuse and M. Mayer, eds. 2011. *Cities for People, Not for Profit:*

Critical Urban Theory and the Right to the City. New York: Routledge.

Brenner, N., J. Peck and N. Theodore. 2010. Variegated Neoliberalization: Geographies, Modalities, Pathways. *Global Networks* 10(2), 182–222. <https://doi.org/10.1111/j.1471-0374.2009.00277.x/>.

Briggs, X. de S. 2005. *The Geography of Opportunity: Race and Housing Choice in Metropolitan America*. Washington, DC: Brookings Institution Press.

Burrows, G. 2014. The New Deal in Puerto Rico: Public Works, Public Health and the Puerto Rico Reconstruction Administration, 1935-1955. Ph.D. dissertation, The City University of New York.

Cabán, P. 2017. Puerto Rico and PROMESA: Reaffirming Colonialism. Latin American, Caribbean, and U.S. Latino Studies Faculty Scholarship. <https://scholarsarchive.library.albany.edu/lacs_fac_scholar/25/>.

Caraveli, H. and E. G. Tsionas. 2012. Economic restructuring, crises and the regions: The political economy of regional inequalities in Greece. Retrieved 4 August 2018. <http://www2.lse.ac.uk/europeanInstitute/research/hellenicObservatory/pubs/GreeSE.aspx/>.

Cebula, R. and R. Vedder. 1973. A Note on Migration, Economic Opportunity, and the Quality of Life. *Journal of Regional Science* 13(2), 205–11. <http://onlinelibrary.wiley.com/doi/10.1111/j.1467-9787.1973.tb00395.x/full/>.

Chalamwong, Y. 1998. The Impact of the Crisis on Migration in Thailand. *Asian and Pacific Migration Journal* 7(2–3), 297–312. <https://doi.org/10.1177/011719689800700209/>.

CLACLS. 2017. Puerto Rico Conference: Savage Neoliberalism, Colonialism, and Financial Despotism. Presented at the Center for Latin American, Caribbean and Latino Studies. 13 April. <http://www.umass.edu/clacls/content/puerto-rico-conference-savage-neoliberalism-colonialism-and-financial-despotism/>.

Clark, C. and J. S. Robey. 1981. The Correlates of Urban Migration Patterns in the United States 1960–1975. *Journal of Urban Affairs* 3(3), 29–38. <https://doi.org/10.1111/j.1467-9906.1981.tb00127.x/>.

Continúa la baja en la población de la isla. 2014. *El Nuevo* Día 2 January.

Corbin, J. and A. Strauss. 2007. *Basics of Qualitative Research: Techniques and Procedures for Developing Grounded Theory*. 3rd edition. Los Angeles: SAGE Publications, Inc.

Cortés Chico, R. 2013. Imparable la emigración. *El Nuevo Día* 15 July.

——. 2015. 72,000 Salen de Puerto Rico. *El Nuevo Día* 1 January.

Creswell, J. W. 2008. *Research Design: Qualitative, Quantitative, and Mixed Methods Approaches*. 3rd edition. Thousand Oaks, CA: SAGE Publications, Inc.

Davis, D. E. 1991. Urban Fiscal Crisis and Political Change in Mexico City: From Global Origins to Local Effects. *Journal of Urban Affairs* 13(2), 175–199. <https://doi.org/10.1111/j.1467-9906.1991.tb00247.x/>.

Diaz, M. 2013. Urge crear empleos bien remunerados. *El Nuevo Día* 3 January.

Dietz, J. L. 1987. *Economic History of Puerto Rico: Institutional Change and Capitalist Development*. Princeton, N.J: Princeton University Press.

El Departamento de Educación anuncia el cierre de 283 escuelas. 2018. *El Nuevo Día* 5 April.

Emigración masiva limita la recuperación económica de Puerto Rico. 2015. *El Nuevo Día* 7 January.

Ezra, M. and G.-E. Kiros. 2001. Rural Out-migration in the Drought Prone Areas of Ethiopia: A Multilevel Analysis1. *International Migration Review* 35(3), 749–71. <https://doi.org/10.1111/j.1747-7379.2001.tb00039.x/>.

Findlay, A., D. McCollum, R. Coulter and V. Gayle. 2015. New Mobilities Across the Life Course: A Framework for Analyzing Demographically Linked Drivers of Migration. *Population, Space and Place* 21(4), 390–402. <https://doi.org/10.1002/psp.1956/>.

Frey, W. H. 2001. The Great American Migration Slowdown: Regional and Metropolitan Dimensions. 30 November. <https://www.brookings.edu/research/the-great-american-migration-slowdown-regional-and-metropolitan-dimensions/>.

_____. 2009. *The Great American Migration Slowdown: Regional and Metropolitan Dimensions*. Washington, DC: Brookings Institution.

Gabriel, S. A., J. Shack-Marquez and W. L. Wascher. 1992. Regional House-price Dispersion and Interregional Migration. *Journal of Housing Economics* 2(3), 235–56. <https://doi.org/10.1016/1051-1377(92)90002-8/>.

Gaffikin, F. and B. Warf. 1993. Urban Policy and the Post-Keynesian State in the United Kingdom and the United States. *International Journal of Urban and Regional Research* 17(1), 67–84. <https://doi.org/10.1111/j.1468-2427.1993.tb00213.x/>.

García-Barrios, L., Y. M. Galván-Miyoshi, I. A. Valsieso-Pérez, O. R. Masera, G. Bocco and J. Vandermeer. 2009. Neotropical Forest Conservation, Agricultural Intensification, and Rural Out-migration: The Mexican Experience. *BioScience* 59(10), 863–73. <https://doi.org/10.1525/bio.2009.59.10.8/>.

Ghosh, B. 2013. *The Global Economic Crisis and the Future of Migration: Issues and Prospects: What Will Migration Look Like in 2045?* New York: Palgrave Macmillan.

Glaeser, E. L. J. D. Gottlieb. 2009. The Wealth of Cities: Agglomeration Economies and Spatial Equilibrium in the United States. Working Paper No. 14806. <https://doi.org/10.3386/w14806/>.

González, J. 2012. Menos gente, menos dinero. *El Nuevo Día* 9 February.

Goodman, L. A. 1961. Snowball Sampling. *The Annals of Mathematical Statistics* 32(1), 148–70. <https://doi.org/10.1214/aoms/1177705148/>.

Government Accountability Office. 2017. GAO-18-160, U.S. Territories: Public Debt Outlook.

Gray, C. L. 2009. Environment, Land, and Rural Out-migration in the Southern Ecuadorian Andes. *World Development* 37(2), 457–68. <https://doi.org/10.1016/j.worlddev.2008.05.004/>.

Gray, C. L. and V. Mueller. 2012. Natural Disasters and Population Mobility in Bangladesh. *Proceedings of the National Academy of Sciences* 201115944. <https://doi.org/10.1073/pnas.1115944109.>.

Harvey, D. 2007a. *A Brief History of Neoliberalism*. First Edition. New York: Oxford University Press.

————. 2007b. *A Brief History of Neoliberalism*. New York: Oxford University Press.

Hatton, T. J. and J. G. Williamson. 2003. Demographic and Economic Pressure on Emigration out of Africa*. *The Scandinavian Journal of Economics* 105(3), 465–86. <https://doi.org/10.1111/1467-9442.t01-2-00008/>.

Hear, N. V., O. Bakewell and K. Long. 2018. Push-pull Plus: Reconsidering the Drivers of Migration. *Journal of Ethnic and Migration Studies* 44(6), 927–44. <https://doi.org/10.1080/1369183X.2017.1384135/>.

Jackman, R. and S. Savouri. 1992. Regional Migration in Britain: An Analysis of Gross Flows Using NHS Central Register Data. *The Economic Journal* 102(415), 1433–50. <https://doi.org/10.2307/2234799/>.

Johnston, L. and J. Merling. 2017. More Trouble Ahead: Puerto Rico's Impending Medicaid Crisis. CEPR. <http://cepr.net/publications/reports/more-trouble-ahead-puerto-rico-s-impending-medicaid-crisis/>.

Kaske, M. 2017. University of Puerto Rico Seeks to Reduce Debt After Aid Drops. *Bloomberg.Com*. 3 August. <https://www.bloomberg.com/news/articles/2017-08-03/university-of-puerto-rico-seeks-to-reduce-debt-as-aid-drops/>.

Katz, M. B., M. J. Creighton, D. Amsterdam and M. Chowkwanyun. 2010. Immigration and the New Metropolitan Geography. *Journal of Urban Affairs* 32(5), 523–47. <https://doi.org/10.1111/j.1467-9906.2010.00525.x/>.

Kennan, J. and J. R. Walker. 2011. The Effect of Expected Income on Individual Migration Decisions. *Econometrica* 79(1), 211–51.

King, R. 2015. *Return Migration and Regional Economic Problems*. New York: Routledge. <https://www.amazon.com/Migration-Regional-Economic-Problems-Routledge-ebook/dp/B00VA7GZ74/ref=sr_1_1?ie=UTF8&qid=1533138065&sr=8-1&keywords=Return+Migration+and+Regional+Economic+Problems/>.

Kline, D. S. 2003. Push and Pull Factors in International Nurse Migration. *Journal of Nursing Scholarship* 35(2), 107–11. <https://doi.org/10.1111/j.1547-5069.2003.00107.x/>.

Kobre & Kim LLC. 2018. The Financial Oversight & Management Board of Puerto Rico.

Koser, K. 2010. The Impact of the Global Financial Crisis on International Migration Through Sovereign Borders: Population Migrations. *Whitehead Journal of Diplomacy and International Relations* 11, 13–20.

Krippner, G. R. 2012. *Capitalizing on Crisis: The Political Origins of the Rise of Finance*. Cambridge, MA: Harvard University Press.

LaCossitt, H. 1958. Our Caribbean Showcase. *Saturday Evening Post* 25 October, 34, 120–2.

Marshall, C. and G. B. Rossman. 2010. *Designing Qualitative Research*. Fifth Edition. Los Angeles: SAGE Publications, Inc.

Martin, P. 2009. The recession and migration: Alternative scenarios. <https://ora.ox.ac. uk/objects/uuid:67cebe30-d8a7-4622-817e-ec6228d0fbf1/>.

Massey, D. S., J. Arango, G. Hugo, A. Kouaouci, A. Pellegrino and J. E. Taylor. 1993. Theories of International Migration: A Review and Appraisal. *Population and Development Review* 19(3), 431–66. <https://doi.org/10.2307/2938462/>.

Mathews, T. G. 1960. *Puerto Rican Politics and the New Deal.* 1st edition. Gainesville: University Press of Florida.

Menjívar, C. 1993. History, Economy and Politics: Macro and Micro-level Factors in Recent Salvadorian Migration to the US. *Journal of Refugee Studies* 6(4), 350–71. <https://doi.org/10.1093/jrs/6.4.350/>.

Mertens, D. M. 1997. *Research Methods in Education and Psychology: Integrating Diversity with Quantitative and Qualitative Approaches.* Thousand Oaks, CA: SAGE Publications, Inc.

Milne, W. J. 1993. Macroeconomic Influences on Migration. *Regional Studies* 27(4), 365–73. <https://doi.org/10.1080/00343409312331347625/>.

Moody's downgrades Puerto Rico general obligation and related bonds to Baa3 from Baa1 and certain notched bonds to Ba1. 2012. *Moody.com* 13 December. <https://www.moodys.com/research/Moodys-downgrades-Puerto-Rico-general-obligation-and-related-bonds-to--PR_262231/>.

Moretti, E. 2011. Local Labor Markets. In *Handbook of Labor Economics.* 1st ed., Vol. 4, eds. O. Ashenfelter and D. Card. Amsterdam: Elsevier.

_____. 2013. *The New Geography of Jobs.* Boston: Mariner Books.

Overman, H. G. 2008. The Geography of Recession. Spatial Economics Research Centre Blog 24 October. <http://spatial-economics.blogspot.co.uk//>.

Pantojas-García, E. 1985. The U.S. Caribbean Basin Initiative and the Puerto Rican Exper- ience: Some Parallels and Lessons. *Latin American Perspectives* 12(4), 105–28.

Partridge, M. D., D. S. Rickman, R. Olfert and A. Kamar. 2012. Dwindling U.S. Internal Migration: Evidence of Spatial Equilibrium or Structural Shifts in Local Labor Markets? *Regional Science and Urban Economics* 42, 375–88.

Peck, J., N. Theodore and N. Brenner. 2013. Neoliberal Urbanism Redux? *International Journal of Urban and Regional Research* 37(3), 1091–9. <https://doi.org/10.1111/1468-2427.12066/>.

Pissarides, C. 2000. *Equilibrium Unemployment Theory.* Cambridge, MA: The MIT Press.

_____. 2013. Unemployment in the Great Recession. *Economica* 80(319), 385–403.

Pissarides, C. and J. Wadsworth. 1989. Unemployment and the Inter-Regional Mobility of Labour. *The Economic Journal* 99(397), 739–55. <https://doi. org/10.2307/2233768/>.

Pohlmann, M. D. 1982. Drawing in the Reins: Political Responses to Fiscal Crisis in America's Cities. *Journal of Urban Affairs* 4(3), 51–63. <https://doi. org/10.1111/j.1467-9906.1982.tb00064.x/>.

Portes, A. 1998. Social Capital: Its Origins and Applications in Modern Sociology. *Annual Review of Sociology* 24(1), 1–24. <https://doi.org/10.1146/annurev.soc.24.1.1/>.

Portes, A. and J. Böröcz. 1989. Contemporary Immigration: Theoretical Perspectives on Its Determinants and Modes of Incorporation. *International Migration Review* 23(3), 606–30.

Puerto Rico v. Franklin California Tax-Free Trust., 579 U.S. 2016.

Quiggin, J. 1999. Globalization, Neoliberalism and Inequality in Australia. *The Economic and Labour Relations Review* 10(2), 240–59. <https://doi.org/10.1 177/103530469901000206/>.

Rivera-Batiz, F. and C. E. Santiago. 1998. *Island Paradox: Puerto Rico in the 1990s.* New York: Russell Sage Foundation.

Roman, E. 1997a. Empire Forgotten: The United States' Colonization of Puerto Rico. SSRN Scholarly Paper No. ID 2997685. <https://papers.ssrn.com/ abstract=2997685/>.

————. 1997b. Empire Forgotten: The United States's Colonization of Puerto Rico. *Villanova Law Review* 42(4), 1119–1211.

Sassen, S. 2001. *The Global City: New York, London, Tokyo.* 2nd Edition. Princeton, NJ: Princeton University Press.

Sánchez Korrol, V. 2006. National Performances: The Politics of Class, Race, and Space in Puerto Rican Chicago. *Journal of Urban Affairs* 28(4), 419–21. <https://doi.org/10.1111/j.1467-9906.2006.00303_1.x/>.

Schultz, C. and T. Sjöström. 2001. Local Public Goods, Debt and Migration. *Journal of Public Economics* 80(2), 313–37. <https://doi.org/10.1016/S0047-2727(00)00113-4/>.

United States Congress. 1950. Puerto Rico Constitution: Hearings Before the Committee on Public Lands. <http://hdl.handle.net/2027/ien.35559007689288/>.

U.S. Department of Treasury. 2018. Puerto Rico's Economic and Fiscal Crisis. <https://www.treasury.gov/connect/blog/Documents/Puerto_Ricos_fiscal_challenges.pdf/>.

U.S. Supreme Court. 2016. *48 U.S.C. §§ 2141(b)(1), (b)(1)(F).*

West, M. J. 1986. Landscape Views and Stress Response in the Prison Environment. Master's Thesis, University of Washington, Seattle.

White, M. J. and G. Kaufman. 1997. Language Usage, Social Capital, and School Completion among Immigrants and Native-Born Ethnic Groups. *Social Science Quarterly* 78(2), 385–98.

Yin, R. K. 2008. *Case Study Research: Design and Methods.* 4th Edition. Los Angeles, CA: SAGE Publications, Inc.

VOLUME XXXIII • NUMBER II • SUMMER 2021

Eso es puertorriqueño:
The Enregisterment of Lateralization Among Puerto Ricans in the United States

ELAINE SHENK

ABSTRACT

This study examines how Puerto Ricans in the United States (USPRs) receive language ideologies produced on the Island. In 2013, the *Academia Puertorriqueña de la Lengua Española* released a publicity campaign about twenty-five linguistic features that appear in some varieties of Puerto Rican Spanish. This paper presented campaign samples to fifteen participants in the U.S. to elicit their reactions and focuses specifically on ideologies about lateralization of syllable-final /-ɾ/, examining the interaction of campaign texts with participants' discourses about those texts, as situated within the sociopolitical realities of USPR communities. The paper analyzes a process of enregisterment whereby lateralization is linked with social identities by agents within an ideological schema that makes this linkage possible. The paper contributes to the study of dialectal diversity awareness among USPRs and offers a greater understanding of speakers' response to prescriptivist and descriptivist discourses that originate both within and outside of their own communities. [Keywords: lateralization, Spanish, Puerto Rico, Puerto Ricans, ideologies, enregisterment]

The author (eshenk@sju.edu) is Professor of Spanish and Linguistics at Saint Joseph's University in Philadelphia, Pennsylvania. Her research centers on symbolic values and ideologies related to language contact and dialectal variation in both the United States and Puerto Rico. Recent publications analyze the perspectives of Puerto Ricans who live in the U.S. regarding Puerto Rican Spanish; metaphors regarding language and status in Puerto Rico; and issues relevant to language policy in U.S. Congressional bills about Puerto Rico's political status.

Puerto Rican Spanish (PRS), among many other dialects of Spanish in the Caribbean and beyond, demonstrates the linguistic creativity that is inherent in all language varieties; various processes of linguistic change, including consonant weakening and deletion, are readily evident (see for example, Beaton 2016; Díaz-Campos and Killam 2012; Emmanuelli 2000; Figueroa and Hislope 1999; Luna 2010; Medina-Rivera 1999; Prosper-Sánchez 1995; Simonet, Rohena-Madrazo and Paz 2008; Valentín-Márquez 2008). Dialectal variation exists on the Island as well as among diasporic communities in the United States, made even more evident as migration from Puerto Rico to the United States has increased due to economic, educational, and social factors (Hinojosa, Meléndez and Severino Pietri 2019). This paper examines perspectives of Puerto Ricans who live in the United States (USPRs) regarding an aspect of dialectal variation that is present in some varieties of PRS—the lateralization of syllable-final /-ɾ/—in response to a campaign that attempts to eliminate this feature in Puerto Ricans' speech. The feature is with some frequency linked with specific social identities, including social class, educational level, and/or rural identity, through processes of enregisterment (Agha 2005; Johnstone 2016). It is clear that some USPRs draw on these processes of enregisterment in their discussion of lateralization, while others delink and re-enregister the feature with alternate identities. In this way, the indexicality of lateralization is shown to be somewhat flexible depending on individuals' personal identities.

Puerto Ricans in Pennsylvania
According to the Center for Puerto Rican Studies (2019), the 5.8 million USPRs in 2018 far surpassed the 3.06 million living on the Island. This demographic pattern can be attributed to multiple reasons, which include regular population growth along with significant socioeconomic pressures in favor of migration off the Island, pressures which were exacerbated in the wake of Hurricane Maria in September 2017 (Figueroa 2020). Socioeconomic pressures have clearly been present throughout the last decade even prior to the hurricane's devastating impact, due to multiple and compounding factors related to Puerto Rico's debt crisis, unemployment rates, housing crisis, increased school closures with a reduction from 1,515 schools in 2006 to 855 in 2018, accompanying academic challenges for children and families, and

declining homeownership rates, which can serve as one indicator of financial stability (Figueroa 2020; Hinojosa, Meléndez and Severino Pietri 2019;
Hinojosa and Meléndez 2018).

According to CPRS (2019) data, Florida's Puerto Rican population
surpassed New York by a small margin as the two states with the highest
numbers of USPRs, followed by New Jersey and Pennsylvania; 8 percent
of the migration from Puerto Rico to the U.S. in 2018 was to Pennsylvania,
second to the 34 percent of Puerto Ricans migrating to Florida, with a total
of 477,312 Puerto Ricans living in Pennsylvania in 2018 (CPRS 2019). Thus,
the USPR population in Pennsylvania, including particularly the southeastern portion in and around Philadelphia and the surrounding region, is quite
diverse, ranging from those whose families have lived in the region for generations to others who have migrated there in the past couple years. Many
are bilingual, on a continuum from Spanish- to English-dominant; others
are monolingual English or Spanish speakers.

Lateralization of (-r)

In all dialects of Spanish, /-ɾ/ can appear as a tap [ɾ] or trill [r], but additional
variants are also available along a continuum including, among others, the
alveolar lateral approximant [l], based on evidence taken from natural-
istic conversational and interview formats (Beaton 2016; Boomershine
2005; Luna 2010; Medina-Rivera 1999; Ramos Pellicia 2007; Simonet,
Rohena-Madrazo and Paz 2008; Willis, Delgado-Díaz and Galarza 2015).
Lateralization has long been documented in PRS, including the use of
visual dialect in texts such as René Marqués' *La carreta* (Canfield 1981;
Maldonado-Cardenales 2008; Navarro Tomás 1948; Nuessel 1997), and we
also see evidence of lateralization beyond PRS in Lope de Vega's historical
work (cited in Ramírez de Arellano 1971, 29). In fact, although the feature
is referred to frequently in the literature as lateralization, scholars have
highlighted the complexity of the phenomenon, with some pointing out that
this is not a mere "neutralization" of differing sounds (Luna 2010; see also
Beaton's (2016) work on "incomplete neutralization"). Lloréns Monteserín,
Narayanan, and Goldstein (2016, 2443) discuss evidence that this feature
goes beyond a categorical neutralization, given that native PRS speakers
"are able to successfully discriminate between" pairs such as *alma/arma*,

whereas speakers of other dialects of Spanish were not as successful in doing so, suggesting that there is a distinction being made to which native PRS speakers are attending. They examined the perception of "naïve" listener-coders (i.e., advanced students of phonetics without "significant, sustained contact with Spanish") and concluded that "L and R have distinct representation in the PRS coda despite variable perceptual lateralization of rhotics" (Lloréns Monteserín et al. 2016, 2446).

Scholars have identified many factors in the rate of lateralization in PRS, including social context, familiarity of interlocutor, topic, task, age, and gender. Lipski (1994) reported greater prevalence among older speakers (as did Beaton 2016) and among those of lower social class, while Prosper-Sánchez (1995) documented the feature across differences of socioeconomic class, age, and sex, finding more lateralization among younger speakers and those with middle educational levels, among both men and women. Beaton (2016) also discounted gender as not being a significant factor in this linguistic variable. Medina-Rivera (1999) found that educational level among young adults in Caguas did not appear significant; all lateralized at some point. Those with higher education produced lateralized variants although they believed that they did not, and speakers lateralized more in groups than in individual interviews; when speaking about childhood or embarrassing moments than about formal topics; and when they were familiar with the interlocutor than when they were not. Medina-Rivera also found that few lateralized variants appeared during oral presentations to university students. Figueroa and Hislope (1999) found that young adult females were less likely to lateralize than young adult males; both were less likely to lateralize when reading than in conversation. Boomershine (2005) found widespread lateralization, especially in informal speech. In Castañer, men lateralized more than women, although this feature was less common in the interior of the Island than in other regions (Holmquist 2008).

Lateralization is also found among USPRs. Bullock, Toribio, Davis, and Botero (2004) reported up to 50 percent lateralization of word-final /ɾ/ in monolingual and code-switching conditions among 18 to 21 year olds. Among USPRs in Michigan, Valentín-Márquez (2008) found that women favored prescribed variants while men, and more generally, middle-age speakers, favored the lateralized variants; in contrast, non-lateralization in

Grand Rapids correlated with lower levels of integration into USPR communities, likely relevant to contact with the Mexican population in that region. Some research has shown the substitution of other variants for /r/ in USPR speech, including retroflex [ɻ] (Ramos Pellicia 2007). Finally, lateralization is not limited to oral registers, as documented in essays and social media posts on Facebook (Medina-Rivera 2014b).

Perspectives on Lateralization of /-r/

Perhaps due to the appearance of lateralization across differences of class, age, sex, and educational background, non-PRS speakers who were asked to imitate PRS tended to exaggerate or ignore rule-based systems of lateralization, that is, regardless of linguistic context (Boomershine 2005; Medina-Rivera 1997; Valentín-Márquez 2008). These oversimplifications are inaccurate and contribute to the ways in which lateralization has been criticized on the Island and in the United States. Salvador Tió, former President of the Academia Puertorriqueña de la Lengua Española (ACAPLE), claimed that lateralization separated PRS from other varieties and portrayed speakers as socially or culturally inferior (Tió 1991; Valentín-Márquez 2008). Likewise, in a speech to bilingual educators in New York, Diana Ramírez de Arellano stated:

Solo dos [fenómenos] habría que extirpar rápidamente y radicalmente del habla de Puerto Rico [...] en realidad no tienen defensa histórica, ni razón de existir. Lo que hacen es afear el idioma y separarnos de la familia sin contribuir nada a la lengua. Los dos fenómenos a los que me refiero son: la -r final de sílaba o final de palabra que se convierte en -l: por ejemplo cal-ne, en vez de car-ne, pol-que, en vez de por-que, correl, en vez de correr, etc. [...] Y hay que estirparla sin chistar. (1971, 28–9)[2]

Ramírez de Arellano was particularly critical of speakers with higher education, indicating that their linguistic behavior should differentiate them from other social groups. In her phonetics lab, she tried to eradicate lateralization among USPRs, sometimes leading to rhotacization (*er muchacho*), which Medina-Rivera (1997) and Valentín-Márquez (2008) have pointed to as examples of hypercorrection.

Although these ideas are at odds with current understandings of the ordinary processes of linguistic variation and change, this kind of negative reaction continues in some circles. Pousada and Poplack (1982) noted that NYC Puerto Ricans' "criteria for 'good Spanish' are pronunciation and vocabulary, not grammatical correctness. This assessment accurately reflects the area in which vernacular Puerto Rican Spanish usage diverges most from that of other dialects" (1982, 234). Medina-Rivera's (1997) survey among Puerto Ricans on the Island showed that only 4 percent held positive attitudes about lateralization; these had completed at least some university education and perceived it as a marker of national identity. Twenty-five percent took a neutral stance, defined in that study as "either related to indifference towards the phenomenon or the opinion of the participant is ambiguous" (Medina-Rivera 1997, 60), and 71 percent held negative attitudes; the latter group claimed that lateralization indicated low education and socioeconomic status, even though they acknowledged that they themselves lateralized. Confirming some contrast between perception and actual usage, Emmanuelli (2000, 215) also found that "los porcentajes de realización de /ɾ/ lateralizada son muy altos, a pesar de la franca actitud negativa hacia el fenómeno." The Academia Puertorriqueña de la Lengua Española (ACAPLE) has criticized lateralization, the velarization of (rr), and the rhotacization of (l), and various educational contexts also impact speakers' perspectives (Valentín-Márquez 2008). Valentín-Márquez (2008, 20) observes that there is a "constant encouragement on the part of teachers to change some features of the speech [the children] acquire at home" (see also Medina-Rivera 1997, 2014b). Nevertheless, patterns of speech that are integrally part of a community are not readily or easily altered, since the members of a community of practice continually make decisions (and form habits) that are outside of the academic pressures or norms, especially since these linguistic features reflect who they are and the communities to which they belong; simply put, an individual will have a strong inclination to speak as their community speaks in order to fit in and have a sense of belonging.

Lateralization represents a divergence between pronunciation and orthography, which, broadly conceived, can be associated with social identities in Latin America (Díaz-Campos and Killam 2012). Díaz-Campos and Killam tested listener attitudes and found that the *deletion* of /-ɾ/ was associated with those from lower socioeconomic status, whereas *retention* was perceived as prestigious; they also found that deletion of intervocalic

/-d-/ was evaluated more neutrally than deletion of /-ɾ/, confirming a different "social stratification" of these variables (2012, 98). Delgado-Díaz and Galarza (2016) present ample evidence of how sociolinguistic factors can play a role in the perception of phonemic categories, and highlight that both the speaker's and the listener's (perceived) characteristics can potentially impact such perception. Suárez Büdenbender (2013) additionally highlights how social stereotypes influence listeners' perceptions of Dominican Spanish in Puerto Rico. Boomershine (2005) found that native speakers of Spanish from Latin America and Spain judged a Puerto Rican speaker to have a low level of education when in fact that speaker had completed a doctoral degree. The sharp focus on the alteration or deletion of some phonemes but not others—even though all represent divergence between orthography and pronunciation—is not restricted to varieties of Spanish, as shown in scholarship on varieties of English that have also received external critique (Lippi-Green 1997, 2011; Rickford amd Rickford 2000).

Stereotypical imitations and attitudes, accompanied by critique from Puerto Rican educators and the ACAPLE, have thus contributed to and shaped perspectives on some features of PRS; "negative attitudes towards the Spanish spoken on the Island prevail all over the Hispanic world" (Valentín-Márquez 2008, 32). USPRs have differing levels of linguistic awareness of these distinctions, particularly those who have grown up in the United States with less exposure to varying registers of Spanish and often a formal education in English (Medina-Rivera 2014a). Nevertheless, USPRs interact with many non-Puerto Rican speakers of Spanish, a potential source of linguistic insecurity if other varieties are perceived as superior (Valentín-Márquez 2008).

Despite evidence of some external and internal negative reaction, it is clear that differing opinions exist among Puerto Ricans. Boomershine indicated that "lateralization seems to be a marker of social identity, and is not stigmatized by speakers of Puerto Rican Spanish" (2005, 56). Some political figures on the Island regularly produce these variants, "quizás para identificarse más con el 'pueblo' y el habla popular de algunos sectores rurales y/o marginales" [perhaps to identify more with the 'people' and the vernacular of some rural and/ or marginal regions] (Medina-Rivera 1999, 533). Cabo Rojo residents preferred lateralization, and its use in words such as *Puerto Rico* and *puertorriqueño* suggests "an emblematic relationship between non-standard features and national identification" (Valentín-Márquez 2008, 11). Valentín-Márquez highlights the lateralization in *reggaetón*, a music style strongly affiliated with Puerto Rico, and among news anchors in informal contexts, when they are interacting with, or interviewing, other speakers. For middle-class USPRs in Orlando, identity is defined among other factors by how well one can speak the Island's vernacular (Duany 2010, 110). Among USPRs, the "practices associated with the linguistic construction of core Puerto Ricanness" may include "the persistent use of distinct stigmatized pronunciations" (Valentín-Márquez 2008, 272). Medina-Rivera (2014b) states that lateralization can also fulfill a ludic function of language, connecting with identity, humor, and solidarity, as USPRs can "play" with lateralization in ways that non-Puerto Ricans cannot, at least not without awkwardness or potential offense. Given that lateralization is strongly associated with PRS, negative reactions are thus perhaps most present specifically when Puerto Ricans interact in Spanish with non-Puerto Ricans.

'El español nuestro de cada día' campaign
Lateralization is one of the features specifically targeted in the 2013 *El español nuestro de cada* día ("Our Daily Spanish") campaign (ENCD), produced by ACAPLE. Twenty-five spots targeted features of PRS as "incorrect" with the final line *"Dilo bien, dilo mejor"* ("Say it well, say it better"), including six features attributed to language contact and the remaining nineteen phonological, morphological, lexical, semantic, or syntactic features, many of which are also found in other dialects of Spanish (e.g., *llegastes, haiga*). The campaign focused on lateralization in words such as *amo*[l], *canta*[l], and *gobie*[l]*no*; in the vignette, a woman tells her partner that she would love him more if he said *amo*[ɾ]. The narrator explains that [ɾ]-[l] leveling in syllable-final position is characteristic of Caribbean Spanish, and that in Puerto Rico it is "much more extensive" than elsewhere. When the man alters his pronunciation, the woman indicates that she loves him even more.

Enregisterment and indexicality
Enregisterment refers to the "processes whereby distinct forms of speech come to be socially recognized (or enregistered) as indexical of speaker attributes by a population of language users" (Agha 2005, 38; see also Agha 2007; Silverstein 1993). Johnstone (2016) observes that links between form and meaning are

made by both linguists and laypeople—one might add the role of traditional and social media in their representations of ways of speaking—and lays out the process of enregisterment in systematic form as schematized in Table 1:

A linguistic form	is enregistered with...
B a register	by...
C an agent	in terms of...
D an ideological schema	because of...
E an interactional exigency *AND*	in which calling attention to the enregisterment serves a rhetorical function
F a sociohistorical exigency	that promotes practices

Source: Johnstone 2016, 633–4.

Bourdieu (1991) argues that speakers respond to the level of congruence (or lack thereof) between their linguistic habitus—the set of dispositions they gain as they acquire language—and the values of the linguistic marketplace. He theorizes that as speakers acquire habitus in given contexts (e.g., families, peers, school), some linguistic products (e.g., lexical items, grammatical structures, pronunciation) are more highly valued in the marketplace, and linguistic differences come to index social positioning.[3] Thus, in Critical Discourse Analysis, where both text and context are taken into account, USPR perspectives on lateralization and public sphere discourse can be represented as shown in Figure 1.

Critical Discourse Analysis (CDA) is an examination of language phenomena that permits the mapping of different kinds of analysis onto each other. It takes into account not only specific linguistic features of what is said and how it is said, but additionally prioritizes the contextualization of these features within a broader historical and sociopolitical framework (see van Dijk 2001; Wodak and Meyer 2009). This study examines how the text about lateralization *within* the ENCD campaign interacts with textual discourses *about* that campaign—namely, what participants articulated about campaign content and beyond. Both "texts" are situated within the broader sociopolitical context in which USPRs function, while yet another layer of the relationship to the broader sociopolitical context of the Island lies beneath all of this.

Figure 1. Critical Discourse Analytical framework of the current study

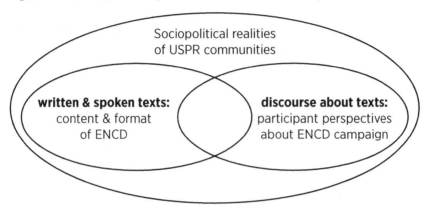

Methodology and Participants

This qualitative study is based on semi-structured interviews with fifteen participants who self-identify as Puerto Rican and who live within a seventy-five mile radius in southeastern Pennsylvania, including Philadelphia and the surrounding region. Initial participants were recruited through the researcher's personal networks, who then suggested names of other potential interviewees through the snowball recruiting method. The study sought demographic diversity, including age, gender, and time of residence in the U.S. (see Appendix A). Nine females and six males ranged in age from 19 to 76 years old and had lived between three and sixty-one years in the U.S. Thirteen were born in Puerto Rico and two in the U.S. Twelve of those born in Puerto Rico moved to the U.S. in their teens or twenties. Thirteen considered themselves native speakers of Spanish; two identified between categories (Appendix A).

The interview topics included both the ENCD and an earlier ACAPLE campaign on uniquely Puerto Rican lexical items, and thus yielded a wide-ranging discussion of many different topics. Each interview was guided by a set of initial prompts and questions (Appendix C), which yielded varying results in terms of each participant's response; the length of the interviews ranged from just under twenty-five minutes to one hour and twenty-six minutes, depending on participants' availability and interest in the topics, and the decision of some participants to comment extensively on specific topics that caught their interest; the average interview length was forty-seven minutes. Each interaction began with a review of the general parameters of the interview format and structure, with participants giving informed consent to participate, along with the confirmation that they could end the interview at any time. Each participant was given a printed list of all items included in each campaign. They listened to several samples, were asked questions related to the samples, and were also invited to comment on any words, pronunciations, or syntactic features that drew their attention. Participants typically discussed several features from the campaigns, but they often raised additional linguistic features that were not included. This article focuses on lateralization, although several additional features are addressed briefly as a point of comparison and contrast. The primary research questions are as follows: (1) How are the language ideologies articulated in the ENCD campaign received and interpreted by USPRs in southeastern Pennsylvania? and (2) What perspectives do these USPRs voice with regard to the campaign's critique of lateralization of (-r)? Although some participants lateralized on occasion, this study makes no attempt to quantify their own *usage* or *frequency*; rather it focuses on their *perspectives*. Participants were informed that the study was not about their own speech, a clarification that was particularly important for one participant who agreed to participate only after this was explained in detail.

Findings and Discussion

This section examines participant discourses in order to document the process of enregisterment that appeared to *link* lateralization with three distinctive social identities (elucidated below); to show how that linkage seems to be facilitated by *agents* internal and external to Puerto Rican communities; to *compare/contrast* participants' reactions to other features that were not part of the campaign; to exemplify how the process of *delinking/ re-enregisterment* was undertaken by several participants; and, finally, to *situate* discourses within cultural norms, values, and identities.

Lateralization linked to social identities

The beginning process of enregisterment in examples (1) through (6) shows how lateralization was linked in these discourses by some participants with three social identities: socioeconomic status, educational level, and/or rural upbringing. It should be noted that participants themselves raised these identities as they discussed the campaign texts, and specifically with regard to the example demonstrating lateralization of /-ɾ/; these identities were not preconceived categories. The ACAPLE campaign itself took a clear ideological stance (i.e., negative) on lateralization of /-ɾ/, a stance which comes across quite clearly in the campaign spot that participants listened to; thus, participants were responding directly to the ACAPLE spot in their discussion. In Example (1), after hearing the spot and being asked her reaction to it, Karla initially states a personal dislike of lateralization, but soon links it to socioeconomic status:

(1)

1   Karla: Pues yo pienso que la pronunciación se debería:: cambiar en:
        Well I think that pronunciation shou::ld be changed in:

2   la mayoría de las palabras. Por ejemplo eso de amol amor (0.5)
        most words. For example that (issue) of amol amor (0.5)

3   a mí no me gusta pero (1.0) esa es mi opinión.
        I don't like it but (1.0) that's my opinion.

4   Como::: pe[r]o usamos el pe[x/χ]o, que a mí tampoco me gusta.
        (1.5) Y
        Li:::ke perro we say el pe[x/χ]o, that I also dislike. (1.5) And

5   se nota más en las—(1.0) las clases más—(0.5)
        that's observed more in the—the classes that are the most—(0.5)

6   (calladita) bajas. Pienso yo en mi familia
        (quieter) the lowest. I think in my family

7   nosotros no usamos—(0.5) y mis amigos no—(0.5) no vamos a—
        we don't use—(0.5) and my friends don't—(0.5) we don't—

8 ES:
                              —decir amo[l]
                              —to say 'amo[l]'

9   Karla: Ajá. Que: sí me gustaría que se cambiara pero. (1.0)
        Right. So: yes I would like that to change but. (1.0)

Karla resists a link between linguistic form and social meaning by framing the issue as one of individual preference (lines 2-3), and offers velarized (r) as a parallel feature (line 4), framing both as a personal, not a social, issue. Nevertheless, in line (5), she switches to a social ideology, hesitating and twice cutting off her statement and pausing before finally referencing social class (line 6). The lowering of her voice (line 6) indicates a potentially problematic stance, as it reduces the possibility of unauthorized listeners to our conversation. Her own familial and social networks are established as non-lateralizing, although this text is also interrupted three times (line 7) and is not completed. When provided with an example of lateralization (line 8), however, she immediately agrees (line 9) that her family, friends, and she would not use this feature. Lateralization was also linked at times in the interview data with lower educational level, as seen in example (2). This participant's discourse first acknowledges a deeply rooted indexicality that links lateralization with PRS generally, not specifically to any particular sub-grouping (line 1), and subsequently establishes a more negative ideological stance related to educational level:

(2)

1	Xiomara:	Eso es puertorriqueño.
		That is Puerto Rican.
2	ES:	Porque el amor—el hombre le dice a la,
		Because "love"—the man says to the,
3		a la mujer—le dice, mi amo[l] te quiero tanto.
		to the woman—he says, 'mi amo[l]' I love you so much.
4	Xiomara:	¡Ay se escucha (risa) horrible! [...] Mira—yo pienso que
		Oh that sounds (laughter) horrible! [...] Look—I think that
5		lo que es el anglicismo es un tema un poquito más (1.0)
		the issue with Anglicisms is a topic that is slightly more (1.0)
6		sensitivo o sea más controversial. Em. (1.5)
		sensitive I mean, more controversial. Um. (1.5)
7		Pero lo que es ESto no hay excusa (risa) para esto
		But THIS there is no excuse (laughter) for this
8		(risa) ¿me entiendes?
		(laughter) do you know what I mean?
9		¡Lo que presenta es falta de educación!
		What it presents is a lack of education!
10		Imagínate cuando vayamos a (1.0) hacer negocios
		Imagine that when we go to (1.0) conduct business

11   en otros países ese que digan aMO[l].
              in other countries that people might say aMO[l].

12   No puedo no puedo. Eso sí de cambiar la r por *l* o sea.
              I just can't I just can't [see it]. *That, yes, changing* r *for* l
              you know.

13   ES   ¿Es algo que se corrige mucho en la escuela también?
              ¿Se comenta?
              Is it something that is also corrected a lot in school? Is it
              discussed?

14   Xiomara: Yo pienso que sí. Por lo menos en mi escula. Era una
              escuela privada.
              I think it is, yes. At least in my school. It was a private school.

15   ¿Em pero en la escuela pública es distinto, ¿no?
              Um but in the public school it's different, you know?

In this example, Xiomara contrasts the perception of lateralization versus the use of Anglicisms (lines 5-6). Added emphasis to "ESto" ("THIS") (line 7) distinguishes the two; laughter (lines 7-8) and the phrase, "no hay excusa" ("there is no excuse"), frame lateralization as unjustified and linked with a lack of control. Xiomara confirms a perceived link between lateralization and lower educational level (line 9); she additionally creates an imagined professional context (lines 10-12), which she sees as a conversational context incompatible with lateralization. She expressed concern by saying, "se va: dañando nuestro idioma" ("It is: harming our language"), noting that she found it "vergonzoso" ("shameful"). The participants in examples (1) and (2) attended private high schools on the Island, a potential indication of familial socioeconomic status. Much of Xiomara's coursework was in English, and she recalled overt correction in her Spanish classes; when asked what would happen if students were to lateralize during class, she stated that this would be addressed publicly:

(3)
1   Xiomara: Uy eso hubiese sido un escándalo exacto
              Wow yes that would have been scandalous

2   el maestro te para no:: amo[ɾ]!
              the teacher stops you no:: amo[ɾ]!

Xiomara's immediate and decisive reaction, seen in her lexical choice of "un escándalo" ("scandalous") (line 1) along with quoting the imaginary teacher through an extended vowel (line 2), confirms a link between a negative response to lateralization and a particular educational context—particularly private, English-language schooling on the Island. The intentional distancing set up in this case from lateralization in the context of education references the dimension of social distance, which varies from one context or community to another (Holmes 1995). Holmes points out that sharing experiences or identities (such as an occupation, membership, gender, educational context) can contribute to the assessment of social distance, which factors into the roles that individuals may have "in relation to" each other. Relationships in the middle of the continuum/axis of social distance (i.e., strangers. casual friends, intimates) may be the most carefully monitored in terms of behavior (and thus speech), whereas the two ends present more "stable" relationships where individuals know what is expected (Holmes 1995; Wolfson 1988). According to Wolfson's (1988) "bulge" model, the middle is more dynamic and open to negotiation, and thus, social distance is a "major factor in determining some aspects of linguistic politeness behavior" (Holmes 1995). Although Xiomara does not reference this directly, it is possible that the private school context sets up the social distance based on class precisely through the teacher's reaction to examples of lateralization in the students' pronunciation, indicating the type of linguistic behavior that is considered (in)appropriate in the classroom.

Xiomara valued the campaign's use of humor and how it addressed an issue that for her was problematic. This distinction between lateralization (unacceptable) and Anglicisms (less problematic) was made by other participants, as we see in example (4), although both have been critiqued:

(4)

1   Fabiola: Pues diría que la pronunciación siempre em: (1.5) tam
                 bién crea—(2.5)

                 Well I would say that pronunciation always em: (1.5) also
                 creates—(2.5)

2   pues, que, no hablamos bie:n o esta:: discusión porque

le quitamos las—
well that we don't speak well or that argument because we
take off the—

3   las eres son ELES
the r's are L'S

4   les quitamos las—(1.0) los endings (sonríe) de las palabras (1.0)
we take off the—(1.0) the endings (smiling) of words (1.0)

5   pero en cuanto a paLAbras NUEvas pues (1.0) a mí (0.5) me
gust—
but in terms of NEW WORDS well (1.0) I (0.5) I like—

6   me gusta que hagamos eso
I like that we do that

7   obviamente la pronunciación y eso a veces—
Obviously pronunciation and stuff like that sometimes—

8   ¡La (1.0) la ele por la ere a mí me vuelve loca! *(smiles)*
The (1.0) the l for r drives me crazy! (smiles)

9   ES: (risa) ¿Te vuelve loca en qué sentido?
(laughter) *It drives you crazy in what sense?*

10   Fabiola: Ay. (sonríe) Me hace pues, no sé. (1.0) No me gusta. (sonríe)
Ay. (smiling) It makes me, well, I don't know. (1.0) I don't
like it. (smiling)

11   No me gusta. Y yo trato de no hacerlo y a veces lo hago pero.
I don't like it. And I try not to do it and sometimes I do
[say it] but.

Fabiola's distinction between pronunciation (lines 3-4), and Anglicisms (lines 5-6) is again one of lesser and greater acceptability, respectively; she legitimated the latter due to connections between Puerto Rico and the United States. She too initially critiques lateralization as personal preference, acknowledging via paralinguistic facial cues that the feature is less than serious (line 8), a perspective that likely contributes to the linguistic insecurity that Zentella (1995, 2007) references, especially among Puerto Rican and Dominican interviewees in New York City. When pressed for reasons, Fabiola did not name factors beyond personal dislike, despite additional paralinguistic cues to some unstated issue (line 10). In spite of this stance, she acknowledged that she too lateralized at times, but several minutes later, returned to link pronunciation with lower educational level:

(5)

1   Fabiola: A mí la pronunciación me importa más que (1.0) las palabras [...]
         Pronunciation is more important to me than (1.0) the words [...]

2   la pronunciación pues pienso que es más (1.0) y también creo
         pronunciation well I think that it's more (1.0) and I also believe

3   que (2.0) uno cuando habla con una persona puertorriqueña también
         that (2.0) when you speak with a Puerto Rican you can also

4   puede ver el nivel de educación, por la pronunciación que usa así.
         see the educational level, by the pronunciation that s/he uses.

5   Pues tú hablas con alguien pues de las montañas que no fue:: a
         So you speak with someone say from the mountains who didn't attend:

6   la high— que también decimos high en vez de escuela superior, pues tú—
         high school— we also say high instead of escuela superior well you—

7   se le nota en el habla. Em y para mí es más importante la pronunciación
         you can hear it in their speech. Um and for me pronunciation is more

8   que (0.5) pues o botar estas palabras o no.
         important than (0.5) well should we throw out these words or not.

The linkage here between lateralization and educational level is explicit (lines 4-7), as Fabiola points out the visibility of the latter in pronunciation. Madsen observes that social class and other categories can be portrayed through "certain cultural and linguistic practices rather than as existing bounded groups reflecting biological, place-related, or socioeconomic facts" (2013, 116). Fabiola reiterated this idea more than once during the interview, indicating that she would not correct use of particular linguistic forms even while linking them to uneducated Spanish.

In addition to linking lateralization with lower socioeconomic status and educational level, it was also linked to rural, or *jíbaro*, speech, as we see in example (6), in which the participant agrees with the campaign's overt correction goals:

(6)

1	Manuel:	Yo estaría a favor de eso porque yo sé que (1.0) am (2.5)
		I would agree with that because I know that, um (2.5)
2		yo entendería que la mujer e::n ese partic— en ese ejemplo
		I would understand that the woman in that partic—in that example
3		en particular, eh: la mujer de hoy puertorriqueña preferiría
		In particular, um a Puerto Rican woman today would prefer
4		que se la dirigiera con— correctamente. Amor.
		to be addressed with—correctly. Amor.
5		Y hasta enfatizarlo. Amo[r::]. [...] Yo creo que todavía
		And even to emphasize it. Amo[r::]. [...] I think that it would still
6		se usaría normalmente en las zonas más rurales entre gente que
		be used normally in more rural areas among people who
7		se entienden y: no tendrían problemas. Pero yo diría que
		understand each other and: wouldn't have difficulties.
		But would say
8		por el nivel educativo del pueblo en general que está subiendo
		that due to the educational level of the community in general
		that is rising
9		y que está a un nivel bastante alto, pues ya se está dejando atrás.
		and that is at a fairly high level, well (this feature) is being left
		behind.

This discourse links lateralization to rural speakers (line 6) and also to lower educational level in that as the latter rises, certain ways of speaking, such as lateralization, are disappearing (lines 8-9). This text also draws on gender distinctions (lines 3-4) that parallel research discussed earlier where lower rates of lateralization were found among women than among men. In summary, the previous six examples show how participants linked lateralization with three social identities.

Agents of enregisterment

In the framework of enregisterment, (A) lateralization is linked with (B) social identities, by (C), agent(s) (Johnstone 2016), as laid out schematically in Figure 2.

Figure 2. Process of enregisterment: Linkage of *A to B by C*

A.	**C.**	**B.**
Lateralization	agent(s) of enregisterment	Lower socioeconomic status Lower educational level Rural upbringing/identity

Participants regularly referenced these agents of enregisterment as being Spanish-speaking individuals who are non-PRS speakers. Although sometimes the linkage is made to Puerto Ricans as a group, not necessarily according to class, education, or urban/rural background, the link often subsumes all Puerto Ricans under one single sociolinguistic identity. The campaign itself did not make the link to class or education directly; nevertheless, the campaign draws on, and indexes, these wider discourses. In example (7), the participant discusses how non-PRS speakers perceive PRS:

(7)

1   Karla: Siempre siempre, no:s (0.5) nos molestan por lo de la ele. Siempre.
              They always always, bother u:s about the l thing. Always.

2   En todos lados he oído que de mi interacción con gente
              Everywhere I go I've heard from my interactions with

3   hispanoamericana, o españoles siempre lo he oído.
              Latin Americans or Spaniards I have always heard that.

4   E::   dicen: ¡Puelto Rico! Así como para hablar del lugar.
              Um:: they say: Puelto Rico! Like that to talk about the place.

5   E: yo estaba ahora en Costa Rica con mi hermana (1.0) y:::
              Um: I was just in Costa Rica with my sister, a:::nd

6   también lo he oído. Yo digo es porque nosotros hablamos tan rápido,

		I also heard it. I think it's because we speak so quickly,
7		que cortamos la ese. Cortamos palabras. Y::: y ellos me decían eso
		that we drop the s. We shorten words. A:::nd and they would tell
		me that
8		que ellos notan el acento de nosotros. Dicen ustedes hablan
		that they notice our accent. They say you all speak
9		bien RÁpido y acortan las paLAbras. Y yo no lo NOto.
		really FAST and you shorten your WORDS. And I don't HEAR it.
10		¡Ya estoy acostumbrada! Pero: ¡pues sí!
		I'm used to it! Bu:t well yes!
11		Nos molestan—no nos molestan pero. Pero es igual—
		They bother us—they don't bother us but. But it's the same thing—
12	ES:	Comentan—
		They mention (it).
13	Karla:	Comentan. Pero yo pienso que todo es igual.
		They mention (it). But I think that it's all the same.
14		Nosotros comentamos con:: los dominicanos los cubanos
		We talk about: Dominicans Cubans
15		y todos los países tienen un acento diferente.
		and all the countries have a different accent.
16	ES	Sí. Y tienen sus rasgo:s en particular:
		Yes. And they have their particular: features:
17	Karla:	Sí. Que al final hay que:: como digo acepTAR también.
		Yes. And in the end one has to:: how would I say it to ACCEPT
		(it) as well.

Karla identifies agents as non-Puerto Ricans (line 3), with the negative linkage evidenced by her lexical choice of "molestan" ("they bother us") (lines 1 and 11), as well as by referencing the marked character of PRS for non-Puerto Ricans (line 8). An ongoing contrast in this text between 3rd- and 1st-person reference demonstrates how outsiders ("they") (lines 1, 4, 7, 8, 11) frame the speaking that insiders ("we" or "I") (lines 6, 7, 9, 10) do. Karla actively resists the outsider discourse, softening interactions from "molestan" ("they bother (us)") to "comentan" ("they comment"), but she also reframes the interactions by acknowledging that Puerto Ricans also discuss others' ways of speaking (lines 14-15). Nevertheless, in spite of the self-defense evident here, she would correct friends' pronunciation, especially lateralization, confirming that some Puerto Ricans also function as agents in the enregisterment process, even though she and others stated that Puerto Ricans did not notice the differences until these were pointed out and compared to other Latin Americans. Xiomara noted other Latin Americans "que hablan pauSAdo y con CALma más coRRECto (laughter)" ("who speak slowly and calmly more correctly (laughter)"), and when asked whether she did in fact believe other versions of Spanish were more correct than PRS, she was hesitant: "E, ¿creo que sí? Siento que: (1.5) no sé." ("Um, I think so? I feel tha:t (1.5) I don't know.")

Ideological schema and interactional/sociohistorical exigencies

The ideological components of enregisterment include access to ideas that lay out the relationship between particular ways of speaking and negative reaction toward these forms. Summarizing from the sections above, (A) lateralization is linked with (B) registers of lower socioeconomic status, lower educational level, and rural identity, by (C) agents including other Latin Americans, Spaniards, Puerto Ricans of higher socioeconomic status, and ACAPLE itself. This process is done in terms of (D) *an ideological schema*, a set of ideas that makes such linkage possible (Figure 3). According to Johnstone (2016), this often includes an assumption that if a phoneme has two variants, one must be correct and the other incorrect; additionally, if differences are perceived between working and middle/upper class, then "incorrect" values are assigned to the working class, and "correct" values to the middle/upper class. When outsiders mimic PRS without regard to linguistic context, the resulting stereotypes contribute to a perception of randomness with features that do not conform to broader Latin American or Peninsular norms. Overt metalinguistic commentary strengthens the connections in the observer's mind between juxtaposed elements (Johnstone 2016); thus, one possibility (as will be discussed in the findings below) is that when outsiders perceive rural identity or hear *lateralization*, the two can potentially become enregistered in the hearers' minds, even when only

Figure 3. Process of enregisterment: linkage of *A to B by C in terms of D* (broader context of E/F)

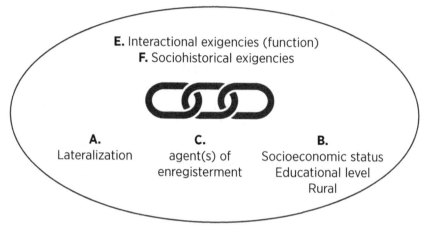

one element is present.

Johnstone (2016, 640–1) points out that these processes are enabled due to interactional exigencies (E), in which calling attention to the enregisterment serves some rhetorical function; this may involve "creating common ground," as individuals work to show they are "part of [a] relevant community," a "narrative evaluation" that points out communication issues, often exaggerated, which, according to Johnstone; "support for a claim in an argument," or "stancetaking," toward the linguistic feature being referenced or discussed (Johnstone 2016, 640–1). Johnstone's framework also incorporates here sociohistorical exigencies (F) that promote these practices, related to the "particular junctures in the lives of individuals and the histories of communities," in a way that makes relevant the language use and forms of adolescents as they grow and mature; the social and geographic mobility which contributes to new ways of speaking, relevant in the context of circular migration to and from the Island; and the processes of enregisterment and re-enregisterment that contribute to individuals' new identities over time.

In the context of Johnstone's (2016) framework, it appears that for some participants, their familial socioeconomic level and private school education in Puerto Rico have been the locus of this process, creating a community of practice which construes Puerto Ricans who lateralize as Other. Scholars such as Tió and Ramírez de Arellano have contributed to the process through discourses such as the latter's speech (analyzed previously in this paper). In addition, social and geographic mobility also places USPRs in contact with other dialects of Spanish and potentially increases exposure to negative metalinguistic commentary from non-Puerto Ricans; nevertheless, Puerto Ricans continue to lateralize for reasons that will be made more evident through examples of the participant discourse below.

Comparison and contrast with treatment of other features of PRS

Although lateralization was overtly addressed in the ACAPLE campaign, participants, with some frequency, also wanted to point out additional features of PRS, including aspiration of /-s/ and elision of /-d-/ (both are common in and beyond the Caribbean region), as well as velarization or posteriorization[5] of (rr) (specific to some sociodialects of Puerto Rico). This next section presents several examples of these portions of the interviews, since the component that clearly unified the discussion of these features with lateralization often centered on how others viewed PRS:

(8)

1   Xiomara: Dicen que nos comemos las palabras (sonríe)
               They say we eat our words (smiling)

2   ES: Ajá (sonríe)
               Yes (smiling)

3   Xiomara: Que les— (0.5) o sea. Lo que es la ese al final las corTA:mos.
               That— (0.5) I mean. The s at the end we cut them OFF:.

4   Hablamos tan y tan rápido que ni— o sea, tú me entiendes
               We speak so so quickly that not even—I mean you understand me

5   pero (1.0) puede ser que otra persona no entienda.
               but (1.0) it could be that someone else would not understand.

Here, the third-person plural perspective is superimposed on first-person plural actions (line 1). Paralinguistic information forms a discourse of quiet resistance in that the problem lies with the outsiders' inability to comprehend.

Notably, aspiration of /-s/ is widespread across differences of socioeconomic status, age, geography, and educational level (Hochberg 1986; Valentín-Márquez 2008), which is likely why ACAPLE did not target this feature despite the fact that it too reflects a disjuncture between pronunciation and orthography. Other participants confirmed this perspective on aspiration:

(9)

1	Diego:	I once tried to map out— like Puerto Ricans' (1.0) s's (0.5)
2		in other words sound like h's. They're aspirated. And (2.0) d's sound
3		like l's (1.0) and so like if you don't know that CODE (laughs)
4	ES:	mhm
5	Diego:	then, it's different.
6	ES:	it's hard to follow what's being said
7	Diego:	So even though it's perfectly good Spanish
8		I'm sure there's plenty of examples on here (gesturing to list) (1.5)
9		Entripao.
10	ES:	Entripao.
11	Diego:	Yeah. (laughter) Everybody knows there's a d in there! (laughter)

Diego's "mapping out" of dialectal differences contributes to a re-enregisterment of these features, and he asserts that nothing is incorrect about Puerto Ricans' "perfectly good Spanish" (line 7). In looking for additional evidence, he references a communal norm "everybody knows" (line 11), with laughter indicating the illogical drive to match pronunciation to what is written on the page. Diego pointed to an urban/rural divide, a distinction that he learned through peers who attended urban universities; he had not experienced this as a child. Overall, participants were not critical of aspiration of /-s/, and like Diego, legitimized this feature as part of PRS, pointing out how speakers of other dialects shared this pronunciation. Héctor drew on a similar ideological schema, demonstrating how pronunciation was part of a cultural identity:

(10)

1	Héctor:	Nosotros siempre hacemos las cosas con ese.

	We always do things with s.
2	Muchas veces, al final muchas veces.
	A lot of the time at the end a lot of the time.
3	Esto es igual que el argentino [ɾ]o el [ɾ]o del argentino.
	This is the same as the Argentinian [ɾ]o the [ɾ]o of the Argentinian.
4	Pero a mí me encanta también. Llegastes ese tipo de cosa (0.5)
	But that also fascinates me. "Llegastes" that type of thing 0.5)
5	porque eso es– YA. Eso es tan tan cultural [...]
	because that is– That is so so cultural [...]
6	ese tipo de pronunciación (1.0) lleva también una motivación.
	that type of pronunciation (1.0) also carries a motivation.

Another participant resisted how Puerto Ricans were singled out, highlighting sociolinguistic variables of geographical distance, migration, and diachronic evolution, as well as referencing Darwin's findings of genetic variation and creating parallels to language as a living organism. In the next example, the participant does not disagree with the campaign's intent, but questions the form in which it was carried out:

(11)

1	Alejandro:	No estoy seguro si lo que va a lograr esa campaña es
		I'm not sure if what that campaign is going to achieve is
2		acomplejar a la gente más de lo que está. [...]
		to give even more of a complex to people than what they already have
3		La idea, de ayudar a gente a hablar (0.5) más correcta mente, es buena
		The idea of helping people to speak more correctly, is a good idea
4		idea pero (1.0) tienen que tener cuidado (1.0) del tono. (1.0)
		idea but (1.0) they need to be careful (1.0) with the tone.(1.0)
5		Si el tono es, a (1.5) crítica (8.0) si lo toman como crítica
		If the tone is, u:m (1.5) critical (8.0) if they take it as a criticism
6		primero que nada es que lo van a rechazar.
		they will simply reject it.

	And I mean [...]
10	pero lo usan como, para, es para (1.5) apreciar el lenguaje y más *but they use it as, to, it's to (1.5) value the language and even more*
11	para uno como, decir ah sí eso eso es bien boricua. Ah: pero *for (us) as if, to say oh yes, that that is really boricua. Uh: but*
12	no necesariamente para educar para que hablemos (0.5) de esta forma. *not necessarily to educate so that we speak that way.*
13	Es más bien para para decir ESTO es parte de nuestra identidad. *It's more to say that THIS is part of our identity.*
14	Pero no necesariamente para luego practicarlo. *But not necessarily to later practice it.*

This discourse points out how particular linguistic forms in PRS are reclaimed/revalorized on Facebook (lines 7, 10) and used to solidify in-group membership (lines 8, 11, and 13). Linguistic "loyalty to the norms of one's own group is a very powerful source of solidarity" (Niño-Murcia 2011, 731). The participants of this study who most clearly re-enregistered features with cultural identity, including both lateralization and additional linguistic features that they themselves brought into the conversation, were typically male, over 30 years of age, and born in/raised through adolescence in rural areas of the Island. Of the six male participants, five grew up outside of the metropolitan area of San Juan. Notably, as seen above, younger female participants varied more in this linkage, often citing the influences of schooling, teachers, or family members on their less favorable evaluation of specific linguistic features. Nevertheless, one younger female participant indicated that (un)intentional changes to pronunciation can be perceived by the community as a loss of identity, as seen in example (15).

(15)

| 1 | Karla: | Y: mira. YO:: e::m mi roommate aquí freshman year era de Miami.
A:nd look. I:: u::m my roommate here freshman year was from |

    Miami.

2   Pero su familia era de Espa—era de Puerto Rico perdón.
       But her family was from Spa—sorry she was from Puerto Rico.

3   Y su español era bien pronunCIAdo:: (0.5) Entonces a mí se
       And her Spanish was really well pronounced:: (0.5) So that way of

4   me pegó. Porque el acento puertorriqueño es bien Débil
       speaking stuck to me. Because the Puerto Rican accent is really
       WEAK

5   y cualquier acento se te pega rápido. Pero luego fui a casa en
       diciembre
       and any accent sticks to you easily. But later I went home in
       December

6   y mi familia (0.5) me comenzó a molestar. Me decía Karla!
       and my family, they started teasing me. They would say Karla!

7   Estás hablando como Univisión. Como Univisión
       You're talking like Univisión. Like on Univisión

8   no tienen aCENto pronuncian todas las paLA:bras—
       They don't have an ACcent they pronounce all the WORDS—

9   ES: de forma neutra
       in a neutral Spanish

10   Karla: Neutra. Y ellos me dicen Karla pero qué— qué tú HACES?
       Neutral. And they say Karla but what—what are you DOING?

11   Y. Tú sabes. Me gufeaban. Como chistes. [...]
       And. You know. They made fun of me. Like joking about it. [...]

12   No fue nada malo ellos lo decían jugando pero— (1.5)
       It was nothing bad they would say it to play around but— (1.5)

13   Fue como raro para ellos
       It was sort of strange for them

Karla's initial slip of the tongue (line 2) is revealing in that while envisioning a "correct" Spanish, what readily came to her mind was Spain, although this was not the dialect in question. Karla's family, however, critiqued her "neutral" Spanish—as if produced by a national cable network—as unacceptable (line 10). The loss of accent—and perhaps the accompanying indexicality of being Puerto Rican—was perceived negatively by Karla's family. Underlying humor softened the critique (lines 11-12), but the dialectal shift was clearly marked (line 13). In this way, despite her enregisterment of lateralization, as in example (1), as well as her sensitivity to agents of enregisterment, in example (7), Karla retains an understanding of pronunciation as indexical of *puertorriqueñidad,* and is sensitive to losing this.

Conclusion and Implications

In conclusion, this paper poses two questions: first, how are the language ideologies, as articulated in the ENCD campaign, received and interpreted by USPRs in southeastern Pennsylvania; and second, what perspectives do these USPRs voice with regard to the campaign's critique of lateralization of /-r/? The intent was not intended to quantify participants' own usage or frequency of lateralization but instead to focus on their *perspectives.* Using a framework of enregisterment, the paper examines the examples presented here and the evidence they provide of some linkages made by participants themselves between lateralization and socioeconomic status, educational level, and/or regional speech, as well as by the various agents (speakers of non-PRS, urban or highly educated Puerto Ricans, ACAPLE) who contribute to the creation of those links. Exaggerated imitations and metalinguistic discourse support an ideological framework that perceives differing variables as correct or incorrect, an overall framework that devalues dialects where pronunciation diverges from orthography.

Not all divergences are treated equally in the public sphere, however, a reality which filters down into the underlying ideologies of these fifteen participants. Lateralization is highlighted by the ACAPLE campaign, and this is reflected in the participants' discourse. In turn, aspiration of /-s/ is not highlighted by the campaign, and likewise, receives much less negative attention by participants; it appears to be less enregistered with lower educational level/socioeconomic status than is lateralization. Perspectives about the aspiration of /-s/ are more likely to reference cultural expression, with fewer underlying moralistic or values-laden ideologies.

It is clear that public campaigns have power to shape ideologies, whether positively or negatively. Prosper-Sánchez (2007), Wolfram (2016), and others have called for increased dialect diversity awareness, supported by research that would contribute to public sphere discourse. Prosper-Sánchez (2007, 190) points out "how illuminating it would be to represent language contrasts and the infinite set of variations, varieties, and voices that they generate without feeling a need to claim authority over them," noting that a lot of time is spent trying to control language instead of acknowledging linguistic creativity. Although many USPRs in this study recognize, and to some extent, engage with language ideologies that devalue and mark features where sounds and orthography diverge, this paper includes evidence that some are actively engaged in re-enregistering lateralization, particularly those raised in rural environments or with some distance from contexts in which prescriptivist discourses are the strongest, such as early education. Upon examining several broader advocacy efforts that are undertaken from, and based on, a sociolinguistic understanding of language variation and change (here related to dialects of English), we see that public service announcements or educational curricula (e.g., North Carolina Language and Life Project) or materials written for readers beyond academia (Rickford and Rickford 2000) can make positive contributions to dialectal diversity awareness and appreciation for those who are exposed to those efforts. Moving forward, the level of creativity and appeal that has been devoted to past prescriptivist campaigns, such as the ACAPLE campaign on Puerto Rican Spanish, could readily be invested in more descriptivist curricula to demonstrate the ways in which Puerto Rican Spanish contributes to the rich dialectal diversity of the Spanish language overall.

NOTES

[1] Many thanks to three anonymous reviewers for their helpful and specific feedback that sharpened the clarity of multiple points in this paper; to numerous participants at the Spanish in the U.S./Spanish in Contact with Other Languages Conference for their questions and comments on a presentation of one portion of this material; and to Melvin González Rivera for his comments on an early draft of this paper. In particular, I appreciate one reviewer's pointed critique and exhortation to present this material without recurring wherever possible to the use of terminology such as "stigmatized," "non-standard," "standard," or "innovative," since this continues to perpetuate negative values related to lateralization, which is specifically not my intention in carrying out and presenting this research. All remaining oversights and errors are my own responsibility.

[2] "Only two phenomena should be removed quickly and radically from the speech of Puerto Rico [...] in reality they have no historical defense, nor a reason to exist. What they do is to ruin the language and separate us from our family without contributing anything to the language. The two phenomena to which I am referring are the syllable-final or word-final –r that becomes –l: for example, <u>cal-ne</u>, instead

of <u>car-ne</u>, <u>pol-que</u>, instead of <u>por-que</u>, <u>correl</u>, instead of <u>correr</u>, etc. [...] And it must be removed without any resistance" (author's translation).

[3] Bourdieu's (1991) discussion of bodily hexis focuses on French, where he points out a contrast between "la bouche" (closed, pinched, censored, and in his words, feminine, characterized by an insecurity and sensitivity to the linguistic market) vs. "la gueule" (relaxed, unashamed, wide open, free, masculine). Although this concept is not explored further here, it offers an interesting perspective on perceptions of dialectal variation in Spanish, given that his theoretical gender distinction is somewhat mirrored in the differences that some scholars have documented in the rate of lateralization of /-ɾ/.

[4] This likely originates from "hablar fino" ("to speak well"); "finodo" could be loosely translated as a person who uses ultra-correct pronunciation.

[5] See Delforge (2013) for a discussion of posteriorization of (rr).

REFERENCES

Academia Puertorriqueña de la Lengua Española (ACAPLE). 2017. Academia Puertorriqueña de la Lengua Española lanza campañas radiales. <http://www.academiapr.org/inicio/academia/capsulas-radio/>.

Agha, Asif. 2005. Voice, Footing, Enregisterment. *Journal of Linguistic Anthropology* 15(1), 38–59.

_____. 2007. *Language and Social Relations.* New York: Cambridge University Press.

Atkinson, J.M. and J. Heritage. 1999. Jefferson's Transcript Notation. In *The Discourse Reader,* eds. Adam Jaworski and Nikolas Coupland. 158–66. New York: Routledge.

Beaton, Mary E. 2016. Revisiting Incomplete Neutralization: The Case of Puerto Rican Spanish. *University of Pennsylvania Working Papers in Linguistics* 22(1), 31–40.

Boomershine, Amanda. 2005. Perceptual Processing of Variable Input in Spanish: An Exemplar-based Approach to Speech Perception. Ph.D. dissertation, The Ohio State University.

Bourdieu, Pierre.1991. *Language and Symbolic Power,* ed. John B. Thompson. Cambridge, MA: Harvard University Press.

Bullock, Barbara, Almeida Toribio, Kristopher Davis, and Christopher Botero. 2004. Phonetic Convergence in Bilingual Puerto Rican Spanish. *WCCFL 23 Proceedings,* eds. Vineeta Chand, Ann Kelleher, Angelo Rodríguez and Benjamin Schmeiser. 113–25. Somerville, MA: Cascadilla.

Canfield, D. Lincoln. 1981. *Spanish Pronunciation in the Americas.* Chicago: University of Chicago Press.

Center for Puerto Rican Studies (CPRS). 2016a. Puerto Ricans in the United States 2014. Accessed 5 November 2016. <https://centropr.hunter.cuny.edu/sites/default/files/PDF/STATE%20REPORTS/PR-US-2016-CentroReport.pdf/>.

_____ 2016b. Puerto Ricans in Pennsylvania: 2010-2016. Data Sheet. Accessed
        18 March 2020. <https://centropr.hunter.cuny.edu/research/data-center/
        data-sheets/puerto-ricans-pennsylvania-2010-2016/>.

_____ 2019. New Estimates of Puerto Rican Migration Post Hurricane Maria
        in 2018: Florida Continues to Grow as the State with the Largest Puerto
        Rican Population. Accessed 18 March 2020. <https://centropr.hunter.
        cuny.edu/sites/default/files/data_sheets/2018_ ACS_1YR_Datasheet-
        DS2019-02_CENTRO.pdf />.

Delgado-Díaz, Gibran and Iraida Galarza. 2016. Sociolinguistic Implications on
        Perception: The Case of the Posterior /r/ in Puerto Rican Spanish. In *Inquiries
        in Hispanic Linguistics: From Theory to Empirical Evidence,* eds. Alejandro
        Cuza, Lori Czerwionka and Daniel Olson. Amsterdam: John Benjamins.

Díaz-Campos, Manuel and Jason Killam. 2012. Assessing Language Attitudes
        through a Match Guise Experiment: The Case of Consonantal Deletion in
        Venezuelan Spanish. *Hispania* 95(1), 83–102.

Duany, Jorge. 2010. The Orlando Ricans: Overlapping Identity Discourses among
        Middle-class Puerto Rican Immigrants. *CENTRO: Journal of the Center
        for Puerto Rican Studies* 22(1), 85–115.

Emmanuelli Muñiz, Mirna. 2000. Valoración social y actuación lingüística hacia
        algunas variantes fonológicas del español puertorriqueño. *Revista de estu-
        dios hispánicos* 27(1), 209–18.

Figueroa, Damayra. 2020. Data Sheet: Puerto Ricans in Florida: 2010-2018. Center
        for Puerto Rican Studies. Accessed 14 May 2020. <https://centropr.
        hunter.cuny.edu/sites/default/files/data_sheets/centro_datasheet_flori-
        da-2010-2018.pdf/>.

Figueroa, Neysa and Kristi Hislope. 1999. A Study of Syllable Final /r/ Neutralization
        in Puerto Rican Spanish. *Romance Language Annual* 10, 563–9.

Hinojosa, Jennifer and Edwin Meléndez. 2018. The Housing Crisis in Puerto Rico and
        the Impact of Hurricane María. New York: Center for Puerto Rican Studies.

Hinojosa, Jennifer, Edwin Meléndez, and Kathya Severino Pietri. 2019. Population
        Decline and School Closure in Puerto Rico. New York: Center for Puerto
        Rican Studies. Accessed 14 May 2020. <https://centropr.hunter.cuny.edu/
        sites/default/files/PDF_Publications/centro_rb2019-01_cor.pdf/>.

Hochberg, Judith. 1986. Functional Compensation for /s/ Deletion in Puerto Rican
        Spanish. *Language* 62(3), 609–21.

Holmes, Janet. 1995. *Women, Men, and Politeness.* London/New York: Longman.

Holmquist, Jonathan. 2008. Gender in Context: Features and Factors in Men's
        and Women's Speech in Rural Puerto Rico. *Selected Proceedings of the
        4th International Workshop on Spanish Sociolinguistics,* eds. Maurice
        Westmoreland and Juan Antonio Thomas. 17–35. Somerville, MA:
        Cascadilla Proceedings Project.

Johnstone, Barbara. 2016. Enregisterment: How Linguistic Items Become Linked with Ways of Speaking. *Language and Linguistics Compass* 10, 632–43.

Lippi-Green, Rosina. 1997/2011. *English with an Accent: Language, Ideology, and Discrimination.* New York: Routledge.

Lloréns Monteserín, Mairym, Shrikanth Narayanan and Louis Goldstein. 2016. Perceptual Lateralization of Coda Rhotic Production in Puerto Rican Spanish. In *Conference of the International Speech Communication Association* (INTERSPEECH). San Francisco, CA.

Luna, Kenneth Vladimir. 2010. The Spanish of Ponce, Puerto Rico: A Phonetic, Phonological, and Intonational Analysis. Ph.D. dissertation, University of California Los Angeles.

Madsen, Lian. 2013. 'High' and 'Low' in Urban Danish Speech Styles. *Language in Society* 42(2), 115–38.

Maldonado-Cardenales, Noemi. 2008. El teatro puertorriqueño: choque, resistencia y negociación lingüística del español de Puerto Rico. Ph.D. dissertation, State University of New York.

Medina-Rivera, Antonio. 1997. Phonological and Stylistic Variables in Puerto Rican Spanish. Ph. D. dissertation, University of Southern California.

———1999. Variación fonológica y estilística en el español de Puerto Rico. *Hispania* 82(3), 529–41.

——— 2014a. El español en Cleveland: Aactitudes lingüísticas y variedades en contacto. *Revista Internacional de Lingüística Iberoamericana* 12(1), 61–76.

——— 2014b. Lateralización de /ɾ/ implosiva: la conciencia fonológica y sus manifestaciones en el español puertorriqueño oral y escrito. In *Perspectives in the Study of Spanish Language Variation,* eds. Andrés Enrique-Arias, Manuel Gutiérrez, Alazne Landa and Francisco O'Campo. 321–40. Santiago de Compostela: Universidad de Santiago de Compostela.

Meléndez, Edwin and Carlos Vargas-Ramos, eds. 2016. *Puerto Ricans at the Dawn of the New Millenium.* New York: Center for Puerto Rican Studies.

Navarro Tomás, Tomás. 1948. *El español en Puerto Rico: contribución a la geografía lingüística hispanoamericana.* Rio Piedras: Editorial de la Universidad de Puerto Rico.

Niño-Murcia, Mercedes. 2011. Variation and Identity in the Americas. In *The Handbook of Hispanic Sociolinguistics,* ed. Manuel Díaz-Campos. 728–46. West Sussex: Wiley-Blackwell.

Nuessel, Frank. 1997. A Linguistic Analysis of the Puerto Rican Dialect of Spanish in René Marqués's *La carreta.* In *Linguistic Studies in Honor of Bohdan Saciuk,* eds. Robert Hammond and Marguerite Goodrich MacDonald. 189–99. West Lafayette, IN: Foreign Language Series.

Pousada, Alicia and Shana Poplack. 1982. No Case for Convergence: The Puerto Rican Spanish Verb System in a Language-contact Situation. In *Bilingual Education for Hispanic Students in the United States,* eds. Joshua Fishman and Gary Keller, 207–37. New York: Teachers College Columbia University.

Prosper-Sánchez, Gloria. 1995. Neutralización homofonética de líquidas a final de sílaba: aspectos sociolingüísticos en el español de Puerto Rico. Ph.D dissertation, University of Massachusetts.

_____ 2007. Transing the Standard: The Case of Puerto Rican Spanish. In *None of the Above: Puerto Ricans in the Global Era,* ed. Frances Negrón-Muntaner. 183–94. New York: Palgrave-Macmillan.

Ramírez de Arellano, Diana. 1971. El español: la lengua de Puerto Rico. Speech, New York City Board of Education in the Puerto Rican Heritage Lecture Series for Bilingual Professionals in Brooklyn, NY. Accessed 10 August 2015. <https://eric.ed.gov/?id=ED084913/>.

Ramos-Pellicia, Michelle. 2007. Lorain Puerto Rican Spanish and 'r' in Three Generations. *Selected Proceedings of the Third Workshop on Spanish Sociolinguistics,* eds. Jonathan Holmquist, Augusto Lorenzino, and Lotfi Sayahi, 53–60. Somerville, MA: Cascadilla Proceedings Project.

Rickford, John R. and Russell J. Rickford. 2000. *Spoken Soul: The Story of Black English.* New York: Wiley.

Silverstein, Michael. 1993. Metapragmatic Discourse and Metapragmatic Function. *Reflexive Language,* ed. John Lucy. 33–58. Cambridge: Cambridge University Press.

Simonet, Miquel, Marcos Rohena-Madrazo, and Mercedes Paz. 2008. Preliminary Evidence for Incomplete Neutralization of Coda Liquids in Puerto Rican Spanish. In *Selected Proceedings of the 3rd Conference on Laboratory Approaches to Spanish Phonology,* eds. Laura Colantoni and Jeffrey Steele, 72–86. Somerville, MA: Cascadilla Proceedings Project.

Suárez Büdenbender, Eva-María. 2013. "Te conozco, bacalao": Investigating the Influence of Social Stereotypes on Linguistic Attitudes. *Hispania* 96(1), 110–34.

Tió, Salvador. 1991. *Lengua mayor: ensayos sobre el español de aquí y de allá.* San Juan: Plaza Mayor.

Valentín-Márquez, Wilfredo. 2008. Doing Being Boricua: Perceptions of National Identity and the Sociolinguistic Distribution of Liquid Variables in Puerto Rican Spanish. Ph.D. dissertation, University of Michigan.

Van Dijk, Teun. 2001. Critical Discourse Analysis. In *Handbook of Discourse Analysis,* eds. Deborah Shiffrin, Deborah Tannen and Heidi Hamilton. 352–71. Oxford: Blackwell.

Willis, Erik; Gibran Delgado-Díaz; and Iraida Galarza. 2015. Contextualized Voicing of the Voiceless Posterior Fricative /h/ in Puerto Rican Spanish. In *Selected Proceedings of the 6th Conference on Laboratory Approaches to Romance Phonology,* eds. Erik W. Willis Pedro Martín Butragueño and Esther Herrera Zendejas. 52–69. Somerville, MA: Cascadilla Proceedings Project.

Wodak, Ruth and Michael Meyer, eds. 2009. *Methods of Critical Discourse Analysis.* London: Sage.

Wolfram, Walt. 2006. Language Diversity and the Public Interest. In *Georgetown*

University Round Table on Languages and Linguistics 06, eds. Natalie Schilling-Estes and Kendall King. 1–14. Washington, DC: Georgetown University Press.

Zentella, Ana Celia. 1995. The 'chiquita-fication' of U.S. Latinos and their Languages, or Why We Need an Anthro-Political Linguistics. In *SALSA III: Proceedings of the Symposium about Language and Society at Austin.* Austin, TX: Department of Linguistics: 1–18.

———. 2003. Recuerdos de una Nuyorican. *Ínsula: Revista de letras y ciencias humanas* 679–680, 37–40.

———. 2007. *"Dime con quién hablas, y te diré quién eres"*: Linguistic (In)security and Latina/o Unity. In *A Companion to Latina/o Studies,* eds. Juan Flores and Renato Rosaldo. 25–38. Hoboken, NJ: Blackwell.

APPENDIX A

Study Participants

Pseudonym	Age	Gender	Place of Birth	Years in PR	Years in U.S.	Educational level	Spanish lang. self-evaluation
Xiomara	19	F	Baltimore	15	4	1st year university	A
Karla	21	F	Ponce	18	3	3rd year university	A
Fabiola	23	F	Ponce	18	5	BA	A
Nayelis	24	F	Jersey City	0	24	BA	B-C
Diego	31	M	Aibonito	16	15	BA	A-B
Bianca	44	F	San Juan	18	26	MA (double)	A
Manuel	58	M	Aibonito	20	38	PhD	A
Héctor	60	M	Coamo	52	8	JD	A
Alejandro	66	M	San Juan	46	20	MA (double)	A
Carmen	66	F	San Lorenzo	15	51	High school	A
Paulina	69	F	Lares	21	48	9th grade	A
María	73	F	San Sebastián	35	38	High school	A
Ismael	73	M	Fajardo	25	48	High school	A
Luis	76	M	Humacao	27	49	7th grade	A
Ana	76	F	Arecibo	15	61	4th grade	A

Spanish Language Self-Evaluation

A: Self-identify as native speakers with no difficulties expressing themselves in Spanish;

B: Are comfortable conversing on wide range of topics in Spanish, but do not consider themselves native speakers;

C: Can carry out basic conversations in Spanish on everyday topics

APPENDIX B

Transcription Conventions

.	Sentence-final falling intonation
?	Sentence-final rising intonation/interrogative
,	Slight pause
(2.5)	Extended pause in the discourse, with length in tenths of a second
a: a:::	Lengthened vowel
ALL CAPS	Increased volume, stress
—	Interrupted or cut-off speech
[...]	Deleted segment
[ɾ]	representation of sound using the International Phonetic Alphabet
( )	Contains information to help the reader interpret the transcript

Transcription conventions are adapted from Atkinson and Heritage (1999).

APPENDIX C

Interview Topics/Questions (listed here in English)

A. Establish participant's preferred language for the interview
(*Spanish, English, both, codeswitching*)

B. Demographic information
   1. Gender
   2. Age
   3. Educational level completed
   4. Place of birth
   5. Current place of residence
   6. Number of years lived in the U.S.
   7. (*If appliwcable*) Number of years lived outside of U.S. and location
   8. Self-assessment of spoken Spanish - With which statement does participant most closely identify?
      a. *I am a native speaker and have no difficulties expressing myself in Spanish.*
      b. *I am comfortable conversing on a wide range of topics in Spanish, but do not consider myself a native speaker.*
      c. *I can carry out basic conversations in Spanish on everyday topics.*
      d. *I can greet people or use an occasional word in Spanish, but am not comfortable with anything further.*
      e. *I do not speak any Spanish at all.*

C. Puerto Rican Spanish - The *¡Atrévete y Dilo!* Campaign
   1. Have you ever heard of the *¡Atrévete y Dilo!* or the *El español nuestro de cada* día campaigns? (*If not, go to Question 2*)
      a. Which campaign have you heard (or heard of)?

      b.   In your opinion, what was the main purpose of that campaign?

      c.   What is your reaction to the content of the campaign?

    2.   Are you familiar with the work of the Academia Puertorriqueña de la Lengua Española? With which aspects? *(If not, go to Question 4)*

    3.   What effect does the Academia have in the lives of Puerto Ricans in the U.S.? And in your life in particular?

D.   *¡Atrévete y dilo!* campaign – provide list of all words included in the campaign (i.e., *revolú, zafacón, yunta, fracatán...*). Play sample campaign spots for participant.

    4.   What connotations do these words hold for you?

    5.   Are the words on this list specifically Puerto Rican words or are they commonly used in Spanish in any region?

    6.   In your opinion, what is the status of Puerto Rican Spanish in relation with other dialects of Spanish? Can you explain your answer?

    7.   What opinion is held in other parts of the Spanish-speaking world about Puerto Rican Spanish?

    8.   In your opinion, is it important to change people's perspectives about Puerto Rican Spanish? Why (not)?
        [ask for clarification if the answer is unclear about direction of change]
        [if the person answers 'yes'] What would be the most effective way of doing so?

    9.   Are Anglicisms part of Puerto Rican Spanish?

      a.   What connotation do words such as *"party, janguiar, wíken, ticket, chequear, enigüei/anyway"* have?

      b.   Are these also Puerto Rican words?

      c.   Why do you think the Academy does not include them in that campaign?

E.   *El español nuestro de cada* día campaign – provide list of all words provided in that campaign. This campaign focuses on words or phrases in Spanish that, according to the Academy, should be corrected in speech (e.g., *estábamos/estábanos, solicitar/aplicar, además/en adición*). Play sample spot for participant.

    10.   What is your reaction to this radio spot? *Ask participant to elaborate if needed.*

    11.   *(If participant speaks Spanish)* Have you ever been corrected on some aspect of your spoken Spanish (e.g., grammar, vocabulary, pronunciation) by someone with whom you were speaking? (If not, go to #12)

      a.   What did they correct you on?

      b.   What was your reaction to that correction?

    12.   Have you ever corrected another Puerto Rican's Spanish (e.g., grammar, vocabulary, pronunciation)?

      a.   If so, what was the correction you suggested?

    13.   Is it important to try to change the way that Puerto Ricans speak Spanish in *[your city/town]*? Why (why not)?

    14.   *[Offer the participant the opportunity to add anything else they feel is relevant to these topics. When they finish, close the interview.]*

VOLUME XXXIII • NUMBER II • SUMMER 2021

High School Student Experiences and Impact of a College Preparatory Program in Puerto Rico During the 1960s

WILLIAM VÉLEZ AND ANTONIO PANIAGUA GUZMÁN

ABSTRACT

The purpose of this article is to look at the history and student outcomes of a college preparatory program for talented students in high school developed by Puerto Rico's Department of Education in the 1960s. This study is based on ten semi-structured interviews of students who participated in the program. Our findings strongly suggest the program was successful in enhancing the academic skills of its students and played a role in the long-term educational and occupational mobility of its students. Students' narratives portray the presence of strong bonds with teachers that led to the accumulation of social and cultural capital leading to the formation of postsecondary educational goals and substantial occupational achievements in our sample. Students obtained cultural capital by participating in extracurricular activities sponsored by the program such as visiting museums and engaging in conversations with poets and novelists. They attended smaller classes and benefitted from an advanced curriculum that challenged their cognitive skills and developed their critical thinking skills. [Keywords: Puerto Rico; model schools; gifted and talented; cultural capital]

William Vélez (velez@uwm.edu) is Professor Emeritus of Sociology at the University of Wisconsin-Milwaukee. He received his Ph.D. in Sociology from Yale University in 1983. His scholarship is broadly focused on educational and housing issues with specialized research interests in Latino urban populations. He has published articles in *Sociology of Education, Social Science Research, Journal of Latinos and Education* and *Urban Affairs Review*.

Introduction

At the beginning of the 1960's public schools in Puerto Rico were facing an institutional crisis. It was a highly centralized system serving both urban and rural areas in the Island, with limited resources and a growing population. Universal school enrollments only existed at the elementary level. Most of the students in the countryside received only about three hours of instruction a day, within buildings in need of serious repair (Quintero Alfaro 1972). Crowded classrooms and scarce instructional materials also contributed to a high dropout rate. Teachers earned meager salaries coupled with bad working conditions (six classes a day) resulted in low job satisfaction and a significant turnover. However, the construction of housing subdivisions targeted to a growing middle class produced a more heterogeneous social mix in the student body of many public schools, with resulting conflicts (Quintero Alfaro 1972). To deal with the changes, the Department of Education of the Commonwealth of Puerto Rico launched a series of reforms or programs (Eliza Colón 1989).

While previous reform efforts had placed more emphasis on the expansion of vocational education in line with the government goals of industrializing an economy based on agricultural production until the early 1940s (Solís 1994), this time educational leaders refocused their attention on preparation for postsecondary attendance. A small number of schools were designated as *escuelas ejemplares* (model schools). The selection process included identifying groups of teachers, school principals and community groups that had approached the central administration with suggestions for improvements at the local level. For example, a model school was built close to a new middle-class subdivision because a group of parents had approached the school superintendent complaining about the area's lack of public schools. These schools received better resources, and higher levels of staff training and supervision as well as intense evaluation of learning outcomes. In addition, new programs were established at the school level: for example, some high schools initiated a special program aimed at students who planned to attend college (Eliza Colón 1989).

Antonio Paniagua Guzmán (paniagu9@uwm.edu) is a sociology doctoral student at the University of Wisconsin-Milwaukee. His research relies on cultural sociology, urban sociology, and ethnographic research methods.

Labeled Programa Especial de Escuela Superior (high school special program) the program modified the usual 6-3-3 format followed by Puerto Rican public schools requiring students to begin high school in 10th grade. It also paid for students to take college classes during their senior year. The main architect and advocate for this program was Angel G. Quintero Alfaro, who was appointed Puerto Rico's secretary of education in 1964, and who, in 1951, as the dean of the School of Education at the University of Puerto Rico developed a partnership with school teachers and principals to offer basic or introductory university classes to talented high school students. His experiences with this experiment persuaded him that practices such as assigning students by grade (rather than skills, interests or knowledge) and offering a uniform curriculum to all students were counterproductive (Quintero Alfaro 1972).

This study is also guided by the importance of cultural capital in mediating the acquisition of educational credentials.

This study is based on the assumption that students succeed in educational environments that support strong social relationships with peers and adults in schools (Portes, Fernandez-Kelly and Haller 2008). Specifically, supportive relationships among adults, friends and family both in and out school provide students with the social capital that leads to acquiring the skills and "funds" of knowledge necessary to navigate successfully academia and the workplace. Social capital is described by Bourdieu (1986) as "durable networks" formed through "institutionalized relationships" intended to distribute resources (e.g., information and opportunities) to individuals with privileged access to these networks. Having a "pro-school" ethos is also crucial to student achievement and is facilitated by affiliation with academically oriented peers (Valenzuela 1999). As we document below, the *Programa Especial* was designed to facilitate the accumulation of social capital through its organizational and pedagogical practices. This study is also guided by the importance of cultural capital in mediating the acquisition of educational credentials. By cultural capital we refer to a taste or disposition to acquire or engage in elite cultural practices and products, linguistic competencies and preferences (Bourdieu 1977).

Often researchers of low-income Latino students start from a cultural deficit perspective and assume their families of origin and communities don't value education (Valenzuela 1999). But under-privileged children can also find valuable cultural resources and aspirational capital through their communities or neighborhoods, as proposed by Tara Yosso (2005). A student's community and/or kinship group can play a central role in engaging rich literacy practices and artistic traditions.

The *Programa Especial* started in the 1962-63 school year included many of the assumptions and features followed by gifted and talented programs in the United States. For example, that gifted and talented students have unique needs requiring a "continuum of services" that could include advanced classes (Kim 2006), full time grouping with students of similar abilities (Van Tassel-Baska 2005), and teachers who received training for working with gifted students (Reiss and Purcell 1993).

The major organizational and academic features distinguishing the program from instruction in regular public schools included the following:

- reduction in the teaching load for teachers working in the program; specialized training for teachers;
- reduction in the hours spent in the classroom for students while requiring them to spend six hours a week on individual research projects;
- a redesigned curriculum that emphasized the development of critical thinking skills;
- a bi-weekly history seminar taught by a university professor and requiring the teachers of English, Spanish and History also to be present;
- modified the usual 6-3-3 format (elementary school goes from first through sixth grade, middle school includes grades seventh through ninth, and high school comprises 10th through 12th grades) by requiring students to begin high school in ninth grade;
- and students enrolled in college classes during their senior year.

Students were selected based on an aptitude test taken during the 8th grade and recommendations from teachers. The *Programa Especial* combined some elements of gifted and talented programs (that are usually implemented in elementary schools) by keeping class sizes small and grouping its students together for all their classes; and features of a college preparatory track (practiced in most high schools) with their emphasis on advanced or honors classes containing a more challenging curriculum. While students in the general track took subject area classes every day, students in the special program attended subject area courses three days a week. The other two days were spent in a seminar jointly taught by a university professor and the Spanish teacher and in the library reading complementary materials and completing research projects. The curriculum was integrated across subjects so that, for example, if the assigned reading for the seminar was the classical Roman story *El rapto de las sabinas* ("The Abduction of the Sabine Women") then the History, Spanish, English, and Social Studies teachers would assign/present additional material surrounding the story.

Dr. Quintero Alfaro and his colleagues envisioned a curriculum that would take advantage of gifted students' faster speed in processing information and their enjoyment of challenging cognitive endeavors (see Meier, Vogel and Preckel 2014). They developed a list of traits or goals a good educational program must promote, including some of the following:

- ability to correctly communicate orally and in written form;
- ability to connect assumptions and reach valid conclusions;
- ability to form a mental image of an object, event, or situation, whether real or imagined;
- ability to correctly assess the quality of a study or scientific statement and understand the underlying principles;
- develop an appreciation of art and literature and understanding the general principles of its creation.

The Department of Education commissioned outside evaluations to test or measure the success of the *Programa Especial* in meeting its programmatic and educational goals. One study compared the growth in knowledge in mathematical and language arts by matching participating students with other students in the same school who had similar initial skills, gender, age, and socioeconomic background (control group). After three years in the program, students manifested growth in mastery of mathematics and language arts that exceeded in a significant and substantial way that of the control group (see Quintero Alfaro 1972, 58). In addition, after three years in the program, average student scores in Spanish were higher than those of private school students, while average scores in English were similar to their private school counterparts. These latter findings are impressive since at that time in Puerto Rico the great majority of private schools enrolled mostly middle and upper middle-class students.

The initial pilot program in the 1962-63 school year was implemented in only six schools with an enrollment of 210 students. By the 1966-67 school year the *Programa Especial* grew to include 19 schools with an enrollment of more than 850 students (Quintero Alfaro 1972). From 1963 to 1967 the Department of Education trained 200 teachers to work in the program. Financial support for the program came from Puerto Rico's Department of Education, the University of Puerto Rico and the Ford Foundation. Although we have not been able to document how many students were served by the program during its seven years of existence, we can safely assume that during its last two years it graduated about 1,700 students across the Island. After the 1968-69 academic year the *Programa Especial* was unfortunately discontinued.

In this article we ask the following questions: Did enrollment in *Programa Especial* increase the college attainment rates among participants? Did it play a central role in participants' occupational achievements? To answer these questions, we explore the experiences of students enrolled in the *Programa Especial* during the 1960s as well as their personal assessment of the impact it had on their subsequent educational and occupational achievements. Our findings are based on a qualitative analysis of ten semi-structured interviews of students who participated in the program in three different high schools.

Historical Context

In order to better understand the political and economic conditions that surrounded the evolution of public education in Puerto Rico from the turn of the century until the 1960s, it is best to examine some of the historical events of that period. At a time when Puerto Ricans had gained increasing political autonomy and representation in Spain's parliament, in 1898 the Spanish-American War returned the Island to a low colonial status with the military in charge under the United States tutelage. Once Puerto Rico was incorporated into the United States, the American government embarked on an assimilationist project. They named English the official language of Puerto Rico and its schools, renamed Puerto Rico to Porto Rico to sound more American, and established schools to teach American culture, including the English language, to native Puerto Ricans (Acosta-Belén and Santiago 2018, 56.). These Americanizing efforts included instruction in English, forcing the students to learn and sing American songs, saluting the flag and uttering the pledge of allegiance as the first activity upon entering school (Osuna 1975). These policies resulted in undermining Puerto Rican history, culture and the Spanish language (Negrón de Montilla 1971). Students were to become familiarized with all things American "through the teaching of U.S. history, the supplanting of Puerto Rican patriots with American ones, the daily ritual of singing the U.S. national anthem and the celebration of U.S. patriotic holidays and parades" (del Moral 2013, 51).

During the first four decades of U.S. control a succession of North American commissioners of education saw their main mission as culturally assimilating inferior racial subjects and manufacturing consent to American rule.

During the first four decades of the 20th century a framework of paternalism guided the founding and governance of the schools under U.S. tutelage, according to Solsiree del Moral (2013). A history book (*Historia de Puerto Rico*, 1922) written by Paul G. Miller, one of the early commissioners of education, decried the terrible conditions of public education under the Spanish colonial regime and lauded the benevolent leadership of the U.S. empire in Puerto Rico—*Historia de Puerto Rico* was included as part of the schools' curriculum. Under Spanish rule, Miller argued, education was mainly focused on elite male boys, while girls, people of color and rural populations were condemned to illiteracy. In contrast, the progressive and modern agenda of the U.S. colonial rule promised equal opportunities to all children without regard to place of residence, gender or color. During the first four decades of U.S. control a succession of North American commissioners of education saw their main mission as culturally assimilating inferior racial subjects and manufacturing consent to American rule. As articulated by Solsiree del Moral, "Puerto Ricans could gain literacy, English-language skills and the ability to comprehend their rights and responsibilities to the US empire (2013, 53).

Under early American control, mass schooling was slowly introduced in the Island, but school attendance was low, and most students dropped out of school between the 4th and 8th grade. In addition to the resistance to the use of English as the medium of instruction, economic necessity forced older children to find some form of work to help support their families (Solís 1994). From the 1910s to the 1930s Puerto Rican teachers mounted a sustained opposition to the Americanizing project through the Teachers Association and continued to advocate Spanish language instruction (Barreto 1998).

In 1917, with the passage of the Jones Act Puerto Ricans were forced into U.S. citizenship. During the first three decades of the 20th century Puerto Ricans saw its economy transformed from a hacienda system focused on coffee production to an agrarian capitalism system dedicated to the production of sugar under the control of a few North American corporations and a smaller group of Puerto Rican *hacendados* (Ayala and Bernabe 2007). In the 1930s worsening economic conditions led to a series of labor strikes and the increasing political strength of a reformist movement (Partido Popular Democratico). The movement was led by a charismatic leader named Luis Muñoz Marín. In 1948 Muñoz Marín became the first Puerto Rican governor elected by popular mandate.

Muñoz Marín's campaign message to the Island voters placed more emphasis on social justice issues while de-emphasizing the quest for political independence from the United States (Scarano 2016). His progressive agenda included an agrarian reform that created agricultural cooperatives; facilitated the creation of trade unions; distributed small plots of land to rural peasants; and attempted to limit the amount of land a single corporation could own. His plans also included the development of locally owned factories and businesses; a minimum wage for workers; and brought electric power and clean water to the rural areas. In 1949, once in power the Populares made Spanish the official language of instruction in the public schools and redirected the curriculum to instill a sense of a common culture, while promising to provide a free public education to all Puerto Rican children through the 8th grade (later expanded to high school).

In 1952 Luis Muñoz Marín and his political party crafted a semiautonomous political status vis-a-vis the United States that would be known as Estado Libre Asociado (Commonwealth) and would be officially approved part of their strategy to attract followers was to assert a distinctive collective identity for Puerto Ricans within the context of a political and economic dependence to the United States. A cultural form of nationalism was sponsored through the schools and other institutions, with the Spanish language as the cornerstone of Puerto Ricanness (Duany 2002). In the mid-1950s his administration created the Institute of Puerto Rican Culture, an organization that would sponsor the study and performance/display of Puerto Rico's folklore, music, literature and plastic arts.

In 1942 one of the initiatives sponsored by the Puerto Rican legislature under the leadership of Muñoz Marín was the creation of the Compañia de Fomento Industrial (Corporation for Industrial Development). Beginning in 1947 Fomento launched a program to boost industrial production under the name Operacion Manos a la Obra (Operation Bootstrap). Generous incentives offered to potential investors included a cheap and pliant labor force, a stable political climate, free access to U.S. markets, low-cost buildings and infrastructure, and a tax exemption period of ten years (later extended to 25 years). By many accounts Operation Bootstrap was very successful (for about three decades) and provided many jobs at a time when agricultural production was in the process of decline and eventual collapse, throwing many farm workers into unemployment (Scarano 2016). The economic transformation from an agricultural to an industrial base led to a demand for more and better schools, and the state tried to meet the demand by building more schools and hiring more teachers. But a highly centralized administration emphasized the teaching of basic skills in a standardized way that ignored the specific needs and learning styles of many students and paid no attention to the input of its underpaid teaching staff (Quintero Alfaro 1972). The curriculum emphasis during the 1940s and 1950s was centered on vocational education, with schools training workers for an industrial labor force that was to learn to live with low wages (Solís 1994). The result was most students attended school only at the elementary level, dropout rates were high, and only a small percentage of students finished high school.

Beginning in the late 1940s the commonwealth administration was determined to expand access to education and constructed dozens of schools, many of them in rural zones (Scarano 2016). It accelerated the training of new teachers by selecting high achieving high school graduates to become rural teachers during the week and attending a teacher certification program on the weekends. In addition, the Department of Education infused the school curriculum with Puerto Rican culture, choosing Puerto Rican authors and materials that better reflected the social and cultural milieu of the students (Scarano 2016). These efforts began to pay off, and by the 1963-64 school year about 84 percent of all school-age children were attending school, compared to only 60 percent in the 1949-50 school year. High school enrollments also increased dramatically, and by the 1963–64 about half of all youth 16 to 18 years old youth were attending school. A higher proportion of students graduating from high school with many aspiring to postsecondary education led to an explosion in college enrollments. Between the late 1940s to the mid-1960s the number of students enrolled at the university almost tripled (from 12,500 students to 33,000). It is under these changing educational pressures that the need to provide more high school students with college-ready skills induced the Department of Education to develop new instructional strategies, such as the *Programa Especial*.

The main objectives of this article are as follows: to get the students' assessment of the program's effectiveness in promoting their academic knowledge and critical thinking skills; identify the features of the program mentioned by the majority of the students as the most enriching in academic and nonacademic skills; and learn their assessment of the impact the program had on their subsequent academic and occupational careers.

The study's findings are presented and discussed within the macro economic conditions produced by the special political relationship between Puerto Rico and the United States. We also consider the socioeconomic background of the parents and their neighborhoods.

Cultural Capital and Community Cultural Wealth

The concept of "cultural capital" was developed by Bourdieu (1977) to make reference to a taste or disposition to acquire or engage in elite cultural practices and products, linguistic competencies, and preferences. The acquisition and development of these sets of elements is closely related to education and the diverse factors and variables it impacts. The study of the relationship between cultural capital and education has been critical as it has influenced education policies in different contexts (Reay 2004; Tzanakis 2011) in part because the student's level of cultural capital is associated with their educational attainment, and in consequence with their professional success (DiMaggio and Mohr 1985; Sullivan 2001). Previous studies have shown the level of cultural capital is a critical variable determining students' willingness and/or probabilities of attending higher education (De Graaf, De Graaf and Kraaykamp 2000; Noble and Davies 2009). Given that this study explores the influence of *Programa Especial* on college attainment rates among participants, as well as its impact on participants' occupational achievements, we consider cultural capital as a central theoretical concept for the analysis not only because, as discussed previously, the program's curriculum was largely focused on strengthening diverse competencies. As previous studies have shown, cultural capital is also related to professional success. Since the influence of *Programa Especial* on participants' educational attainment and occupational achievements is central, one of the areas in which we put particular attention was in the social mobility outcome. We assume there is a positive association between level of education/occupational attainment and social mobility (Matthys 2012; Plewis and Bartley 2014).

The theoretical contributions by Tara Yosso (2005) to the study of education are also central in this study. To challenge traditional interpretations of Bourdieu's cultural capital in explaining educational outcomes, Yosso developed an alternative theoretical model. She positioned cultural capital as just one component of what she called "community cultural wealth" defined as "an array of knowledge, skills, abilities, and contacts possessed and utilized by communities of color to survive and resist macro and micro-forms of oppression" (2005, 77). According to Yosso (2005; see also Oliver, Shapiro and Shapiro 2006) cultural, aspirational, familial, social, navigational, resistant and linguistic capitals are contained in "community cultural wealth." This theoretical approach has been primarily used in the United States context to analyze aspects of minorities' education such as color-based inequalities in academic fields (Martínez, Chang and Welton

2017), performance and educational attainment among minority students (Espino 2014; Pérez II 2017), and teaching performance (Burciaga and Kohli 2018). It has also been used in the Latin American context. For example, drawing on Yosso (2005), a recent study by Trigos-Carrillo (2019) based on Mexico, Costa Rica and Colombia shows that families and communities play a central role in engaging rich literacy practices, and derives in a stronger performance in college. Similarly, Webb and Sepúlveda (2020) conducted an analysis in the Chilean context showing that community cultural wealth, along with aspirational and resistant capital, are instrumental in indigenous students' higher educational motivations. As Kouyoumdjian et al. (2017) have suggested, the community cultural wealth model can be employed to analyze not only the sources of support students have, but also the challenges they face. Therefore, given that one of the fundamental elements of this study is the examination of the multiple factors impacting educational and occupational attainment, Yosso's (2005) community cultural wealth model appears to be a strong theoretical tool to guide our analysis.

Data and Methods

Participants

This study aims to answer the following questions: (1) Did *Programa Especial* increase the college attainment rates among participants? (2) Did it play a central role in participants' occupational achievements? It draws on interviews with ten individuals who were part of the *Programa Especial* and graduated between 1967 and 1969 from three different high schools in Puerto Rico.

Seven of the participants were enrolled in the Dr. Pila High School in the city of Ponce. Dr. Pila at that time sat between a middle-class subdivision called San Antonio to its west and a public housing complex to the east.

Two of the students were enrolled in the Ernesto Ramos Antonini High School in the city of Yauco near a barrio or neighborhood by the name of Barinas. At that time the school was located in a section of the city reserved for educational institutions, with an elementary school and a middle school nearby. The only other buildings located in the proximity of the school were an evangelical church, a bakery and a fraternal lodge. An abandoned train station lay across from the school, and the long-abandoned sugar cane mill, Hacienda Florida, was also located in the vicinity. And last we interviewed one student who attended the Dra. Maria Cadilla de Martínez High School in the city of Arecibo. The school at that time was located in front of a middle-class subdivision and had recently been built (it was later closed and moved to another part of town).

Collectively, their educational attainment ranged from some college to postgraduate degrees, with eight of the participants completing at least a bachelors' degree.

Six of the participants were females, four were males. Collectively, their educational attainment ranged from some college to postgraduate degrees, with eight of the participants completing at least a bachelors' degree. Two of the students started college but dropped out. Fernando dropped out after his first semester in college but subsequently completed an associate degree in computer technology that helped him get a job with digital equipment. He had a long and successful career in the computer electronics industry as a manager including rising to the position of vice president of a California company that manufactures compact disks.

Francisco received an honor scholarship to study chemical engineering at the University of Puerto Rico, Mayagüez campus. In 1970 in the middle of his sophomore year he enlisted in the U.S. Army. In 1972, while serving in the personnel office at Fort Eustis, Virginia, Francisco attained the highest Military Occupational test score in his field at that base. In 1974 he was promoted to Staff Sargent and in April 1978, the Department of the Army promoted him to Warrant Officer I. Following that promotion, he attended the Military Personnel Officer course at Fort Benjamin Harrison, Indiana, where he finished first in his class with one of the best percentages ever (99%). During his 23-year Army career he excelled in numerous assignments at different Army installations: as Detachment Commander, Personnel Officer and Data Processing Officer, including an affiliation with the XVIII Airborne Corps at Fort Bragg, North Carolina, and the 8th Infantry Division (Mechanized) in Germany. In June 1993, following the conclusion of his three-year tour with the 21st Sustainment Command (TAACOM) in Germany, he retired having achieved the level of a Chief

Warrant Officer IV (CWO-4). After his military retirement, Francisco spent nine years with the U.S. Postal Service, during which he rose to the position of Post Office Manager. He then pursued his love for the game of chess by working in many capacities for the U.S. Chess Federation (e.g., as national tournament director), and the World Chess Federation (e.g., as International Arbiter). Although he never obtained a formal college degree, the training (and experience) he received in the U.S. Army allowed him to pursue a successful career as an administrator/manager first in the Army, then with the U.S. Postal Service, and finally with the U.S. Chess Federation.

Regarding occupational status, five of the participants are still active in their professional activities while the remainder have retired and, in some cases, started new professional or personal projects. Since participants' occupations are very diverse, we classify them into four professional sector categories: business and private sector (N=2); public sector and government (N=3); education and academia (N=3); and culture and entertainment (N=2). All participants are Puerto Ricans and eight still live on the Island.

Data Collection and Sampling
The principal investigator conducted the data collection process. A snowball sampling strategy was used to recruit ten participants for this study. Using social media, the researcher contacted a high school classmate who agreed to participate in the study and provided additional information for contacting other graduates from the *Programa Especial* in Puerto Rico. Five interviews were by phone and five were in person, either in participants' homes or in public spaces like restaurants or shopping malls in Puerto Rico. Interviews were conducted between January and March 2019 and lasted approximately one hour each. The second author assisted in the transcriptions of the interviews, translations to English, and took the lead in the analysis of the data and the reporting of the results.

Most interview questions were broad, open-ended, and designed to elicit information and stories from the respondents about their program experiences, subsequent educational careers, and work histories. In each interview, participants were asked about three primary aspects. First, individual program experience and the ways both academic and extracurricular experience influenced participants' personal and professional lives.

In addition, we asked questions to learn about participants' assessment of the program and their perceptions of faculty's performance, institutional design, and its benefits and potential drawbacks. Second, their post-graduation professional careers and the extent to which their experience in the program helped them succeed in their fields. We devoted special attention to the evolution of their professional careers since they graduated from Escuela Superior up to present day. This includes highest educational level achieved, economic sectors in which they worked, positions they occupied, and degree of positive impact on their communities and country. To assess intergenerational mobility, we asked about parental educational level and occupation, pre- and post-graduation neighborhood/residential characteristics and mobility, and international experience.

Data Analysis

Interviews were conducted in Spanish by the principal investigator. All interviews were transcribed and translated into English by both investigators, who are proficient in Spanish and English. In order to gather and process the data necessary to answer the research questions, we coded the interviews by questions (13 questions in total) and grouped them into the four areas of analysis previously described. Then, using NVivo 12, we coded each student's response to contrast differences and similarities between their responses to identify patterns (Campbell et al. 2013). The inter-participant comparison we generated with the software was critical to identify specific patterns in each area of analysis and answer the research questions. Also, the software-based analysis allowed us to identify key words/terms that were fundamental for the results presented later. In addition to the software-based analysis, the researchers conducted a discourse analysis of the interviews capturing additional information of participants in an analytic memo that they used to compare and contrast participants' responses and professional profiles. In the following section, we present results derived from such analysis. Quotes presented were originally in Spanish and translated into English. The students referred to the *Programa Especial* as *"grupos especiales"* and we use the two terms interchangeably throughout the paper.

Table 1: Participants' Professional and Educational Background

Name	Professional Sector	Gender	Level of Education	*Year	**City	Occupational Status
Fernando Díaz	Business & Private Sector	M	Associates Degree	1968	Ponce	Retired
Ramón Caquías	Business & Private Sector	M	Bachelor's Degree	1968	Ponce	Active
Migdalia Fraticelli	Public Sector & Gov.	F	Doctoral Degree	1967	Ponce	Retired
Francisco Guadalupe	Public Sector & Gov.	M	Some College	1968	Ponce	Retired
Hirám Sánchez	Public Sector & Gov.	M	Doctoral Degree	1968	Yauco	Retired
Linda Colón	Education & Academia	F	Doctoral Degree	1969	Arecibo	Active
Marta Lopez	Education & Academia	F	Master's Degree	1968	Yauco	Retired
Ada Hilda Martínez	Education & Academia	F	Doctoral Degree	1967	Ponce	Retired
Carmen Gaud	Culture & Entertainment	F	Doctoral Degree	1967	Ponce	Active
Carmen Nydia Velázquez	Culture & Entertainment	F	Bachelor's Degree	1968	Ponce	Active

* Year of graduation from escuela superior.
** City in which their escuela superior was (or is) located.

Results

As Table 1 displays, participants (N=10) are distributed across four different professional categories. The professional sector with lower educational attainment is "business and private sector"; in the other three it ranges from bachelor's to doctoral degrees. Regarding gender, while only one of the four male participants holds a doctoral degree, four of the six females hold doctor-

Students at the Dr. Pila High School in Ponce (1966). From left: María Teresa Mena, José Luis Medina, Ada Hilda Martínez Vélez, Nelson Ithier, Noemí Bigas, Carlos Caraballo and Annette Mattei. Photograph courtesy of William Vélez. Reprinted by permission.

al degrees—and in some cases more than one master's degree. While our study was not designed to test for gender effects, census results for Puerto Rico have consistently shown women to earn proportionately more college degrees than men (see Puerto Rico: Data USA 2019). In addition, it is important to highlight that while the sectors "education and academia" and "culture and entertainment" are fully dominated by females, the "business and private sector" is a male-dominated one; the only one in which we observe a mixed gender composition is "public sector and government". Finally, another interesting aspect about participants' professional and educational characteristics is that half are still active in their field, or after retiring started new careers in other fields. For example, Hiram, who retired from the public sector started publishing fiction ten years ago and now is a very prolific and well-known writer in Puerto Rico. Ada Hilda Martínez, after retiring as a professor of Hispanic Literature, serves as a member of selection committees of literary prizes, is in

Hiram Sánchez Martínez (2017), one of the program participants, is a former judge and writer. In 2008 one of his books won the Premio Nacional PEN Club de Puerto Rico. Photograph courtesy of William Vélez. Reprinted by permission.

Recent reunion of former participants, Manatí, Puerto Rico. From left: William Vélez, Fernando Díaz and José Artemio Torres. Photograph courtesy of William Vélez. Reprinted by permission.

the editorial board of a university journal, regularly writes and recites poetry, and offers public lectures. Another respondent started as a volunteer in his son's school organizing a chess club and ended up serving in both volunteer and paid positions with the U.S. Chess Federation, who in 2009 named him US Chess Tournament Director of the Year.

Our interviews revealed that a close student-teacher relationship was central in this process.

Experience and Assessment of Program

According to Bourdieu (1986), there are three components of social resources that determine individuals' positions within the social ladder: social, cultural and economic capital. Social scientists have widely explored the impact of these three forms of capital on access to education, educational outcomes, institutional design of educational organization, among others. However, they have devoted special attention to the study of the influence of cultural and social capital on students' performance and programs' outcomes. While social capital refers to group membership and individuals' "network of connections" (Bourdieu 1986, 249), cultural capital comprises a wide array of elements such as accumulation of knowledge, linguistic competencies, preferences, orientations, manners, etc. (Bourdieu 1977, 82–4). The relevance of these forms of capital in education is that, as previous research has shown, the acquisition and/or strengthening of those resources (both in educational and non-educational settings) is a driver of social mobility and play a central role in individuals' class and economic circumstances (Monkman, Ronald and Theramene 2005; see also Reay 2004). Also, specifically, social capital allows children and young adults to access information, language skills, physical goods, and additional social networks (McNeal 1999).

One of the main objectives of the *Programa Especial* was to offer an advanced academic curriculum covering subjects and fields that regular programs did not. Apart from getting exposed to a wider range of disciplines and subjects with a larger academic load, this program was instrumental in increasing students' cultural and social capital. Our interviews revealed that a close student-teacher relationship was central in this process. Teachers' lectures, as well as the active role students had in the classroom and other academic activities (e.g., debates, field trips, and group projects), were central in the creation of an impactful experience that largely determined students' post-graduation professional paths. While participants' overall program experience varied depending on their areas of interest or individual professional projects, all of them highlighted the relevance of the teacher and the strong bonds they created with the students. Being a teacher of this program, according to one of our participants, was a very "prestigious" position that gave the teachers the opportunity to explore with students disciplines and fields not part of the regular curricula. As Carmen Nydia, an actress and TV/radio announcer highlights:

"Uno de los beneficios de haber formado parte de los grupos especiales es que teníamos maestros especiales. Sus clases nos prepararon para lo que después sería la vida universitaria". (One of the benefits of having been part of the grupos especiales was that we had *maestros especiales* [special teachers]. Their classes prepared us for college.)

Students considered teachers' role and social position as very prestigious and in turn reported that teachers were highly influential in their lives. When answering the question, Who were your favorite teachers and why? Migdalia, a jurist and law professor asserts:

"Socorro Girón de Segura [maestra de español y literatura] era la poetisa residente del Municipio de Ponce. Ella fue como un paradigma, yo dije, 'yo quiero ser como esa señora'". (Socorro Girón de Segura [Spanish and literature teacher] was the poet laureate of Ponce. She was like a paradigm for me...I just wanted to be like her.)

Another feature of the program that generated a positive and beneficial experience for students, as well as the enlargement of social and cultural capital, was the extra-curricular activities, mainly cultural and academic, and mostly designed and executed by teachers, which were a central and a fundamental complement of classroom work. These activities ranged from field trips and movie clubs to debates and even summer internships (e.g., museum guide in the summer); apart from allowing students to interact both with their peers and teachers in non-academic settings, they embodied an opportunity for many students—mainly the ones coming from economically disadvantaged communities—to get access to cultural experiences for the first time. When we asked to identify two enriching or exceptional moments from their days in the "grupos especiales," Hirám, a jurist, law professor and writer, mentioned the relevance of being exposed to elite cultural products and expressions for the first time (in this case a museum). This experience, according to him, had a huge impact in his experience in the program, and consequently, in his life:

"Antes de ser parte de los grupos especiales yo jamás había ido a un museo. Claro, había visto fotografías y reproducciones de obras de arte, pero jamás una pieza original colgada en la pared. Recuerdo cuando lo vi por primera vez fue una experiencia estremecedora—es difícil describir lo que sentí". (Before being part of the grupos especiales I had never gone to a museum. Of course, I had seen pictures and art reproductions in magazines and books, but I remember that when I saw a genuine piece of art hanged on the wall of the museum, it was an extraordinary experience—it is difficult to describe what I felt.)

The importance of acquiring cultural capital within the process of social mobility among Latino urban students has been documented in previous studies (see Monkman, Ronald, and Theramene 2005). The *Programa Especial* enabled students attending an urban public school to engage in high status cultural activities more common in elite private schools. These cultural activities, coupled with the materials consumed and discussed in class, influenced students' program experience in the short run, and also in some cases were pivotal in students' professional future, to the degree of determining their future careers. Hirám's case illustrates this as he decided to go to law school in the wake of a debate around Sophocles' tragedy: *Antigone*. When describing that moment he says:

"Esa lectura [*Antígona*] me impresionó al punto que quise estudiar derecho...eso fue durante los seminarios de los grupos especiales. Trataba sobre el choque que hay entre la ley humana y la ley divina, porque a Antígona le habían prohibido enterrar a su hermano y ella tenía que tomar una decisión sobre si cumplir con la ley de Dios o cumplir con la ley de los hombres". (That reading [*Antigone*] impressed me to the point that I decided to study law...it was in the seminars, in the grupos especiales. It dealt with the clash between human law and divine law because Antigone had been prohibited to bury her brother and she had to decide whether to obey God's law or man's.)

As Monkman, Ronald, and Theramene suggest, "By helping children build social networks and acquire access to social and cultural capital as well as to revalue existing resources, teachers make it possible for these children to benefit from their successes in schools and in society" (2005, 30). In the case of *Programa Especial*, both extracurricular and in-class activities were designed to promote the development of critical thinking and the development of students' social and cultural capital. Thus, coupled with the big influence teachers had on students, students were able to develop skills and habits that allowed them to strengthen their social and cultural capita, and by doing so, became more likely to succeed in their careers.

As the above examples illustrate, most participants acknowledge their experience in grupos especiales was positive overall and benefited largely from its institutional design—different curricula that exposed them to a wide variety of topics, disciplines, and teachers. The two aspects that emerged in all the interviews we conducted were the positive influence of teachers on students—that was strong due to the position of privilege the teachers had among students and strong student-teacher bonds—and extra-curricular activities that exposed students to high status cultural practices that could be used for social advantage.

Our respondents also recall the influence their families had on their educational aspirations. Linda Colón, who grew-up in a poor rural neighborhood, was inspired by her mother's heroic struggles to get a college education. This is how she describes her mother's pursuit of a teacher's credential:

"Yo venía de una familia donde mi mamá, por ejemplo, era una eterna estudiante. Durante toda mi niñez yo veía a mi mamá estudiando. Empezó a estudiar en la universidad los sábados. En los grupos de las clases de extramuros que se daban de la Universidad de Puerto Rico en Arecibo los sábados. Y se tardó un montón de años en llegar a ser maestra. Cuando tuvo que hacer la práctica pues, tuvo que venirse a Río

Piedras y coger una licencia y estar un semestre completo. Y entonces también yo venía a Río Piedras con ella los veranos". (I come from a family where my mother was an eternal student. She started studying at the University on Saturdays. In the extension courses that were offered at the University of Puerto Rico in Arecibo on Saturdays. It took her many years to become a teacher. When she had to do the practicum (student teaching) she had to travel to Rio Piedras. And obtain a license (leave) and spend the whole semester. I accompanied her to Rio Piedras during the summers.)

Linda developed her own college aspirations from observing her mother's love for studying, confirming Yosso's community cultural wealth ideas. Her mother provided modelling for the kinds of literacy practices and study habits crucial to succeed in educational institutions.

Marta Pérez López, who grew up in relative poverty with her widowed mother and four sisters in a poor neighborhood in Yauco also recalls the support she received from her neighbors. They would often gift vegetables and fruits from their small gardens to her household, and they would meet in small groups to have a "tertulia" or a group discussion:

"Tambien yo recuerdo que se reunían en diferentes casas a tertuliar de los diferentes acontecimientos del día. Aunque no había televisión, la radio era clave en todo hogar. Hasta daban programas donde cantaban en décima (a poetic form with roots in Spain and used in Puerto Rican oral and musical traditions) los sucesos que ocurrían". (I also remember they would meet in different houses to discuss the news of the day. Although we did not have television, radios were key in every household. They would even offer programs where they will sing in decima the latest news).

From her community Marta and her family received material assistance, intellectual stimulation and camaraderie. This is another example of the community cultural wealth model proposed by Yosso (2005).

All of them acknowledge that their main motivation to pursue higher education was rooted in their years as students of this program.

Post-graduation Experience

Apart from analyzing participants' program experience and subjective assessment of the program, this study also focuses on the program's impact on the post-graduation professional careers of participants. To evaluate the impact of the program on participants' professional performance, we asked participants to describe in detail, first their professional activities within five years after graduating, and then the rest of their careers. As displayed in Table 1, six participants hold a postgraduate degree—five a Ph.D. and one a master's degree. Even though these participants received postgraduate degrees in different disciplines, and at different stages of their professional careers, some received such degrees several years after graduating from *Escuela Superior*. All of them acknowledge that their main motivation to pursue higher education was rooted in their years as students of this program. According to the participants, it was both the critical role of teachers in encouraging students to pursue higher degrees and the atmosphere of academic and intellectual challenge, which pushed students to keep studying after graduating from Escuela Superior. For example, Migdalia, suggests:

"Todos los estudiantes que estábamos ahí, todos éramos buenos estudiantes, y aunque había rivalidades normales propias de la edad, el hecho de que todo el mundo estaba enfocado en estudiar, en sacar buenas notas, y en ir a la universidad y seguir estudiando, era un tremendo estímulo...todos estábamos enfocados, y bueno, en esa época no había drogas y era un ambiente completamente sano, así que lo único que teníamos en mente era seguir adelante en nuestros estudios". (We were all good students and while there were rivalries typical of our age, the fact that everyone was focused on studying, getting good grades, and continuing our studies by attending college was a great stimulus...we were all focused, and, well in those days there were no drugs and it was a completely healthy environment, so the only thing we had in mind was to further our studies.)

Carmen Gaud, who had a long career with the Methodist Church is another student who recalls with fondness the intellectual stimulation she enjoyed from her classmates. This is how she describes their interactions:

"Para mí lo más importante en esos grupos era el diálogo con personas que estaban a cierto nivel intelectual... con una cierta curiosidad intelectual... y nos sentábamos a hablar de Freud y de Marcuse y nos sentábamos a hablar de los últimos libros, discutiendo toda clase de temas, explorando todo el asunto". (To me the most important aspect of the grupos especiales was the dialog with people who were at a certain intellectual level... who had intellectual curiosity... and we sat down to talk about Marx and Marcuse and the latest books and we would discuss/explore many different themes and issues.)

Apart from showing the effectiveness of the program in pushing students to pursue postgraduate degrees, this study also finds that, regardless of their field, occupation, or highest educational level achieved, participants appear to be central actors in the cultural, economic and social development of their communities. From different fronts, and at different degrees, all of them were involved in and/or promoted initiatives that benefited third parties. One of the questions we included in the interview was, What have been your most important professional and educational achievements? In response, most mentioned specific activities, programs, and/or initiatives in which they participated. The fact that they consider their contributions to their community as part of their most important achievements professionally, reflects the community values learned in grupos especiales, as the program not only prepared students to grow individually but also to turn into positive externalities capable of improving other people's lives. As shown in the following passage, Marta, who worked in the public and educational fields, acknowledges that her most important professional achievement was a public cultural project that she coordinated:

"Parte de mi trabajo como autoridad académica era coordinar diversos certámenes y actividades extracurriculares para niños estudiantes. Yo podría decir que mi mayor logro fue fundar en mi ciudad el 'concurso de niños trovadores', el cual dirigí por 17 años y en el cual le dimos oportunidad a muchas generaciones de niños para desarrollar sus habilidades artísticas y musicales. Este fue un legado que dejé y afortunadamente se ha perpetuado". (Some of my work as a school administrator involved coordinating a number of contests and extracurricular activities for students. I would say my biggest achievement was starting the 'children's folk singers' competition in my city, which I directed for 17 years and gave many generations of children the chance to develop their musical and artistic abilities. That's a legacy I left and fortunately still continues.)

One relevant finding derived from this study is that although previous research has shown higher levels of education—specifically post-graduate degrees—are positively associated with class and economic prosperity (e.g., Archer 2005; Archer, Hutchings and Ross 2005), in the case of this program, students who decided not to pursue post-graduate degrees also had prominent professional careers, experienced high levels of social mobility (discussed in next section), and accumulated economic capital. This was evident in the interviews with those individuals who did not pursue advanced degrees. They acknowledged that, although their fields were highly competitive and, in some cases, they had to compete with people with higher academic credentials, their communication and leadership skills, as well as their overall professional performance and curiosity, were highly valued by their employers. These skills were acquired during their days in the grupos especiales. As Fernando, an expert in computer technology suggests, he was conscious he had to work hard in order to be competitive and get access to better positions, as he did not have a post-graduate degree:

"En Puerto Rico, en los años en los que yo comencé a trabajar, había un problema grande en la industria, como había tanta demanda de empleados, había gente que se movía de un trabajo a otro con la única finalidad de subir salarios. Mi intención no era esa, mi intención era que donde yo estuviera, aunque ganara menos, yo quería ser feliz, ser útil, desarrollarme profesionalmente. Yo siempre pensaba, quizás inconscientemente, que por el hecho de que yo no tenía grados universitarios avanzados, tenía que trabajar más y buscar conocimiento para competir con gente que tiene eso. Siempre buscar el conocimiento es una habilidad que adquirí en los grupos especiales". (In the years I started working in Puerto Rico there was a big problem in the industry; since there was such a demand for workers, there were many who moved from job to job with the only goal of raising their salary. My intention was not that; my intention was that no matter where I was, I wanted to be happy, be useful, and develop professionally. I always thought, perhaps unconsciously, that since I lacked advanced university degrees, I had to work harder and seek knowledge to compete with those who had. Always seeking knowledge is a skill I acquired in the grupos especiales.)

Fernando's case is particularly interesting because, apart from benefiting from this program, he was positively impacted by the program Operation

Bootstrap. This was a set of economic projects launched and and implemented in Puerto Rico from 1947 into the 1970s to boost the Island's economy mainly by expanding the industrial sector and develop infrastructure that could be conducive to the growth of the manufacturing and technology industries (see Cabán 1989; Leonard 1998). After Fernando graduated from high school, he started working at a company that was part of this program; he moved to other companies as he was acquiring more experience in the technology industry. He became vice-president of operations of an international technology company and moved to the United States.

All participants regardless of their level of education, occupied high positions in their respective fields, and all of them acknowledge that the skills—cultural and social capital—they acquired in the grupos especiales was central in their professional success.

Results derived from the analysis of participants' post-graduation experience show two clear patterns. First, given that teachers of grupos especiales were highly qualified and that most of them had postgraduate degrees in their fields, students were particularly prone to follow the same pattern as teachers had a considerable influence on them. All participants regardless of their level of education, occupied high positions in their respective fields, and all of them acknowledge that the skills—cultural and social capital—they acquired in the grupos especiales was central in their professional success. This is illustrated in the following passage by Carmen Nydia:

"Desde mis días en los grupos especiales, yo siempre estuve segura de que quería estar en el ámbito artístico. Después de graduarme [de los grupos especiales], entré a la universidad y me entregué a lo que es y sigue siendo mi vida [el arte]...después, yo empecé a trabajar como actriz y nunca pensé en volver a la escuela, me entregué por completo. Desde ahí no he parado y nunca me ha faltado el trabajo". (From my days in the grupos especiales I was always sure that I wanted to be in artistic circles. After I graduated [from the grupos especiales] I entered college and dedicated myself to what is and will continue to be my life [the arts]...later, I started working as an actress and never thought of coming back to school. I was completely dedicated. Since then, I never stopped and had never lacked work.)

Second, regardless of their educational attainment, professional field, or economic/social background—before they joined the program—all of them acknowledge the program as one of their most important professional and/ or educational achievements activities, and/or initiatives in which they participated and benefited specific communities or groups. This pattern shows that while they highly benefited from the *Programa Especial*—and sometimes by current political and/or economic circumstances of the country, as in the case of Fernando—they became "positive externalities" for their communities and country as they promoted and/or pushed projects that benefited third parties.

Intergenerational Mobility

Previous studies have shown that education is a powerful driver of intergenerational mobility (Bourdieu 1977). To evaluate this outcome, we asked participants about paternal educational level and occupation. In addition, we asked them to provide a detailed description of the neighborhood they lived in when they were part of the grupos especiales; this included community life, infrastructure and public services, dominant economic activities in the neighborhood, goods and services available and leisure. This information, coupled with the description of their current occupational status, place of residence and other characteristics such as international experience, helped us determine the degree of social mobility observed in the sample.

Seven of the ten participants belonged to working class families living in highly segregated and poor neighborhoods. Their parents' educational attainment ranged from having finished 4th to 8th grade and all of them had blue-collar jobs such as truck driver, factory worker, custodial, etc. From those families, only two had stay-at-home moms, while the remaining mothers were also part of the workforce with blue collar jobs as well. Three of the participants belonged to middle class families whose income came from family-operated business and/or high-qualified jobs. These students grew up in neighborhoods with good public services and low crime rates. In addition, one reported having a stay-at-home mother, while the other two had mothers who were high-qualified professionals.

Results derived from this analysis suggest that this program might have been a positive factor in the students' socioeconomic achievement, as all students reported a substantial socioeconomic status improvement compared to their childhood circumstances. For example, this is how Fernando (who now lives in a penthouse condominium overlooking the ocean) describes his family's economic circumstances when he was a student:

"En el año en que nos graduamos [1968] yo no fui a la fiesta de graduación. Una de las razones por las que no asistí fue por la situación económica que mi familia afrontaba en ese momento, no tenía dinero para comprar un traje, y no quería forzar a mi madre o hacerla sentir mal, así que decidí decirle, 'no, yo no quiero ir'". (In the year we graduated [1968] I did not attend my graduation party. One of the reasons why I didn't attend was my family's economic situation. At that point, I did not have money for a suit, and did not want to force my mother or make her feel bad, so I decided to tell her 'No, I don't want to go.')

To summarize, we found all the study participants experienced social mobility. While all participants' socioeconomic status increased at different levels, we also found that increase was associated either to acquiring advanced educational degrees, or with skills and/or habits developed based on their experience in the grupos especiales. Although we realize social mobility is a product of many personal, community and historical factors, our findings suggest participation in the program may have contributed to the overall chances of upward mobility of its students.

Discussion
Our findings strongly suggest the 1960s *Programa Especial* developed by Puerto Rico's Department of Education was successful in enhancing the academic skills of its students and played a role in the long-term educational and occupational mobility of its students. Students' narratives portray the presence of strong bonds with teachers that led to the accumulation of social and cultural capital leading to the formation of postsecondary educational goals and substantial occupational achievements.

Students obtained cultural capital by participating in extracurricular activities sponsored by the *Programa Especial* such as visiting museums and engaging in conversations with poets and novelists. They attended smaller classes and benefitted from an advanced curriculum that challenged their cognitive skills and developed critical thinking skills. The program instilled intellectual preferences in its students, and these "habits of the mind" served them well after they left high school and pursued educational and occupational careers. Many of our respondents have made big impacts in their communities and continue to do so in retirement.

However, the law has never been implemented.

Although most of our respondents came from working class backgrounds, all of them acquired moderate to considerable socio-economic mobility. For example, two students later became lawyers and eventually judges, and another two became university professors. And two of our respondents had very successful careers in the business world. All of them credit their formation in the *Programa Especial* as an important factor in their occupational success. Our respondents also attained high levels of education, with seven out of ten students completing at least a bachelor's degree. By contrast, in 2018 only 18 percent of Puerto Ricans ages 65 or older (our respondents' average age was 68) had achieved similar levels of education (U.S. Census 2018) We conclude that the program was a contributing factor of intergenerational mobility amongst its students.

Our students also report their communities of origin provided cultural capital crucial to their academic success, in accordance with Yosso (2005). For example, neighborhood *tertulias* encouraged intellectual curiosity and parents provided aspirational capital.

Unfortunately, it appears that after the 1968-69 academic year the *Programa Especial* was discontinued by the Department of Education. In 1980 a group of parents initiated a class action lawsuit against the Department of Education. The parents argued the public schools had failed to provide legally mandated services to special education students. At the time this article was written the lawsuit had still not been settled (López Cabán 2013). In the summer of 2019, the Puerto Rican legislature approved the sum of $123 million to be spent on special education, but the Fiscal Board appointed by the U.S. Congress to monitor government spending has indicated it will block the disbursement (López Alicea 2019). In 2012 the Puerto Rican legislature approved a law establishing a pilot program targeted at gifted and talented children. In addition to establishing a definition of a gifted and talented child, the law mandated the Department of Education to keep a registry of gifted and talented students enrolled in public schools and encourages public schools to offer a more advanced curriculum to these students (Ortiz-Cartagena 2012). However, the law has never been implemented.

Some of the features of the *Programa Especial* were continued by Puerto Rico's Department of Education after the *Programa Especial* was discontinued. Advanced or honors classes are offered to high school students with college aspirations. Educational exchange trips to other countries are offered to students free of charge through a partnership between municipal governments and the Department of Education. And teachers certified to teach in a subject matter (e.g., English, Sciences) receive additional professional preparation in pedagogical practices (as reported by Marta Pérez López, who was a teacher, a principal and a curriculum supervisor in Puerto Rico until her retirement in 2005).

We conclude that well-designed high school programs providing accelerated curricula and effective and caring teachers like the *Programa Especial* produce short- and long- term benefits for public school students. Public schools in Puerto Rico are in a state of crisis. An economic recession that started in the first decade of this century, culminating in an austerity plan caused by a $73 billion government debt, and a combination of hurricanes and earthquakes have produced an exodus of students from the Island. Enrollments declined 44 percent between 2006 and 2018. The academic performance of its students, as measured by the National Assessment of Educational Progress, is so dismal that in 2017 not a single grade 8 student in Puerto Rico reached the Proficient or Advanced level in the mathematics test (see Holzman 2019). Local and federal authorities in Puerto Rico should work together to adequately fund the implementation of services and pedagogical practices that are needed to fully develop the academic, social and emotional needs of all students in the Island's public schools.

REFERENCES

Acosta-Belén, Edna and Carlos E. Santiago. 2018. *Puerto Ricans in the United States: A Contemporary Portrait*. Boulder: Lynne Rienner Publishers.

Ayala, Cesar and Rafael Bernabe. 2007. *Puerto Rico in the American Century: A History Since 1898*. Chapel Hill: University of North Carolina Press.

Barreto, Almílcar A. 1998. *Language, Elites, and the State: Nationalism in Puerto Rico and Quebec*. Westport, CT: Praeger.

Bourdieu, Pierre. 1977. Cultural Reproduction and Social Reproduction. In *Power and Ideology in Education*, eds. Jerome Karabel and A. H. Halsey. 487–511. New York: Oxford University Press.

————. 1986. Forms of Capital. In *Handbook of Theory and Research for Sociology of Education*, ed. John Richardson. 241–58. New York: Greenwood.

Burciaga, Rebeca and Rita Kohli. 2018. Disrupting Whitestream Measures of Quality Teaching: The Community Cultural Wealth of Teachers of Color. *Multicultural Perspectives* 20(1), 5–12.

Cabán, Pedro A. 1989. Industrial Transformation and Labour Relations in Puerto Rico: From 'Operation Bootstrap' to the 1970s. *Journal of Latin American Studies* 21(3), 559–91.

Campbell, John L., Charles Quincy, Jordan Osserman and Ove K. Pedersen. 2013. Coding In-Depth Semistructured Interviews: Problems of Unitization and Intercoder Reliability and Agreement. *Sociological Methods & Research* 42(3), 294–320.

De Graaf, Nan Dirk, Paul M. De Graaf and Gerbert Kraaykamp. 2000. Parental Cultural Capital and Educational Attainment in the Netherlands: A Refinement of the Cultural Capital Perspective. *Sociology of Education* 73(2), 92–111.

del Moral, Solsiree. 2013. *Negotiating Empire: The Cultural Politics of Schools in Puerto Rico, 1898-1952*. Madison: The University of Wisconsin Press.

DiMaggio, Paul and John Mohr. 1985. Cultural Capital, Educational Attainment, and Marital Selection. *American Journal of Sociology* 90(6), 1231–61.

Duany, Jorge. 2002. *The Puerto Rican Nation on the Move: Identities on the Island and in the United States*. Chapel Hill: University of North Carolina Press.

Eliza Colón, Sylvia. M. 1989. Colonialism and Education in Puerto Rico: Appraisal of the Public Schools during the Commonwealth Period—1952 to 1986. Ph.D. dissertation, Washington University, Saint Louis, MO.

Espino, Michelle. M. 2014. Exploring the Role of Community Cultural Wealth in Graduate School Access and Persistence for Mexican American PhDs. *American Journal of Education* 120(4), 545–74.

Holzman, Michael. 2019. Educational Achievement in Puerto Rico. *Daily Kos* 22 July. <https://www.dailykos.com/stories/2019/7/22/1873614/-Educational-Achievement-in-Puerto-Rico/>.

Kim, Sally. 2006. Meeting the Needs of Gifted Mathematics Students. *Australian Primary Mathematics Classroom* 11(3), 27–32.

Kouyoumdjian, Claudia, Blanca L. Guzmán, Nichole M. Garcia and Valerie Talavera-Bustillos. 2017. A Community Cultural Wealth Examination of Sources of Support and Challenges among Latino First-and Second-generation College Students at a Hispanic Serving Institution. *Journal of Hispanic Higher Education* 16(1), 61–76.

Leonard, Thomas. M. 1998. Teodoro Moscoso and Puerto Rico's Operation Bootstrap. *The Journal of American History* 85(1), 301.

López Alicea, Keila. 2019. Junta de Supervisión no daría paso a asignación de $123 millones para Educación Especial. *El Nuevo Dia* 3 September. <https://www.elnuevodia.com/noticias/locales/nota/juntadesupervisionnodariapasoaasignaciond e123millonesparaeducacionespecial-2515643/>.

López Cabán, Cynthia. 2013. Gobierno se compromete a cumplir con la sentencia de Educacion Especial. *El Nuevo Dia* 5 April. <https://www.elnuevodia.com/noticias/locales/nota/gobiernosecomprometeacumplirconlasentenciadeeducacionespecial-1484728/>.

Martinez, Melissa. A., Aurora Chang and Anjalé D. Welton. 2017. Assistant Professors of Color Confront the Inequitable Terrain of Academia: A Community Cultural Wealth Perspective. *Race Ethnicity and Education* 20(5), 696–710.

Matthys, Mick. 2012. *Cultural Capital, Identity, and Social Mobility: The Life Course of Working-class University Graduates*. New York: Routledge.

Meier, Elisabeth, Katharina Vogel and Franzis Preckel. 2014. Motivational Characteristics of Students in Gifted Classes: The Pivotal Role of Need for Cognition. *Learning and Individual Differences* 33, 39–46.

Miller. Paul. G. 1922. *Historia de Puerto Rico*. New York: Rand McNally.

Negrón de Montilla, Aida. 1971. *Americanization in Puerto Rico and the Public School System*. Río Piedras, PR: Editorial Universitaria.

Noble, John and Peter Davies. 2009. Cultural Capital as an Explanation of Variation in Participation in Higher Education. *British Journal of Sociology of Education* 30(5), 591–605.

Oliver, Melvin. L. and Thomas M. Shapiro. 2006. *Black Wealth, White Wealth: A New Perspective on Racial Inequality*. New York: Taylor & Francis.

Ortiz Cartagena, Miguel. A. 2013. Los derechos de los niños dotados en Puerto Rico. *Revista Juridica de la Universidad Interamericana de Puerto Rico* 47(3), 769–92.

Osuna, José. J. 1975. *A History of Education in Puerto Rico*. Río Piedras, PR: Editorial Universitaria.

Pérez II, David. 2017. In Pursuit of Success: Latino Male College Students Exercising Academic Determination and Community Cultural Wealth. *Journal of College Student Development* 58(2), 123–40.

Plewis, Ian and Mel Bartley. 2014. Intra-generational Social Mobility and Educational Qualifications. *Research in Social Stratification and Mobility* 36, 1–11.

Portes, Alejandro, Patricia Fernandez-Kelly and William Haller. 2008. The Adaptation of the Immigrant Second Generation in America. Working Paper #09-

02. Princeton, N.J: Center for Migration and Development.

Puerto Rico: Data USA. 2019. <https://datausa.io/profile/geo/puerto-rico/>.

Quintero Alfaro, Ángel G. 1972. *Educación y cambio social en Puerto Rico: una* época *crítica*. San Juan: La Editorial Universidad de Puerto Rico.

Reay, Diane. 2004. Education and Cultural Capital: The Implications of Changing Trends in Education Policies. *Cultural Trends* 13(2), 73–86.

Reis, Sally. M. and Jeanne H. Purcell Jeanne. 1993. An Analysis of Content Elimination and Strategies Used by Elementary Classroom Teachers in the Curriculum Compacting Process. *Journal for the Education of the Gifted* 16(2), 147–70.

Scarano, Francisco. A. 2016. *Puerto Rico: Cinco Siglos de Historia*. Fourth Edition. San Juan: McGraw-Hill Interamericana.

Solís, José. 1994. Public *School Reform in Puerto Rico: Sustaining Colonial Models of Development*. Westport, CT: Greenwood Press.

Sullivan, Alice. 2001. Cultural Capital and Educational Attainment. *Sociology* 35(4), 893–912.

Trigos-Carrillo, L. 2019. Community Cultural Wealth and Literacy Capital in Latin American Communities. *English Teaching: Practice & Critique* 19(1), 3–19.

Tzanakis, Michael. 2011. Bourdieu's Social Reproduction Thesis and the Role of Cultural Capital in Educational Attainment: A Critical Review Of Key Empirical Studies. *Educate~* 11(1), 76–90.

U.S. Census Bureau. 2018. Educational Attainment – Table S1501. <https://data.census.gov/cedsci/table?q=education&d=ACS%201-Year%20Estimates%20Subject%20Tables&g=0400000US72&tid=ACSST1Y2018.S1501&t=Education&hidePreview=true/>.

Valenzuela, Angela. 1999. *Subtractive Schooling: U.S.-Mexican Youth and the Politics of Caring*. Albany: State University of New York Press.

Van de Werfhorst, Herman. G. 2010. Cultural Capital: Strengths, Weaknesses and Two Advancements. *British Journal of Sociology of Education* 31(2), 157–69.

VanTassel-Baska, Joyce. 2005. Gifted Programs and Services: What are the Nonnegotiables? *Theory into Practice* 44(2), 90–7.

Webb, Andrew and Denisse Sepúlveda. 2020. Re-signifying and Negotiating Indigenous Identity in University Spaces: A Qualitative Study from Chile. *Studies in Higher Education* 45(2), 286–98.

Yosso, Tara. J. 2005. Whose Culture Has Capital? A Critical Race Theory Discussion of Community Cultural Wealth. *Race Ethnicity and Education* 8(1), 69–91.

Colonial Migrants at the Heart of Empire: Puerto Rican Workers on U.S. Farms

By Ismael García-Colón
Berkeley: University of California Press, 2020
ISBN: 978-0-5203-2579-1
352 pages; $29.95 [paper]

Reviewer: Aldo Lauria Santiago (alauria@lcs.rutgers.edu) Rutgers University, New Brunswick.

Colonial Migrants uncovers the history of Puerto Rican seasonal (and permanent) agricultural workers in the U.S. and farm worker policies since the 1940s. This 350-page book is based on extensive research in multiple collections, including important archival materials, most of them previously unused. It is one of the few publications to use the collection of the Labor Department's Migration Division held at the Center for Puerto Rican Studies and at the Puerto Rico General Archive. As such, the book represents an outstanding contribution to multiple fields, including farm worker, Puerto Rican and migration studies, and a breakthrough in the study of the experience of Puerto Ricans farm workers in the U.S.

The book is ambitious in scope. It integrates and balances shifting actors, goals, and policies over various decades and states. The overarching focus is on the five to twenty thousand seasonal migrant workers that came to Northeastern and other farms yearly under the terms of Puerto Rico's Department of Labor contract with U.S. farmers, as well as those that came on their own. He follows the ones who stayed, the ones who were satisfied, and the many problems and issues with both the labor sites and conditions and the shifting role of government agencies (especially the Migration Division). Along the way, he sketches variations across various states in farm structure and employment trends, as well as a comparative perspective with Mexican and Jamaican labor migration.

The text is organized into an introduction, seven substantive chapters, and an epilogue. The introduction explains the basics of the Puerto Rico's colonial trajectory as a U.S. territory and considers past works and approaches to Puerto Rican migrant farm workers. The first chapter discusses the legal basis and trajectory of Puerto Rican migration to the U.S. from 1897 to WWII. Chapter two introduces the origins of Puerto Rico's Labor Department farm labor program in the context of the Island's economic trajectory and the U.S.'s larger policies toward contracted migrant workers from inside and outside the territorial U.S. The chapter established how Puerto Rico's colonial government sought to place farm workers during the war years and then sought to regulate the growing and exploitative private labor contracting that emerged once the war ended. It explains how the innovative program differed from Mexican and Jamaican labor programs, and the complex motivations that combined protection with exposure to exploitation and harsh conditions. The text traces carefully the policy decision that shaped the start of the program between 1945 and 1948, and the astute negotiation that Puerto Rican colonial officials pushed and lobbied for.

The third chapter examines the first few years of the programs operation and how colonial officials continued to lobby and pressure for access to formal recognition and support from federal employment and farm labor regulation programs and legislation. It notes the persistence of Puerto Rico's officials in gaining access, and breaking prejudices and resistance, to place farm workers in context, where deportability and alienness were seen as intrinsic and necessary characteristics of the economics and culture of hiring migrant farm workers. The chapter also traces how the contract developed and the administration of enforcement through the migration division's regional offices. It concludes with the fullest treatment yet of the fiasco experienced by workers sent to Michigan to harvest beets in 195X, the only part of the farm labor program to have received significant previous attention.

Chapter four emphasizes the experiences of migrants themselves as they travelled and worked in northeastern farms from Delaware to Massachusetts, harvesting vegetables, fruits, and tobacco. The chapter discusses wages, housing conditions, and the myriad of disputes and complications that emerged from sending five to fifteen thousand laborers to work seasonally   n remote and dispersed workplaces, under a myriad of employers and working conditions. As in other chapters, the book connects the experience of Puerto Ricans specifically to larger trends in agriculture and policy and to specifically local issues. The next chapter extends this discussion to emphasize the larger residential camps in which large groups of workers concentrated. Worker life in camps included cooking, cleaning, worshipping, and celebrating, and the chapter covers these in detail and with illustrations. Camps also offered workers an opportunity to discuss and organize responses to conditions. The demand for adequate and familiar food emerged as a critical issue for homesick workers, as well as relations with local and other migrant workers. The text emphasizes the diversity of conditions and responses, as well as the management strategies of both workers and Migration Division staff.

In the sixth chapter the text zooms away from work and the camps to the larger question of permanent Puerto Rican settlement in a myriad of small towns that began in the 1950s. The chapter considers resistance and integration of Puerto Ricans to small town life, the rise of farm workers as a labor and civil rights issue in U,S. national attention, and the welfare service intervention of local government and allies in support of farm workers or their families. It also discusses the 1966 North Collins protest in which farm workers confronted local police after various abuses (published earlier as a longer article). The final chapter reviews attempts in the 1970s and 1980s to organize and politicize the permanent and migrant farm workers, especially in New York, Connecticut, and New Jersey, including attempts by Puerto Rian leftist and nationalist organizations to extend their organizing to this sector.

These efforts sought to gain better conditions, including medical services and higher wages for the workers. In its final years the Migration Division's contract program faced legal and political obstacles and challenges, as well as a declining pool of migrating workers. The demise of the program in 1993 marked the end of Puerto Rico's government efforts to manage and protect farm workers through its labor contract program. The epilogue considers more recent trends in Puerto Rican migration, farm workers trajectories, and the deportation crisis in the U.S., and presents more recent work on recurrent farm labor migrants as a result of Puerto Rico's multiple and ongoing crises. The author also restates the criticism, expressed in other publications as well, that Puerto Rican migrants are unreportable citizens but also *colonial* in origin and status and therefore not easily understood as *transnational*—a concept more applicable to migrants who originate in sovereign states.

Especially valuable is how the author provides carefully researched empirical material and how the text takes seriously the need to provide larger contextual and historical frames and historical precision, something that seems lost to many anthropologists recently. Garcia Colon favors thick description and a complex narration of the forces that produced patterns in workers' experiences instead of grand theoretical or abstract formulations. Yet the book has important implications, perhaps not sufficiently drawn out in the conclusion, for debates about U.S. colonialism, racialized labor, and work conditions in U.S. agriculture.

Sometimes the text leaves the reader wondering what the author thinks beyond the material and narratives presented, as they could potentially be interpreted or inserted in various debates in different ways. Also, the density of the material is such that the reader gets the sense that many themes could have been studied more extensively and the many thematic (and archival materials) could be followed in further detail with similarly productive results. But the book is extraordinary in that it develops in a well-structured and flowing narrative a rich map across decades, institutions, and states, and suggests a framework for further study. With a book this ambitious, one can always find shortcomings and criticisms, but the balance that the book strikes in its coverage of complex and dense materials is impressive. It should be at the top of the reading list of any scholar working on Puerto Rican studies; with other recent contributions, it is the latest contribution of a wave of historically framed *and researched* studies that will reimagine our understanding of the Puerto Rican experience.

Race and nation in Puerto Rican folklore: Franz Boas and John Alden Mason in Porto Rico

By Rafael Ocasio,
Rutgers University Press, 2020
ISBN: 978-1-9788-1020-4
252 pages; $34.95 (paper & ebook)

Reviewer: Efraín Barradas (barradas@latam.ufl.edu), University of Florida

El impacto intelectual del gran antropólogo alemán/estadounidense Franz Boas (1858-1942) se hizo sentir más allá de las fronteras de los Estados Unidos, donde estableció una escuela de antropología con cede en la Universidad de Columbia pero que impactó a toda la nación y su huella se evidencia aún más allá de las fronteras nacionales. Quizás México fue el país que más directamente sintió ese impacto ya que allí Boas no sólo hizo y dirigió excavaciones arqueológicas y estudios etnográficos sino que llegó a fundar un instituto internacional de antropología que no duró mucho pero que sirvió de estímulo para que los propios mexicanos, sobre todo por el esfuerzo de Manuel Gamio (1883-1960), discípulo suyo, crearan una escuela de antropología independiente de la estadounidense que, a su vez, influyó en toda América Latina.

Sin recibir el mismo gran impacto que México, la escuela de Boas también impactó la arqueología, el estudio del folklore, la etnografía y la antropología en general en Puerto Rico. El estudio de ese impacto es en verdad el tema central del nuevo libro de Rafael Ocasio, *Race and nation in Puerto Rican folklore: Franz Boas and John Alden Mason in Porto Rico* [sic], libro al que hay que darle la bienvenida por la contribución que hace a los estudios puertorriqueños en general y, en particular, al estudio de la literatura, a través del examen del folklore. Ya Jorge Duany en ensayos que recoge en *The Puerto Rican Nation on the Move: Identities on the Island and the United States* (2002) había estudiado la contribución de Boas y de Mason, entre otros antropólogos que trabajaron en Puerto Rico. Pero Ocasio vienen a ampliar lo ya apuntado por Duany al enfocar el tema desde otra perspectiva. Y como es de suponer en el caso de un estudioso responsable, cita con frecuencia los trabajos del otro intelectual que ya había estudiado el tema. Pero Ocasio se interesa por un aspecto específico de los estudios sobre Puerto Rico hechos por estos antropólogos, particularmente por Mason quien es en verdad el foco del libro. Aunque trata ligeramente los estudios etnográfico de Boas y los arqueólogos del propio Mason en la Isla, su interés principal reside en las colecciones del folklore puertorriqueño hechas por este último quien, como discípulo de Boas, hizo su trabajo de campo en la Isla bajo la guía, directa e indirecta, de su maestro. Pero, aunque el centro de la atención de Ocasio está en los cuentos recogidos por Mason en Utuado y Loíza, su libro se puede leer como un estudio de la amplia labor de estos dos antropólogos en Puerto Rico.

La recopilación de cuentos folklóricos hecha por Mason se publicó en la década de 1920 en el *Journal of American Folklore*, revista dirigida por Boas. Por ello esa colección es hoy de difícil acceso. Ricardo Alegría, quien en muchos sentidos siguió los pasos de Boas y Mason y quien fue marcado por Boas a través de sus estudios en la Universidad de Chicago, otro centro que sintió directamente el impacto de este gran antropólogo a través de otros discípulos suyos, particularmente Edward Sapir (1884-1939), trató de hacer accesible a los lectores boricuas esos textos, pero sólo logró reeditar las adivinanzas que Mason recogió en la Isla: *Folklore puertorriqueño. I: Adivinanzas* (1960). Nótese que en el título aparece un número romano que indirectamente promete otros volúmenes. Pero este fue el único tomo que se volvió a publicar. Mason, quien regresó en 1956 a Puerto Rico invitado por Alegría, estaba muy dispuesto a darle a este para publicación y conservación los materiales que había recogido en Puerto Rico, incluyendo sus notas de investigación. Pero mucho de estos se habían perdido o estaban en manos de otros investigadores. Por ello, nos hemos quedado sólo con este tomo de adivinanzas. Para leer hoy los cuentos hay que volver a los viejos números de la revista de Boas. Valdría la pena tener esos cuentos recogidos por Mason. Quizás el mismo Ocasio se anime a volver a publicarlos o, al menos, a dar de nuevo a la luz pública una selección, que ya a su vez, estos fueron una muy limitada selección de los que Mason recogió.

Y en este proceso entra una tercera figura que, creo, que por su importancia en todo este proceso habría que añadir al título junto con los nombre de Mason y Boas. Este fue Aurelio Espinosa (1880-1959). Es que la mano, muchas veces deformadora, de Espinosa moldeó la muestra de nuestro folklore que Mason recogió. Por ello hay que prestarle atención a quien fue el editor de los materiales reunidos por Mason y quien determinó qué se publicaba y cómo aparecía impreso.

Espinosa nació en Nuevo México y este dato es muy revelador. Esta área de los Estados Unidos se considera la más directamente colonizada por españoles. Por ello, en una carta a Boas Espinosa establece: "I am pure Spanish and can trace my ancestry to the nobility of Spain." (citado por Ocasio, p. 65) En esta declaración no sólo se nota el reclamo de una rancia y noble herencia hispánica que marca profundamente toda la obra de Espinosa sino un temor a que se le identifique como mexicano, como mestizo. La hispanofilia claramente expuesta en esta declaración, que no deja de tener tonos racistas, es un elemento central en la obra de Espinosa quien aboga por el estudio de un folklore que pruebe la retención de elementos españoles en el hispanoamericano y en el de las comunidades de Nuevo México y California que estudió. Esa visión marca su interpretación del material recogido por Mason. Espinosa, como otros estudiosos del momento, estaba interesado en hallar lo que permanecía de la cultura europea, en su caso española, y no en la transformación de esa herencia en algo nuevo. Dicho llanamente, Espinosa se interesaba por la retención y no por el cambio, no por el mestizaje cultural. Y esta visión de la cultura y el folklore reflejan su propia autodefinición como descendiente directo de nobles españoles, no como mestizo.

A esto hay que añadir un sentido de superioridad frente a Mason, no a Boas a quien Espinosa le dedica una colección de cuentos que recogió en España. Ocasio lo establece claramente: "...Espinosa was difficult to deal with and often did not accept suggestions without conflict" (p. 59). Y más directamente establece que para entender el proceso editorial de los materiales recogidos en Puerto Rico hay que contar con "...Espinosa's profound dislike of Mason compilation techniques" (p. 59). Sumémosle a esto el hecho que Espinosa insiste en que lo que se publique tiene que estar en lo que él llama "correct Castilian" (p. 60) y que eliminó muchos cuentos, poemas, canciones y adivinanzas recogidos por Mason porque creía que contenían temas escabrosos y lenguaje soez, lo que para él era ofensivo. Lo que se publicó de lo recogido por Mason fue transformado, tergiversado, deformado por Espinosa. Lejos estamos de una verdadera actitud de objetividad antropológica. Por ello y a pesar de estas innegables posturas conflictivas, creo que el nombre de Espinosa —a quien trato aquí mucho más duramente que Ocasio, quien es más comedido y diplomático que yo — debería aparecer en el subtítulo del libro. Lo digo a pesar, muy a pesar de reconocer la influencia negativa que tuvo en todo el proceso de edición y publicación de estas muestras de folklore boricua. Su impacto en el material de Mason se dio en el momento de publicación del mismo y hasta aún más tarde porque pudo ser que Espinosa, quien no contestaba a las cartas de Mason, se negó a devolverle los materiales que este le había entregado para la edición y publicación o se había deshecho de los mismos. Mason quería entregarle a Alegría estos materiales para su publicación y conservación.

Pero, a pesar de que no tenemos las notas de campo de Mason, a pesar de que este no manejaba bien el español, a pesar del tono de superioridad que se detecta en todos estos estudiosos que a principio del siglo XX llegan a Puerto Rico para "observarnos" —el subtítulo de uno de los capítulos del libro de Duany es revelador: "Puerto Rico in the gaze of American anthropologists, 1898-1915"—, tenemos que estar agradecidos a Mason por su trabajo de recopilación. ¡Algo al menos tenemos!

¿Qué tenemos? Tenemos, entre otras muestras de nuestro folklore, los cuentos que Ocasio estudia en el cuarto capítulo de su libro: "Telling a story about class and ethnicity through fairy tales, cuentos puertorriqueños, and leyendas". Creo que este es uno de los capítulos más importantes del libro. Ocasio, como señala el título de este, trata de ver cómo se refleja la identificación de clase del campesino y su autodefinición étnica en esos cuentos. Olvidemos por un momento la mano deformadora de Espinosa y aceptemos que este material puede servir de base para tal exploración. Ocasio ve en estas narraciones reflejos de los conflictos sociales que afectaban en ese momento a los campesinos boricuas, especialmente a los jíbaros de Utuado. Dado su interés por este pueblo en particular, pueblo que Mason consideró idóneo para su trabajo, la investigación histórica de Fernando Picó le es de gran ayuda para explorar este tema. Pero el autor se vale también de los aportes de muchos otros estudiosos y escritores de principio de siglo XX para matizar el cuadro que nos presenta. Para mí una de las sorpresas de este libro fue descubrir la obra de muchos intelectuales de ese momento que usualmente no se citan en los trabajos históricos y literarios que se enfocan en estos años. No me cabe duda de que este capítulo es una de las contribuciones mayores de Ocasio.

A la vez aquí hallo una de sus fallas: la ausencia de una mayor diversidad de enfoques críticos que le hubieran servido para entender aún mejor estas narraciones, especialmente los cuentos de hadas y de aparecidos. Por ejemplo, Ocasio pudo emplear muy fructíferamente el análisis sicoanalítico de Bruno Bettelheim sobre ese tipo de narración folklórica o el acercamiento formalista de Vladimir Propp o la lectura reveladora de la crueldad en los cuentos de los hermanos Grimm hecha por María Tatar para sacarle más provecho a su ya provechoso análisis de estos cuentos. No se trata de seguir al pie de la letra esos acercamientos sino aprovecharse de los mismos para ver mejor el tema que se quiere explorar. Este, pues, es una tarea por hacerse que habrá que explorar aún más detalladamente.

Pero ya lo que Ocasio nos ofrece sobre estos cuentos es mucho y valioso. Aunque nos hace ver lo que se perdió cuando este material pasó por las manos de Espinosa, Ocasio ve el valor de estas narraciones. Por ejemplo, parte del material perdido es toda la información lingüística, medicinal y religiosa que Mason obtuvo de un informante de Loíza. Melitón Congo dice Mason que se llamaba esta enciclopedia viva que había nacido en África y había sido esclavo en Puerto Rico. Mason lo encuentra en Loíza y lo entrevista. De todo el material recogido de Melitón Congo pueden haber quedado algún cuento que Espinosa juntó con los recogidos de los jíbaros de Utuado y que "limpió" para hacerlos aceptable según sus criterios lingüísticos y estéticos. Al leer lo que Ocasio nos dice sobre Mason y Melitón Congo sólo puedo pensar en Esteban Montejo, el cimarrón cubano que Miguel Barnet entrevistó detenidamente y sobre el cual escribió una "autobiografía" que es hoy trabajo esencial para conocer la cultura afrocubana. Las notas de las entrevistas de Melitón Congo se perdieron y con ellas se perdió un poco de lo mucho que este ex esclavo pudo habernos revelado sobre nuestra herencia africana.

Por todos estos deslumbrantes descubrimientos hechos con un ejemplar rigor académico e intelectual es que hay que leer este nuevo libro de Rafael Ocasio. Lo leí con interés, con asombro y, sobre todo, con agradecimiento.

OBRAS CITADAS

Duany, Jorge. 2002. *The Puerto Rican Nation on the Move: Identities on the Island and in the United States.* Chappel Hill: Univresity of North Carolina Press.

Mason, John Alden. 1960. *Folklore puertorriqueño. I: Adivinanzas.* San Juan: Instituto de Cultura Puertorriqueña.

Parenting Empires: Class, Whiteness, and the Moral Economy of Privilege in Latin America

By Ana Y. Ramos-Zayas
Duke University Press, 2020
ISBN: 978-1478008217
296 pages; $27.95

Reviewer: Guillermo Rebollo Gil (grebollogil@gmail.com) Universidad Ana G. Méndez, Recinto de Carolina

There's a Black Lives Matter mural on the roof of the Hiram Bithorn Municipal Stadium in San Juan. There's another painted across the pavement in Condado's Ashford Avenue, right in front of the Ventana al mar plaza. The murals were painted at the behest of the city's mayor, Carmen Yulín Cruz, in a special collaboration with local rapper and international superstar Bad Bunny. If you want to have a look at the one atop the stadium, you have to catch a plane out and then come back. The one on the avenue is considerably more accessible. It just happens to have been painted in one of the most inaccessible parts of the city. In terms of who can afford to live there, I mean. Or who can afford to go for a stroll in the area without being harassed by state police or private security guards. In either case, both are infinitely more accessible to tourists flying in and booking a room at one of Condado's many signature hotels. Which begs the question: How exactly do Black Lives matter here?

II

There is no more ideal place to read Ana Y. Ramos-Zayas' new book *Parenting Empires: Class, Whiteness, and the Moral Economy of Privilege in Latin America* than parked on a side street in Condado, waiting for the traffic on Ashford Avenue to ease up. Except maybe in Ipanema. But, as a reader, you often stick with what you know.

In this illuminating ethnographic study, Ramos-Zayas explores the making and meaning of racial and class privilege as put to work—and put in place—by the choices that make up, and the beliefs and values that underpin, parenting amongst white elites in Puerto Rico and Brazil. Over a five-year period, the author interviewed, shared space, and established relationships with thirty participants (mothers, fathers, grandparents, teachers, and community organizers) in Condado and 39 interlocutors (mothers, fathers, and grandparents) in Ipanema. These two sites are bonded by the imperial markings of the U.S. across their respective socio-political terrains, and also by the signature elements of the present political moment: economic crisis, austerity politics, precarity, governmental corruption, the rise of the right and repression of dissent. Specifically, the book highlights how:

As agents of empire, the upper-class parents in this ethnography engaged in spaces and circuits of affinity and sociability that produced forms of personhood rooted in aesthetics of affect and morality, which effectively dovetailed with projects of austerity and perspectives of "crisis" and "corruption" in Brazil, Puerto Rico, and the Americas more broadly. (p. 4)

Moreover, the author, in agile, informed, and engaging prose, argues that "Parenting—with all its neoliberal intensities, aspirations, languages, claims to expertise and science, and emphasis on inner-world cultivation—has become an effective, morally legitimate imperial formation" (p. 5).

III

Another question: If you're going to commission a Black Lives Matter mural anywhere in Puerto Rico, why not do it in Spanish? That Yulín Cruz, who during her two terms in office made it a point to erase the traces of the previous pro-statehood, English-privileging administration, would opt—in collaboration with a Spanish-exclusive rapper—to stick to the English original is telling. It is as if anti-racist struggle has no possible Spanish translation. Or, worse, that the struggle against racism better not find an adequate Spanish translation in the Puerto Rican archipelago. At least not here, on Ashford Avenue, in front of Ventana al mar, a water front plaza, between the exclusive Condado Vanderbilt hotel and a small strip of eateries, featuring a Ben & Jerry's. The plaza, with a generous patch of grass where one could ostensibly play with one's dogs, and where children could ride their bikes, used to be the idyllic setting for a monthly series of free jazz concerts, sponsored by Heineken. The series was cancelled some time ago. And it just so happens that neither dogs nor bicycles are allowed on the premises. That's what the private security guard standing right next to the waffle shop will surely tell you, as he dutifully warned the author when she showed up with her son and his bicycle:

As Sebastián and I approached the park, a young dark-skin security guard approached us, almost timidly, to let us know that "bikes were not allowed in the park." My face must have shown disbelief, because the guard tilted his head and made a facial gesture almost shrugging and agreeing with what I was thinking: How could it be that one of the few green areas with cemented lanes in the neighborhood could forbid kiddie bikes? I felt bad for the security guard, who looked obviously uncomfortable at trying to justify something he viewed as ridiculous. Hesitantly he told me, "They don't want to have an accident of people bumping into bikes...You know, the tourists and all the new people moving in."

The author then told one of her participants, a white Condado parent, of the encounter:

When I expressed my surprise to Manolo, he was sympathetic but adamant that the no-bike policy was "unfortunately, a necessity." He explained, "This rule was really not directed to forbid young kids from riding their bikes, but unfortunately, that's the byproduct of it. Here in El Condado, we're having an issue with young men from Lloréns [public housing complex, los muchachitos de Lloréns] riding bikes, very aggressively and recklessly. They rob, grab cell phones, and when you're with your kids that makes you very vulnerable. As parents, we had to get involved in that." (pp. 85–6)

That, as Ramos-Zayas astutely chronicles, explores and interprets, refers to the requisite formal and informal policing of spaces and bodies upon which individual and collective notions of whiteness depend on. Whiteness is a tricky privilege to enforce and enjoy in purported racial democracies where racial distinctions are understood to be messier or more ambiguous or not-so-determining of people's life chances. Parenting, on the other hand, is almost universally regarded to be a life-determining enterprise, especially in social contexts—like the Puerto Rican and Brazilian— marked by extreme inequality. As Ramos-Zayas demonstrates throughout her study, the individual and collective anxiety of being part of a culture that imagines itself free of the formal, brutal structures of racism is channeled by the white and wealthy into their child-rearing practices and routines, which, taken together, shape both the private and public sphere in their image. In other words, the choices elite parents make for their children (where to study, where to play and who to do it with) amount to a nation-building project through which they seek to ensure a prosperous future for their children. And their children's children.

In this context, the question of who can ride their bike across the lawn is a question of who gets to take part in this future-in-the-making and in what capacity.

IV.

White people in Condado, though as white as me, do not move the same, walking down the avenue pushing baby strollers with one hand, holding a Starbucks cup with the other. They even seem to "lose" themselves in vigorous runs, dressed impeccably like storefront mannequins.

As a child of gated communities, I've run like this before, certainly, but from the front of my house to the guard station and back. In looking at them I also notice that this sense of white freedom is not a product of the surrounding space. While, yes, Condado can overwhelm the visitor with its architecture of leisure, wealth, and privilege, it is impossible—today—to not also take into account the many run down, abandoned structures that housed restaurants, residences, and assorted businesses. It is impossible to not notice the considerable number of people without a home. Condado, in this regard, looks no different from most urban sectors in Puerto Rico. In considering this, it occurs to me that what maintains the area's aura of prosperity and prestige are precisely white locals' bodies. Ramos-Zayas refers to this quality as "a palpable sense of ease, entitlement and comfort" (p. 63), which must be protected, without putting—or at least, not showing—pressure on the white body.

Participants in Ramos-Zayas' study are very much engaged in self-care. While respondents acknowledge investing considerable time and energy into working on their inner selves, becoming (and surrounding themselves with) *personas sencillas*, and slouching toward a "moral way of being wealthy," what Ramos-Zayas highlights is a self-care work of a different sort: "Being an Ipanema resident came to be described as a set of cultivated cultural, social, and affective practices that required trekking a fine line between hierarchy and informality, democracy and elitism, heterogeneity and exclusivity, self-discipline and *despojamento* ([being] laid back)" (p. 58). And so, the book details how aware white elites are of their presence in neighborhood cafés and stores, making sure to be extra nice to employees; how they agonize over the painstaking process of first selecting somebody worthy enough to care for their children and then having to stress over how to keep their children from attaching themselves to their [mostly black and/or immigrant] nannies. They are also extremely careful not to waste possible "teaching moments" for their young ones so they learn how to relate with "difference" in the world; how, especially in Puerto Rico, participants ended up with wives or husbands who could very well pass for their brothers and sisters; how, especially in Brazil, respondents make sure to have caring and working black bodies close by, but always right behind them, pushing the stroller, wherever they may go.

While these details might astound some and surely enlighten us all, where *Parenting Empires* reveals itself as a trail-blazing text within critical race studies in Latin America is in the author's knack for picking up, and keenly reflecting, on the anxiety and uncertainty that sit at the root of white identities. Whiteness, at least in these parts, requires—feeds on—validation. You are only as white as the social circles you belong to, and even then, questions may linger as to any and all members' claim to authenticity. It's a question of color, yes. But also of family history, and wealth and "by the way, where did you go to school?," and hair color and texture, and assorted physical features and styling choices, and a wide array of manners and gestures, and how you go about moving your body, and what kind of Spanish you speak, and how good your English is, and where you live and how, and when all these other boxes are checked, it still depends on the individual's will to whiteness; on how much a person is invested—and how anxious and eager they continue to be about increasing their investment—in continually playing the part as the social, cultural, and political parameters of whiteness shift and change over time, however slightly. Participants' stories, as collected and organized in Ramos-Zayas' book, would seem to suggest that whiteness in Latin America entails a multifarious array of policing ticks, tricks, and techniques of both the outer and inner world because it's never enough to keep the "wrong" people out, one always has somebody whiter to look up to and strive toward:

> "Being white" was not enough; they had to create a range of choices about how to "be white" and what that meant for their racial privilege across various scales, including the neighborhood, the region of the country, the nation, and transnational or global referents. (p. 144)

V

A third and final question: What are the politics of such a mural in such a place? On the one hand I would like to say that the mural is a righteous affront to the policy of the plaza. One could argue that it makes visible the racial segregation and surveillance that Afro-Puerto Ricans are subjected to on a regular basis. The mural, then, brings some attention to this historically ignored social fact—so long as you can read English, of course. And attention, as they say, leads to awareness, which might bring about eventual social and political change. Perhaps this is what the mayor and the rapper had in mind. Hopefully so.

Still, one would have to wonder about the efficacy of the gesture. What good is the mayor signing off on Black Lives Matter as street art, if a black Puerto Rican boy in a bicycle can ride by the yellow letters, and still not be able to cross through the plaza on the way to the public beach, as the security guard would surely intercept him to inform him about the no-black-boy policy. Only the guard will not say it like that. But it will, chances are, be understood that way by both parties. Because, as Ramos-Zayas notes:

> While race is traditionally thought about in terms of people, ultimately and historically, the politics of race become comprehensible only when considered in territorial terms. Thus, race is always, more or less explicitly, the racialization of space and the naturalization of segregation. (p. 59)

In this precise sense, "no bicycles allowed," as uttered by a dark-skin private security guard, is a much more forceful, clear, widespread, socially

significant, and life-determining message about the state of black lives in
Puerto Rico than the mayor commissioning a Black Lives Matter mural on
Ashford Avenue. *Parenting Empires* tells the story about how a small group
of people's shared desires to live simply and "do good" by their children both
create   and are sustained by these exclusionary policies and practices. Safe
to say, these people's children should not matter so much.1 And yet, at least
in Puerto Rico, they are the only ones that count as *somebody's* child. The
rest are simply *muchachitos.*

VI

Perhaps a more adequate, context-specific, life-affirming, politically con-
tentious, and infinitely more hopeful rendition of the mural would be *Los
muchachitos de Lloréns importan.*

---

[1] These people are, to an extent, my people. Which is to say, I was parented in a
similar way: "Interlocutors in the El Condado sample led virtually the same lives
that their own parents and even grandparents had led; they attended the same
schools and clubs, grew up in the same neighborhoods, had the same occupations,
knew the same families, married people they knew since childhood, and had dense
social networks. I have never seen a more perfect example of what classical sociology has called "social reproduction" than what I witnessed in El Condado." (p. 30)

La Nueva Dramaturgia Puertorriqueña: trans/acciones de la identidad

By Laurietz Seda
San Juan: Nuevos Cuadernos del Ateneo Puertorriqueño, 2018
ISBN: N/A
140 páginas; N/A [papel]

Reviewer: Lawrence La Fountain-Stokes (lawrlafo@umich.edu), University of Michigan, Ann Arbor

En su nuevo libro, la investigadora, crítica teatral, gestora y catedrática Laurietz Seda se posiciona fuertemente dentro de un campo muy específico de los estudios teatrales puertorriqueños. Este campo incluye, como la autora señala en su introducción, la crítica teatral de investigadores tales como Roberto Ramos-Perea, Rosalina Perales, Grace Dávila-López, Carmen Montañez, Priscilla Meléndez y Bonnie H. Reynolds (pp. 13–5) y favorece el análisis del movimiento identificado como la "Nueva Dramaturgia Puertorriqueña" que surge a mediados de los años setenta, integrada principalmente por Roberto Ramos-Perea, Carlos Canales, Teresa Marichal y José Luis Ramos Escobar. La autora discute sus obras usando el novedoso concepto de "trans/acción", proponiendo las "trans/acciones de la identidad" como manera de repensar ciertos discursos sobre la puertorriqueñidad.

Laurietz Seda ha enseñado en el Departamento de Literatura, Cultura y Lengua de la Universidad de Connecticut, Storrs, desde 1997. Cursó estudios universitarios de pregrado en la Universidad de Puerto Rico, Recinto Universitario de Mayagüez (1983), pasando a obtener una maestría en Rutgers University (1989) y un doctorado de la Universidad de Kansas (1995). Entre sus libros anteriores se encuentra la antología *La Nueva Dramaturgia Puertorriqueña* (2003; segunda edición, 2007) y con Jacqueline Bixler, *Trans/Acting: Latin American and Latino Performing Arts* (2009). Seda es miembro del consejo editorial de varias revistas especializadas incluyendo *Latin American Theatre Review* y *Boletín del Archivo Nacional de Teatro y Cine del Ateneo Puertorriqueño*.

La Nueva Dramaturgia Puertorriqueña: trans/acciones de la identidad incluye un breve prefacio, una introducción, cuatro capítulos principales, una breve conclusión y una lista de obras citadas. También incluye como apéndice la obra teatral *El adiestramiento* de Teresa Marichal Lugo y cuatro fotos en blanco y negro. En cada capítulo, la autora ofrece información biográfica sobre los dramaturgos y se enfoca en el análisis de una obra. Como señala Seda, "Este libro explora cómo se enfrentan algunos dramaturgos de la autodenominada Nueva Dramaturgia Puertorriqueña a las transformaciones de los modos de pensar las identidades", añadiendo que "las obras analizadas proponen que los individuos de una nación son complejos, contradictorios, heterogéneos y ambiguos" (p. 11).

En la introducción ("La Nueva Dramaturgia Puertorriqueña: Cruzando Fronteras"), Seda define trans/acción "como el uso consciente de la actuación y de la negociación como estrategias para vivir en un espacio fronterizo, fragmentado, entre culturas, etnicidades, naciones, profesiones y/o géneros", añadiendo que "La practican aquella o aquél que reta los conceptos binarios tradicionales" (p. 16). Seda cita el trabajo crítico de Néstor García Canclini, Jorge Duany, Carlos Pabón y Arlene Dávila para contextualizar el fenómeno de la globalización y la manera en la que Puerto Rico se encaja en estos procesos desestabilizadores.

En el primer capítulo ("¿Aquí o allá? Esa es la pregunta: *Malasangre* de Roberto Ramos-Perea"), Seda discute una obra de 1987 en relación a "un grupo de textos teatrales que hablan sobre la emigración del puertorriqueño a Estados Unidos" (p. 28), indicando que "en *Malasangre* se presenta el nuevo tipo de emigrante que va a Estados Unidos en busca de un mejor porvenir económico, el profesional que llega con puestos en la NASA, la IBM y otras grandes corporaciones" (p. 30), es decir, la migración de clase media profesional puertorriqueña. En *Malasangre*, "los discursos sobre la emigración del puertorriqueño a Estados Unidos se enfrentan a una disyuntiva: el deseo o la necesidad de regresar a Puerto Rico para luchar por los ideales independentistas o nacionalistas... versus el deseo de progresar económicamente y de formar parte del 'sueño americano'" (p. 31). Seda argumenta que Ramos-Perea se opone a las nociones nacionalistas patriarcales que René Marqués expone en *La carreta* (1953) y contextualiza su análisis de la migración contemporánea en diálogo con Jorge Duany, Alberto Sandoval-Sánchez, Luis Felipe Díaz y Luis Rafael Sánchez ("La guagua aérea").

Malasangre presenta la historia de una pareja puertorriqueña que se muda de Mayagüez a El Paso, Texas, debido a las oportunidades laborales de la protagonista, quien es ingeniera. Como señala Seda, "Contrario a *La carreta* donde las mujeres siguen las riendas del hombre, en *Malasangre* la mujer es quien maneja su propia vida" (p. 35). Desafortunadamente, este empoderamiento también lleva a la desintegración familiar. El análisis de Seda sobre la migración de clase media puertorriqueña tiene puntos de contacto con las investigaciones de Ana Y. Ramos Zayas (*National Performances*) y Elizabeth M. Aranda (*Emotional Bridges to Puerto Rico*), quienes también exploran este fenómeno; sería valioso profundizar este paralelo.

El segundo capítulo ("¡Trans/acciones de la identidad?: *Indocumentados* de José Luis Ramos Escobar") se enfoca en una obra de 1989 que también problematiza la migración caribeña a Estados Unidos, pero en este caso desde la República Dominicana. Seda ve la obra de Ramos Escobar como una reacción a *La carreta*, en la que el protagonista también muere. Valiéndose del análisis de Yolanda Martínez-San Miguel sobre el prejuicio puertorriqueño antidominicano, Seda analiza los retos psicológicos que el protagonista de *Indocumentados* experimenta al tratar de pasar por puertorriqueño para poder trabajar en la ciudad de Nueva York de manera legal. También discute la centralidad de la selección de actores. El fracaso del protagonista refleja su inhabilidad de trans/accionar en un contexto nuevo y cambiante.

El tercer capítulo ("La identidad construida: *Bony and Kin* de Carlos Canales") analiza una obra de 2001 que explora la influencia de los medios de comunicación masiva. Seda entiende que "Canales traza un panorama en el que pone de manifiesto ciertos mecanismos de apropiación, selección, resemantización y trans/acción de imágenes relacionadas con la construcción de una identidad nacional mediante figuras y temas del cine norteamericano que han penetrado en el ambiente cultural de la isla" (p. 58). Seda discute los elementos metateatrales y brechtianos en *Bony and Kin*, una autoficción dramática sobre dos criminales que buscan la fama y sólo la adquieren después de sus muertes. Como señala la autora, "A Canales no le interesa definir qué es ser puertorriqueño, sino descubrir y socavar los mecanismos que las generaciones anteriores, los líderes sociales, el gobierno y aún los medios de comunicación masiva han utilizado para proclamar, en un intento de homogenización cultural, una identidad nacional pura" (p. 58).

El cuarto capítulo ("¿Nuevas formas de ser ciudadano?: *El adiestramiento* de Teresa Marichal") se enfoca en una obra de 1997 que fue estrenada en 1998 por el grupo de teatro Agua, Sol y Sereno bajo la dirección de Israel Lugo. Seda indica que *El adiestramiento* "plantea cuestionamientos al sistema capitalista que excluye a los desposeídos" y propone "que el puertorriqueño es un trans/ actor en el sentido de que negocia conscientemente estrategias para subvertir la invasión cultural y administrativa de Estados Unidos en la isla" (p. 73). En *El adiestramiento*, dos vagabundos viven escondidos en el sótano o almacén de una tienda por departamentos en un centro comercial y "Al finalizar el día... emergen... para comenzar un adiestramiento en el cual emulan los comportamientos de los empleados y los consumidores en una sociedad capitalista" (p. 73). La obra incorpora juegos teatrales e interacción directa con el público y cuestiona el espacio social de los centros comerciales o "malls" en la sociedad puertorriqueña. Seda dialoga con *El Mall: del mundo al paraíso* de Rubén Dávila Santiago; este tema también ha sido explorado por Arlene Dávila (*El Mall*).

El libro de Seda complementa de manera valiosa el trabajo de investigadores tales como Camilla Stevens (*Family and Identity*), Lowell Fiet (*El teatro puertorriqueño reimaginado*), Sara V. Rosell (*Dramaturgas puertorriqueñas de 1990 a 2010*) y Carlos Manuel Rivera (*Para que no se nos olvide*, ganador del Premio de Literatura del Instituto de Cultura Puertorriqueña en 2013), quien se enfoca en la obra de Myrna Casas, Lydia Milagros González, Víctor Fragoso, Antonio Pantojas, Zora Moreno, Abniel Marat y Oscar Giner. *La Nueva Dramaturgia Puertorriqueña: trans/acciones de la identidad* es una aportación útil en la medida que documenta y analiza con gran detenimiento a cuatro dramaturgos como representantes de un movimiento muy específico, ofreciendo interpretaciones informadas por una valiosa bibliografía secundaria. Una limitación del libro es que no reconoce la labor de críticos que cuestionan, critican o no celebran la Nueva Dramaturgia Puertorriqueña (Lowell Fiet), o que se aproximan a ella con un interés marcado en otros dramaturgos como Abniel Marat (Carlos Manuel Rivera). Seda tampoco posiciona a los dramaturgos de la Nueva Dramaturgia Puertorriqueña en relación al teatro de Luis Rafael Sánchez (de sus obras como *Quíntuples* o *La pasión según Antígona* Pérez) o de Myrna Casas. ¿No hay diálogo entre la Nueva Dramaturgia Puertorriqueña y estas figuras claves contemporáneas? La lectura del libro de Seda junto a otros textos, por ejemplo, a la reciente antología editada por José-Luis García Barrientos *Análisis de la dramaturgia puertorriqueña actual* (2019), nos facilita una visión más abarcadora.

OBRAS CITADAS

Bixler, Jacqueline y Laurietz Seda, eds. 2009. *Trans/Acting: Latin American and Latino Performing Arts*. Lewisburg, PA: Bucknell University Press.

Dávila, Arlene. 2016. *El Mall: The Spatial and Class Politics of Shopping Malls in Latin America*. Berleley: University of California Press.

Dávila Santiago, Rubén. 2005. *El Mall: del mundo al paraíso*. San Juan: Ediciones Callejón.

Fiet, Lowell. 2004. *El teatro puertorriqueño reimaginado: notas críticas sobre la creación dramática y el performance*. San Juan: Ediciones Callejón.

García Barrientos, José-Luis, ed. 2019. *Análisis de la dramaturgia puertorriqueña actual*. Madrid: Ediciones Antígona.

Ramos-Zayas, Ana Y. 2003. *National Performances: The Politics of Class, Race, and Space in Puerto Rican Chicago*. Chicago: University of Chicago Press.

Rivera, Carlos Manuel. 2014. *Para que no se nos olvide: ensayos de interpretación sobre un teatro puertorriqueño marginal*. San Juan: Editorial del Instituto de Cultura Puertorriqueña.

Rosell, Sara V. 2010. *Dramaturgas puertorriqueñas de 1990 a 2010*. Lewiston, NY: Edwin Mellen Press.

Seda, Laurietz. 2007 [2003]. *La Nueva Dramaturgia Puertorriqueña*. Segunda edición. San Juan: LEA.

Stevens, Camilla. 2004. *Family and Identity in Contemporary Cuban and Puerto Rican Drama*. Gainesville: University Press of Florida.

CARIBBEAN STUDIES

Revista bianual del Instituto de Estudios del Caribe
Universidad de Puerto Rico

ÍNDICE • CONTENTS • SOMAIRE
Vol. 45, Nos. 1-2 (January-December 2017)

Special Issue: Language Contact, Creoles, and Multilingualism:
Stigma, Creativity, and Resilience

Suscripción Anual

Instituciones $50.00 / Individuos $25.00

Cheque o giro postal pagadero a

Universidad de Puerto Rico

INSTITUTO DE ESTUDIOS DEL CARIBE
UNIVERSIDAD DE PUERTO RICO
9 AVE UNIVERSIDAD STE 901
SAN JUAN, PR 00925-2529

Tel. 787-764-0000, ext. 87738
caribbean.studies@upr.edu

New release from CSRC Press ...

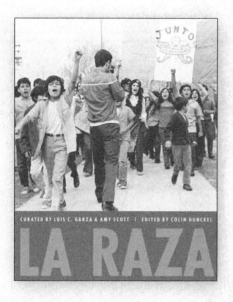

La Raza

Edited by Colin Gunckel

Exhibition curated by Luis C. Garza and Amy Scott

La Raza, launched in 1967 in the basement of an Eastside Los Angeles church, was conceived as a tool for community-based organizing during the early days of the Chicano movement. The photographers for the newspaper and subsequent magazine played a critical role as artists, journalists, and activists, creating an unparalleled record of the determination, resilience, and achievements of the Chicana/o community during a period of profound social change.

This volume presents over one hundred photographs drawn from the more than 25,000 images in the CSRC's *La Raza* Photograph Collection and from the exhibition *La Raza*, curated by Luis C. Garza and Amy Scott, at the Autry Museum of the American West. The accompanying essays offer not only scholarly assessments of the role of Chicana/o photographers in social movements and art history but also personal perspectives from *La Raza* photographers.

Design by William Morosi

Distributed by the University of Washington Press

 UCLA Chicano Studies
Research Center Press
www.chicano.ucla.edu

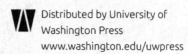 Distributed by University of
Washington Press
www.washington.edu/uwpress

Centro Publications

2021 CATALOGUE

Patria: Puerto Rican Revolutionary Exiles in Late Nineteenth Century New York
Edgardo Meléndez
$24.99

Patria examines the activities and ideals of Puerto Rican revolutionaries exiles in New York City at the end of the nineteenth century. The study is centered in the writings, news reports, and announcements by and about Puerto Ricans in the newspaper *Patria*, of the Cuban Revolutionary Party. The book looks at the political, organizational and ideological ties between Cuban and Puerto Rican revolutionaries in exile, as well as the events surrounding the war of 1898. The analysis also offers a glimpse into the daily life and community of Puerto Rican exiles in late nineteenth century New York City.

Liberalism and Identity Politics: Puerto Rican Community Organizations and Collective Action in New York City
José E. Cruz
ISBN 9781945662089 | LCCN 2017006438
$24.99; $9.99 Kindle

This book is a recollection and analysis of the role of ethnic identity in Puerto Rican community institutional development and collective action in New York City between 1960-1990. The book demonstrates that through institutional development and collective action, Puerto Ricans articulated and promoted a liberal form of identity politics in which ethnic identity and the idea of group rights provided a platform for the production of both individual and collective goods.

Not the Time to Stay: The Unpublished Plays of Víctor Fragoso
Víctor Fragoso; Edited, Translated and with an Introduction by Consuelo Martínez-Reyes
ISBN 9781945662249 | LCCN 2018034538
Pbk. 2018; 244 pages
$24.99; $9.99 Kindle

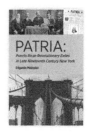

Not the Time to Stay brings to light for the first time the marvellous work of Puerto Rican playwright Víctor Fragoso. Eight plays, edited and translated by Consuelo Martínez-Reyes, portray the socio-cultural issues Fragoso sought to expose: the choice and difficulties of migration, the clash between American and Puerto Rican societies, the oppression suffered by Latinos in the USA, homelessness, and domestic violence, among others. Fragoso played a key role in the New York City theatre scene in the 1970s, and in the overall interrogation of Puerto Rican and Latino identities in the USA.

Centro Publications

2021 CATALOGUE

Race, Front and Center: Perspectives on Race Among Puerto Ricans
Edited by Carlos Vargas-Ramos
ISBN 9781945662003
LCCN 2016030601. Pbk. 2017; 403 pages **$24.99**

Race, Front and Center is a collection of essays that captures in a single volume the breadth of research on the subject of race among Puerto Ricans, both in Puerto Rico, in the United States and in the migration between the two countries. Its twenty-two chapters divided into seven sections address the intellectual, aesthetic and historical trajectories that have served to inform the creation of a national identity among Puerto Ricans and how race as a social identity fits into the process of national identity-building.

Before the Wave: Puerto Ricans in Philadelphia, 1910–1945
Víctor Vázquez-Hernández
ISBN 9781945662027
LCCN 2016047262. Pbk. 2017; 129 pages **$19.99**

This book recounts the genesis of the Puerto Rican community in Philadelphia during the interwar years (1917–1945). It connects the origins of this community to the mass migration of the post-WW II years when Puerto Ricans consolidated their presence in Philadelphia (1945–1985). This study compares the experiences of Puerto Ricans with that of the Italians, the Polish, and African Americans in Philadelphia during the early twentieth century.

Rhythm & Power: Performing Salsa in Puerto Rican and Latino Communities
Edited by Derrick León Washington, Priscilla Renta and Sydney Hutchinson
ISBN 9781945662164
LCCN 2017038687. Pbk. 2017; 88 pages **$12.00**

The story of New York salsa is one of cultural fusion, artistry, and skilled marketing. A multi-disciplinary collective of scholars illuminate how immigrant and migrant communities in New York City—most notably from Puerto Rico—nurtured and developed salsa, growing it from a local movement playing out in the city's streets and clubs into a global phenomenon.

Centro Publications

2021 CATALOGUE

State of Puerto Ricans 2017
Edited by Edwin Meléndez
and Carlos Vargas-Ramos
ISBN 9781945662126
LCCN 2017021705. Pbk. 2017; 138 pages   **$20.00**

This book provides an updated overview of some of the most salient subjects
and themes about the Puerto Rican population in the United States at present.
It highlights the continued mobility and expansion of the Puerto Rican population throughout the country, including state-to-state migration, migration from
Puerto Rico in light of the economic crisis in the island, as well as the role of
service in the armed forces in anchoring new areas of settlement.

Almanac of Puerto Ricans in the United States
Editors Jennifer Hinojosa and
Carlos Vargas-Ramos
ISBN 978-1945662072
LCCN 2017002040. Pbk. 2016; 167 pages.   **$20**

Learn more about the recent changes in the Puerto Rican community on the
mainland United States through national and state-specific demographic
data. The almanac compiles information on social, economic, and civic
conditions of the Puerto Rican population in nine key states, and includes
maps, tables, and descriptions of the population nationwide.

The Bodega: A conerstone of Puerto Rican Barrios
(The Justo Martí Collection)
Carlos Sanabria
ISBN 978-1945662065. Pbk. 2016; 43 pages.   **$15**

This photo book is a compilation of photographs of bodegas in 1960s New
York City shot by Cuban photographer Justo Martí. The photos are part of
Centro's Justo Martí collection, which documents the life and activities of
the individuals, families and organizations that made up the Puerto Rican
experience in New York.

Centro Publications

2021 CATALOGUE

Gilberto Gerena Valentín: My Life as a Community Activist, Labor Organizer, and Progressive Politician in NYC

Edited by Carlos Rodríguez Fraticelli; Translated by Andrew Hurley; With an Introduction by José E. Cruz
ISBN 9781878483744; 2013; 315 pages.   **$20**

Gilberto Gerena Valentín is a key figure in the development of the Puerto Rican community in the United States, especially from the forties through the seventies. He was a union organizer, community leader, political activist and general in the war for the civil-rights recognition of his community. In his memoirs, Gilberto Gerena Valentín takes us into the center of the fierce labor, political, civil-rights, social and cultural struggles waged by Puerto Ricans in New York from the 1940s through the 1970s.

Puerto Ricans at the Dawn of the New Millennium

Edited by Edwin Meléndez
and Carlos Vargas-Ramos
ISBN 978187848379-9. Pbk. 2014; 319 pages.   **$24.99**

This edited volume features chapters by Centro researchers and outside scholars presenting new research on social, economic, political and health conditions of the Puerto Rican population in the United States and highlighting the improvements and the challenges in this rapidly changing and growing community.

Soy Gilberto Gerena Valentín: memorias de un puertorriqueño en Nueva York

Gilberto Gerena Valentín; Edición de Carlos Rodríguez Fraticelli
ISBN: 9781878483645—ISBN: 9781878483454 (ebook); 2013; 302 pages.
$20 (print); $6 (ebook)

Gilberto Gerena Valentín es uno de los personajes claves en el desarrollo de la comunidad puertorriqueña en Nueva York. En sus memorias, Gilberto Gerena Valentín nos lleva al centro de las continuas luchas sindicales, políticas, sociales y culturales que los puertorriqueños fraguaron en Nueva York durante el periodo de la Gran Migración hasta los años setenta.

http://www.centropr-store.com

Centro Publications

2021 CATALOGUE

The AmeRícan Poet: Essays on the Work of Tato Laviera
Edited by Stephanie Alvarez and William Luis
ISBN: 9781878483669; 2014. Pbk. 2014; 418 pages. **$24.99**

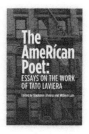

A collection of thirteen essays, an introduction and a foreword by fifteen established and emerging scholars. The essays discuss diverse aspects of Laviera's life and substantial body of work that includes five published collections of poetry, twelve written and staged plays, and many years of political, social, literary and healthcare activism. The book also includes four unpublished poems and the play King of Cans.

The Stories I Read to the Children: The Life and Writing of Pura Belpré, the Legendary Storyteller, Children's Book Author, and New York Public Librarian
Pura Belpré; Edited and Biographical Introduction by Lisa Sánchez González
ISBN: 9781878483805—ISBN: 9781878483454 (Kindle). 2013; 286 pages.
$20 (print); $7.99 (Kindle)

The Stories I Read to the Children documents, for the very first time, Pura Belpré's contributions to North American, Caribbean, and Latin American literary and library history. Thoroughly researched but clearly written, this study is scholarship that is also accessible to general readers, students, and teachers. Lisa Sánchez González has collected, edited, and annotated over 40 of Belpré's stories and essays, most of which have never been published. Her introduction to the volume is the most extensive study to date of Belpré's life and writing.

The State of Puerto Ricans 2013
Edited by Edwin Meléndez
and Carlos Vargas-Ramos
ISBN: 9781878483720; 2013; 91 pages.   **$15**

The State of Puerto Ricans 2013 collects in a single report the most current data on social, economic and civic conditions of the Puerto Rican population in the United States available from governmental sources, mostly the U.S. census Bureau.

http://www.centropr-store.com